Photographing Newborns

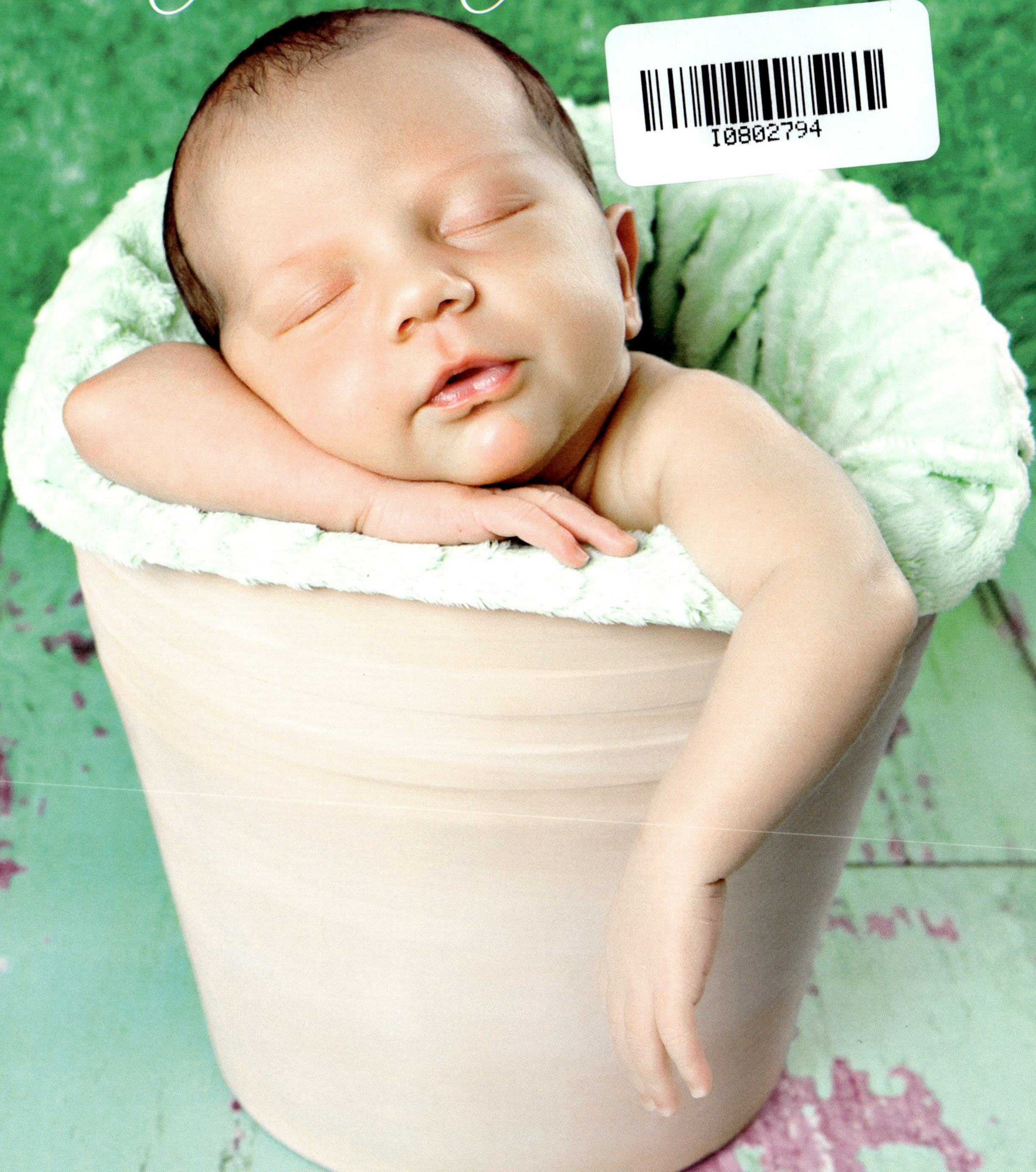

For Boutique Photographers

Mimika Cooney

Amherst Media, Inc. ■ Buffalo, NY

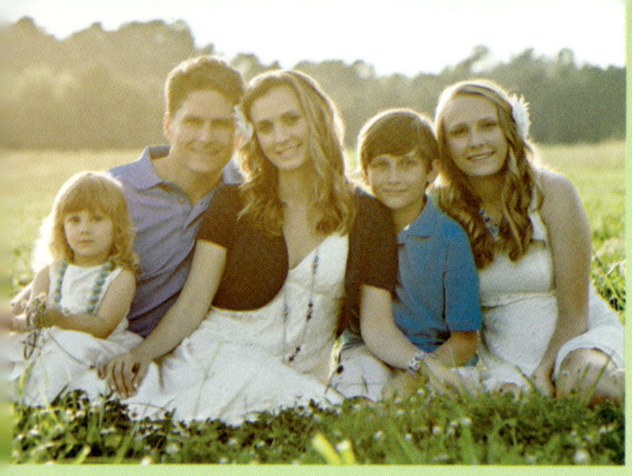

Image courtesy of Crystal Stokes Photography.

Dedication

To my wonderful family—you make my world complete. You bring the sunshine into my life. Thank you for your patience and understanding every time I've been occupied with another great idea. Most importantly, I thank the Lord for His good grace, patience, and guiding hand for allowing me this blessed life.

In Support of Now I Lay Me Down to Sleep

A portion of the proceeds from this book will be donated to Now I Lay Me Down to Sleep (NILMDTS), an organization that provides free remembrance photography to parents suffering the loss of a baby. NILMDTS trains, educates, and mobilizes professional photographers to provide beautiful heirloom portraits to families facing the untimely death of an infant. We believe these images serve as an important step in the family's healing process by honoring the child's legacy.

Published by:
Amherst Media, Inc.
P.O. Box 586
Buffalo, N.Y. 14226
Fax: 716-874-4508
www.AmherstMedia.com

Publisher: Craig Alesse
Senior Editor/Production Manager: Michelle Perkins
Editors: Barbara A. Lynch-Johnt, Harvey Goldstein, Beth Alesse
Associate Publisher: Kate Neaverth
Editorial Assistance from: Carey A. Miller, Sally Jarzab, John S. Loder
Business Manager: Adam Richards
Warehouse and Fulfillment Manager: Roger Singo

ISBN-13: 978-1-60895-739-2
Library of Congress Control Number: 20149533300
10 9 8 7 6 5 4 3 2 1

Contents

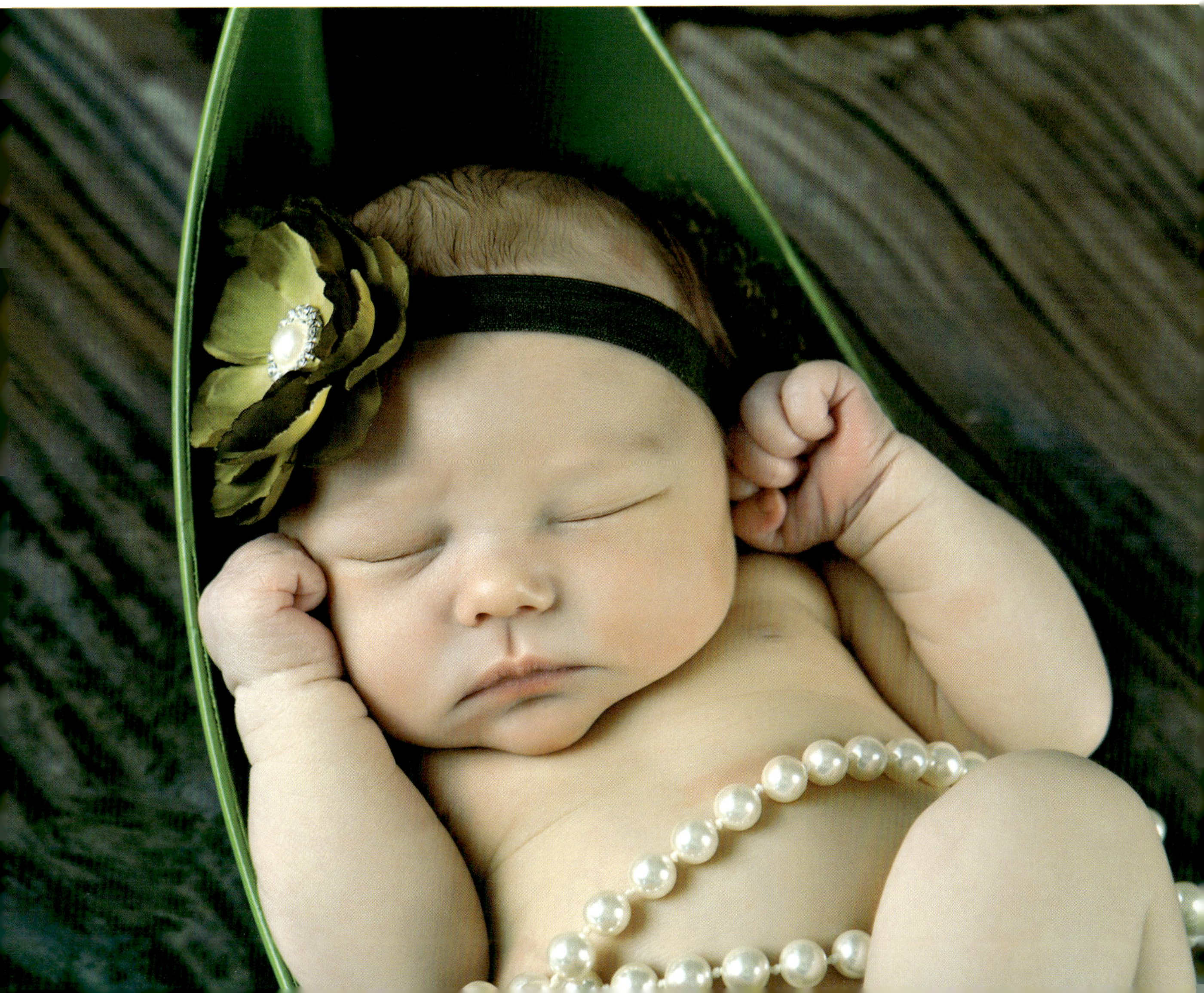

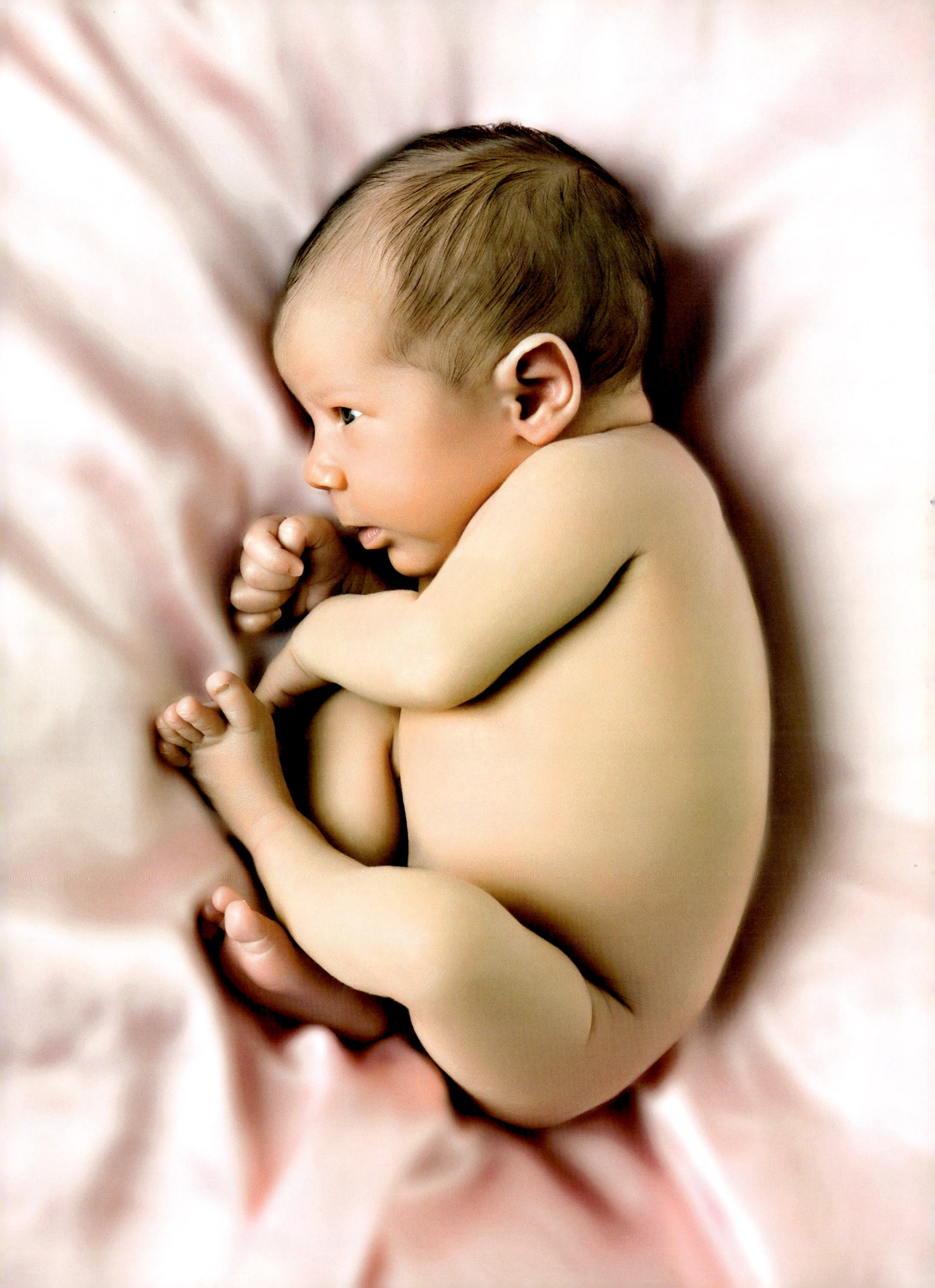

About the Author

Mimika Cooney is an international-award-winning photographer, published author, speaker, and small business marketing expert. She enjoys sharing her business marketing and photography knowledge, both online and at workshops, with other professional photographers and small-business owners. She owns a residential portrait studio specializing in beauty, glamour, and baby portraiture based in Charlotte, North Carolina.

Born in South Africa, Mimika received her photographic training in England and is an accredited licentiate by the British Institute of Professional Photographers (BIPP) and the Society of Wedding and Portrait Photographers (SWPP).

Mimika's first book, *Boutique Baby Photography: The Digital Photographer's Guide to Success in Maternity and Baby Portraiture* (Amherst Media, 2011), is now available on Amazon and in bookstores worldwide. Mimika's photography work has appeared on an American PBS TV documentary titled *Newborn Birth Injuries: The Untold Story.* She travels the world to speak at professional photography conventions, training other professional photographers and small business owners in both the United States and United Kingdom. She has spoken several times at the prestigious SWPP photographic convention in London, England.

Mimika, along with her husband, has worked and owned four businesses in South Africa, England, and the United States. She has experience in website design, public relations, and business administration in South Africa and England and spent ten years specializing as a portrait photographer. Mimika also worked as a live-on-air television broadcaster hosting a morning breakfast magazine show, *York Today,* in York, England, and has experience in the modeling and TV industry. She received television presentation training in South Africa from Nadia Bilchick (current CNN news anchor). Her training in public speaking, makeup application, and posing has proven useful in applications throughout her career. With her signature CaptureSchool.com, Mimika now focuses on teaching, speaking, and writing to share her knowledge with the world.

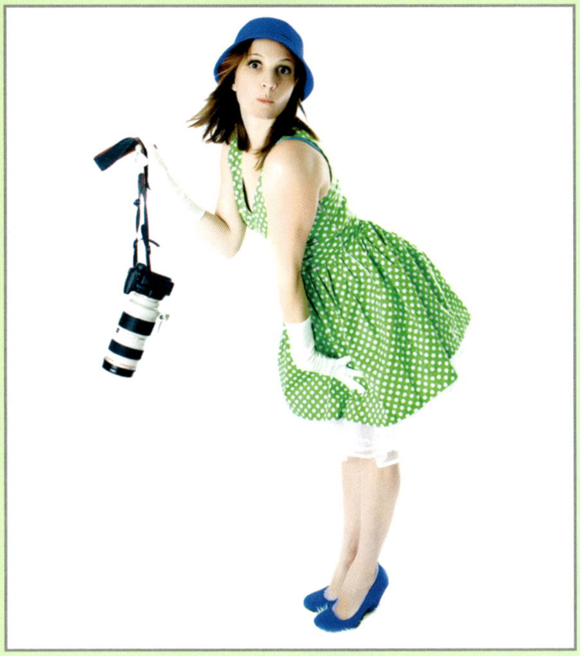

Mentoring and Workshops

Mimika teaches business, marketing, and sales techniques especially for photographers both online and in live workshops. For more information, visit www.mimikacooney.com and www.captureschool.com.

Mimika on Social Media

www.facebook.com/mimikacooneyfans
www.twitter.com/mimikacooney
www.instagram.com/mimikacooney
www.pinterest.com/mimikacooney
www.linkedin.com/in/mimikacooney
www.plus.google.com/+MimikaCooney
www.youtube.com/user/mimikacooneytv

1. Business Foundation

"Anyone can take a picture, but it takes an artist to envision and capture the perfect moment."

Building the Business

I remember the very first time I experienced a darkroom. The pungent smell of the chemicals made me lightheaded. The anticipation as my photo started to appear under the red lights was so thrilling! I was giddy to see something I had envisioned and created come to life. It was immediate—I was in love.

It's difficult to pinpoint the exact moment when my photography hobby became a business; I guess it was when I started getting paid. It seemed surreal that someone was paying me to do what I loved! The leap from passion to profit can be a big one, especially if we don't have a business background. That is why it's so important to have a plan. Let's face it, no one really wants to be a starving artist.

My business background isn't based in the halls of a university; rather, it came from the school of hard knocks. I had a serial entrepreneur for a father, but genetic disposition isn't a requirement for business success. I believe if you have the nose to sniff out an opportunity, the guts to give it a go, and a passion for what you do, you're golden. Do what makes you happy!

There is no better time than the present to start a business, and there are many opportunities available if you're willing to grab them. Before you go out and buy that fancy camera and register that domain name to set up shop, however, you must establish your direction and build your foundation.

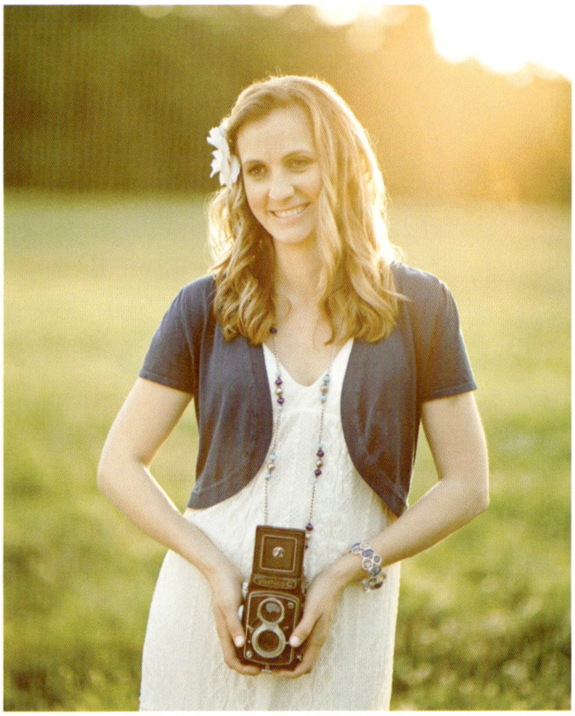

▲ Image of Mimika, courtesy of Crystal Stokes Photography.

Having a business plan really does help in setting a firm foundation. I'm sure many of you cringe at the thought of having to force yourself to put pen to paper—you just want to take pictures! A business plan doesn't have to be a complicated, laborious undertaking. It's simply a written summary of your goals that will help you to measure your success. As the saying goes, if you aim for nothing, that is surely what you'll get!

Taking the time now to figure out your thoughts, likes, and preferences will go a long way to helping you stay on track in the future. The "SWOT Analysis" is worth the effort in helping establish what you should focus your attention on and what you should ignore.

SWOT Analysis

If you don't know where to start, you can draw out some ideas with a single exercise. A SWOT Analysis is a strategic method for analyzing the strengths (S), weaknesses (W), opportunities (O), and threats (T) inherent in a project or business venture. This analysis can help you figure out your thoughts and preferences, which will go a long way toward helping you stay on track in the future.

So take out a piece of paper and an easy-flowing pen and list the following: your strengths, your weaknesses, opportunities for your business, and threats to your business. Under each category, fill in as many words as possible—anything that comes to mind. Figuring out what makes you unique, what drives you, and where your talents lie will help solidify your brand in years to come. Armed with this kind of information, you can make educated decisions about what will work best for your business—so you don't run yourself ragged taking jobs just

▼ There is more to newborn portraiture than taking photos of babies—you'll need to polish your business skills too.

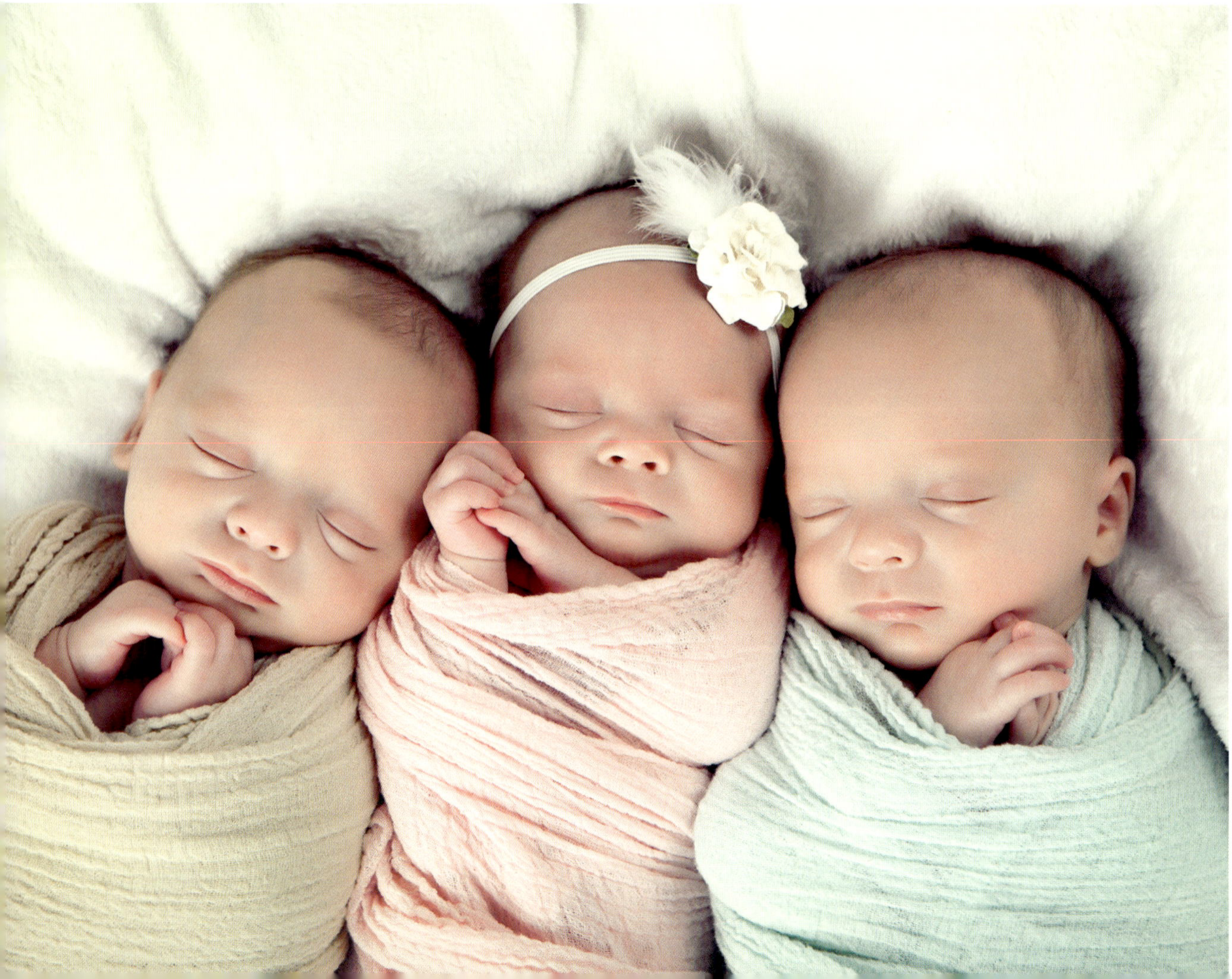

➤ Complete the Ideal Customer Profile and SWOT analysis to put your best foot forward for every client.

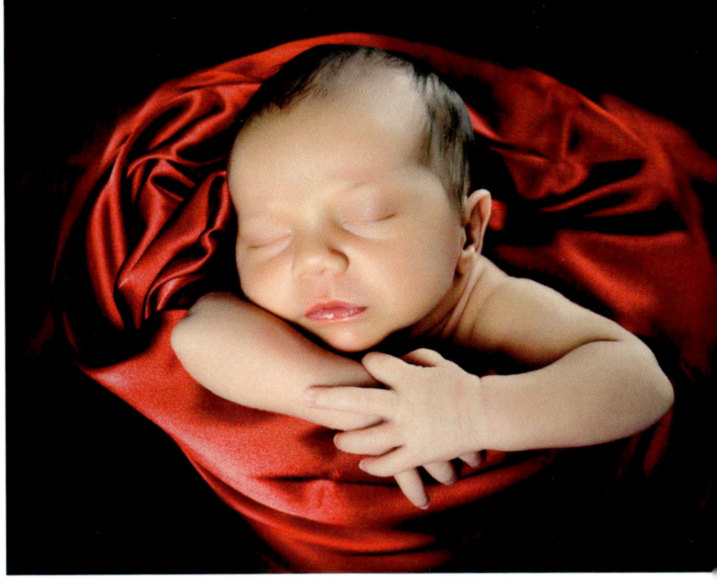

because the opportunity presents itself. Being a jack of all trades and a master of none will eventually come back to bite you on the behind.

The Three Tiers of Buying Behavior

There are three general tiers in the business landscape when it comes to affordability and motivation. It's important to decide what tier you are aiming for so you don't waste time, energy, resources, and money. Each tier has its own advantages and disadvantages, so determine what tier you will put your efforts into. Marketing to your target audience will greatly increase your odds of success.

Tier One. If it is your goal to do a high volume of business and you want to keep yourself busy with a never-ending stream of clients, then tier-one clients would probably suit you. Bear in mind that this demographic is quite budget conscious—you most likely will experience the apples-to-apples comparison since competition in this area is fierce and oversaturated. These are the clients who call and ask "How much are your 8x10-inch prints?" There is often no brand loyalty, and they are easily swayed by a good deal when they hear "50 percent off" or "free." These clients want to grab the CD and run to the nearest kiosk to print their own prints as cheaply as possible with no regard to how they turn out. If you start out competing in this category, you will find it very hard, if not impossible, to increase your prices without losing clients.

Understandably, if you're just starting out, you probably don't have the confidence and experience to charge what you believe you are worth and feel you have to in order to begin in this tier. There is no harm in exploring this market to discover your mojo, as there is room to make mistakes. Be prepared to entertain the demands of this budget-conscious bunch that will drive you down for a good deal—they can be downright mean! They may question your abilities and complain about price. To them, you will always be expensive. If you're the sensitive type, you will need the fortitude and thick skin to survive the sharp claws of the competition. You'll also need the wits to continually come up with special offers that will keep your clients coming back.

Tier Two. This level of clientele—generally the middle-class suburban family looking for a good value—is easier to work with. They are

Ideal Customer Profile

Who is your perfect client? By evaluating the following criteria, you'll come up with a pretty good idea of exactly the kind of customer you'll need to target:

- Demographics (age/kids/zip code)
- Ideals (beliefs/values)
- Favorites brands (style/price)
- Where to find her

easy to please and are enthusiastic referral-givers, telling their friends about their good find (that's you). They too love a good deal, so you have to show them the value in your work. They trust your judgment as an artist and look to your expertise for direction. You can charge more for your work than the lower tier expects, so this is a good market to get comfortable in. However, if a financial crisis hits, prepare yourself for the chance that you may not see them for long periods of time. Although they love what you do, money talks, and if they have to cut down on their family budget, the first on their list will be luxuries like photography. The way to survive this is to build a bigger clientele pool and keep that marketing engine running. This is where you can benefit from the experience of others. Buy templates and duplicate the marketing strategies that established photographers are selling. Do keep in mind that your competitor has access to the same resources, so your potential client may be conflicted when faced with the same offer from two photographers. This is where brand loyalty becomes very valuable.

Tier Three. With a high-end clientele, you can live the "work-less-earn-more" adage. Of

Clients value quality.

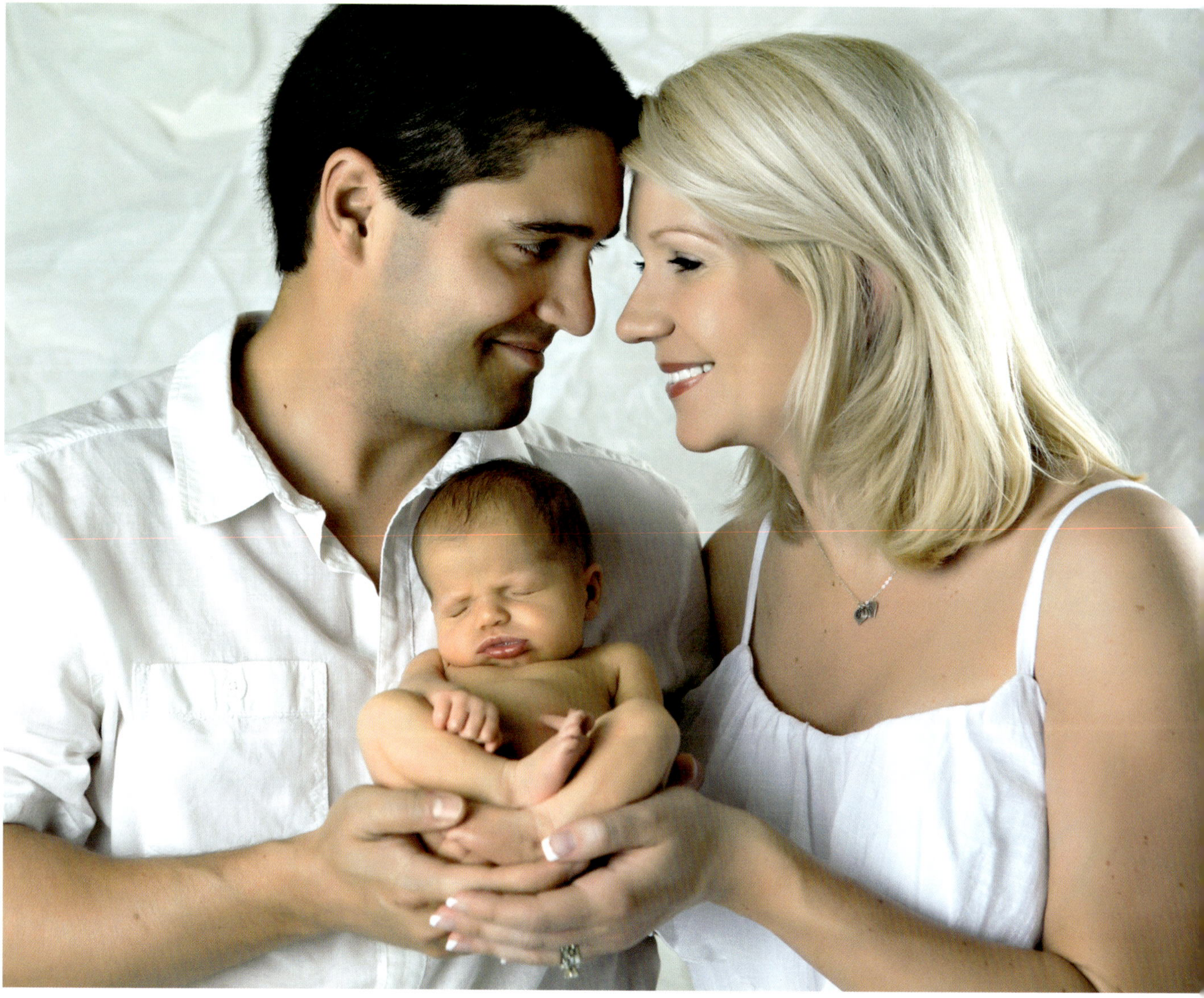

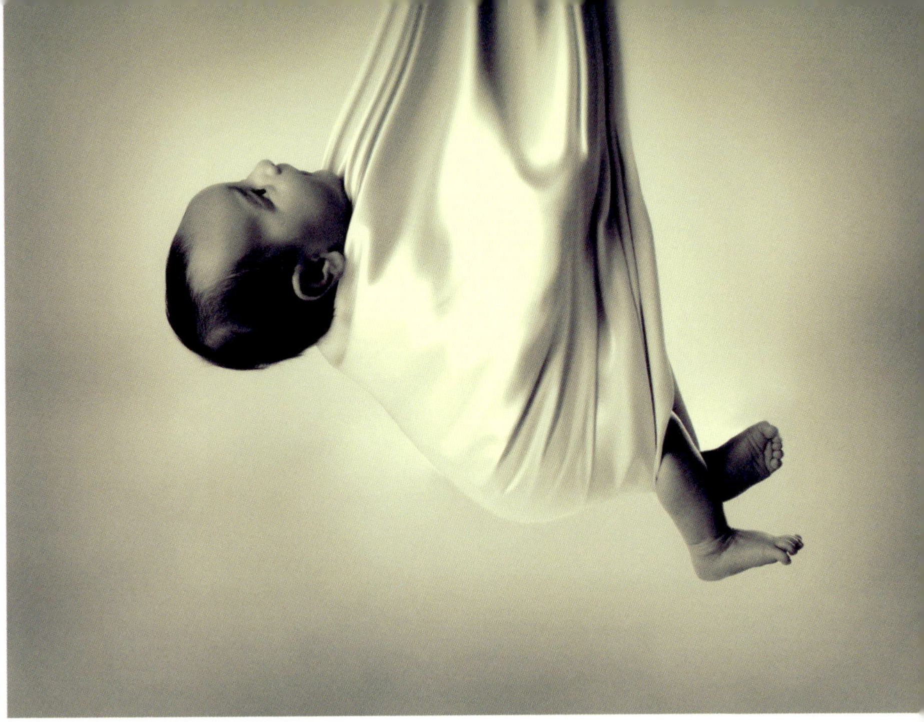

➤ Clients who develop brand loyalty will invest in your art.

course, there is no get-rich-quick way to build a business; it always takes blood, sweat, and tears. However, with fewer higher-paying clients, you will inevitably earn more per sale since you can charge more for your work. This group gives you lots of room for creativity, so you can come up with unique ideas as they trust you emphatically as the professional and look to you for direction. Brand loyalty runs deep, as it is the artist that they are investing in—they are in love with you.

These clients will seek you out for your uniqueness, artistic vision, and style. Most often, they are prepared to travel the distance to come to you so that they can experience your must-have brand. Delivering a quality product takes time, and they are prepared to wait. However, this market has a smaller pool of clients and they are much harder to find. Many of these clients won't want to share you with others. They want to be the only one amongst their friends to have your artwork decorating their walls, so getting referrals is tricky. They have high expectations and demand perfection, so you cannot afford to cut corners in quality and delivery.

Pretty ribbons and bows go a long way in making them happy (think Tiffany's or Gucci). You are expected to deliver stellar, high-quality products. In this book, we'll focus on developing a boutique brand around the middle and upper-class market.

Just Because You *Can* Doesn't Mean You *Should*

When we start out, we have little or no money to pay ourselves, let alone pay someone else. We invest everything we earn straight back into the business to keep it afloat. There comes a time I like to call the tipping point. This is when you realize that you just can't fit everything into a 24-hour period. You're spending too much time behind the computer editing photos and not enough time bringing in business. You feel very busy, but you can't seem to get on top of your to-do list. This is when you have to make the decision to delegate or drown!

When you force yourself to take a good look at your situation, you will identify the areas of your life that need work. If you break down your hourly rate by including all the tasks you squeeze in, you will realize that you're worth a pretty penny! If you can charge $100 per hour to photograph a session, why would you spend five hours cleaning your house—cleaners would charge you $100 for all five hours! Handling the job yourself does not make good business sense.

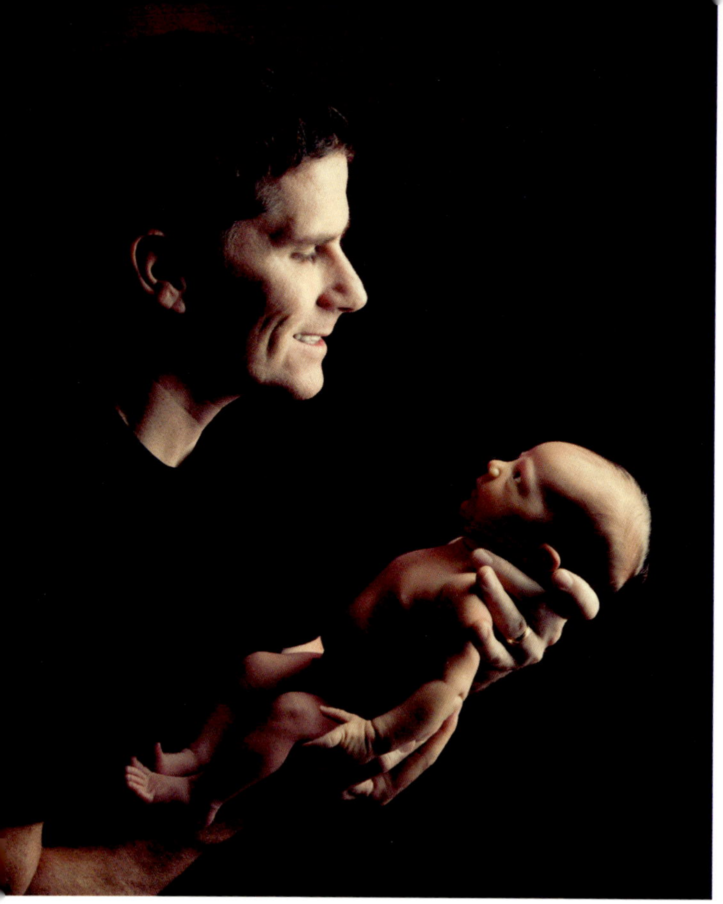

My family is the reason why I became my own boss.

The same goes for retouching. Many photographers actually like to spend hours perfecting their images using every conceivable tool, template, or action they can get their hands on. I prefer taking pictures and marketing to spending hours on my computer retouching. Just because I have the skills to do the retouching doesn't mean I necessarily should.

After years of spending his evenings alone, my husband gave me an ultimatum: fix it or find something else to do. My family is the reason I became my own boss. I wanted to be in control of my time, but I found that my business was running me, I was not running my business. Something had to change; I had to buy myself time to do the things I really wanted to do. I decided that my time is too valuable to spend it on things I can pay someone else to do faster and cheaper. I'd rather spend my evenings with my family than retouching until midnight!

I could have kicked myself when I did my research and found that graduating students from the local Arts Institute were willing to work for next to nothing just to have the opportunity to work in a photography business. Finding such great talent was such a revelation! What I could pay a student to do was ten times less than what I would equate to spending myself. In fact, the skills they are taught could show me a thing or two! I finally had my life back.

Now, I'm sure many of you are thinking, "Yeah, that's fine if you have the business to pay for help, but I don't have enough money to feed myself." This is where you have to change your mind-set. From now on, you have to charge for retouching time and build it into your cost of sales. I can guarantee that you will stop wasting so much time doing the unnecessary when you realize that time literally is money.

Something to note: if you find yourself having to "fix things" in Photoshop, you're not capturing the images right the first time. I cannot emphasize enough how important it is to get things right in the camera. Photoshop is there to enhance our work, not to salvage a bad job. If you find yourself in this position, perhaps you need to spend more time perfecting your technique. We will cover this in greater detail in later chapters.

The best way to get ahead is to have systems and tools in place to shorten the time it takes to finish tasks. There are many software programs available that you can use to minimize the time spent on doing repetitive tasks. For example, during my first year of shooting weddings, I used to edit by opening each and every image individually in Photoshop to fine-tune the color

Specialization

The Jack-of-all-trades general practitioner doesn't appeal to clients today. Consumers want to know that they are investing their money in someone who knows what they are doing and understands their needs. Painting everyone with the same broad brush will not produce the desired results, as not everyone is into the same shade of green. Become the best you can be in your area of expertise, own it, and people will find you.

"It's not the camera that makes the artist but the person behind the camera that makes the art."

and exposure. Today, I use Lightroom and sync settings to a batch of images, thereby minimizing the time spent in postproduction. There are other tools to get you organized. Google calendar is free, and you can share your calendars with others so you can get help making appointments. Other do-it-yourself tools like BrownBookIt allow customers to pick and pay for their preferred appointment date online. Also, you can use studio management software like Successware and ShootQ to keep you on top of your business so you can accurately determine your prices, know your numbers, set your goals, and plan your finances with the click of a button. Only once you have your systems in place will you have the peace of mind and confidence that you are running your business, it is not running you!

Tools of the Trade

Don't you just love it when someone says to you "What a great picture! You must have a great camera"? It's like saying to a painter, "Nice masterpiece! You must have nice brushes!" Uh-huh, right. It's not the camera that makes the artist but the person behind the camera that makes the art.

When it comes to selecting your gear, a lot comes down to personal preference. However, my advice is to buy the best quality and most recent equipment models you can afford. The two biggest players in the camera market, Canon and Nikon, offer

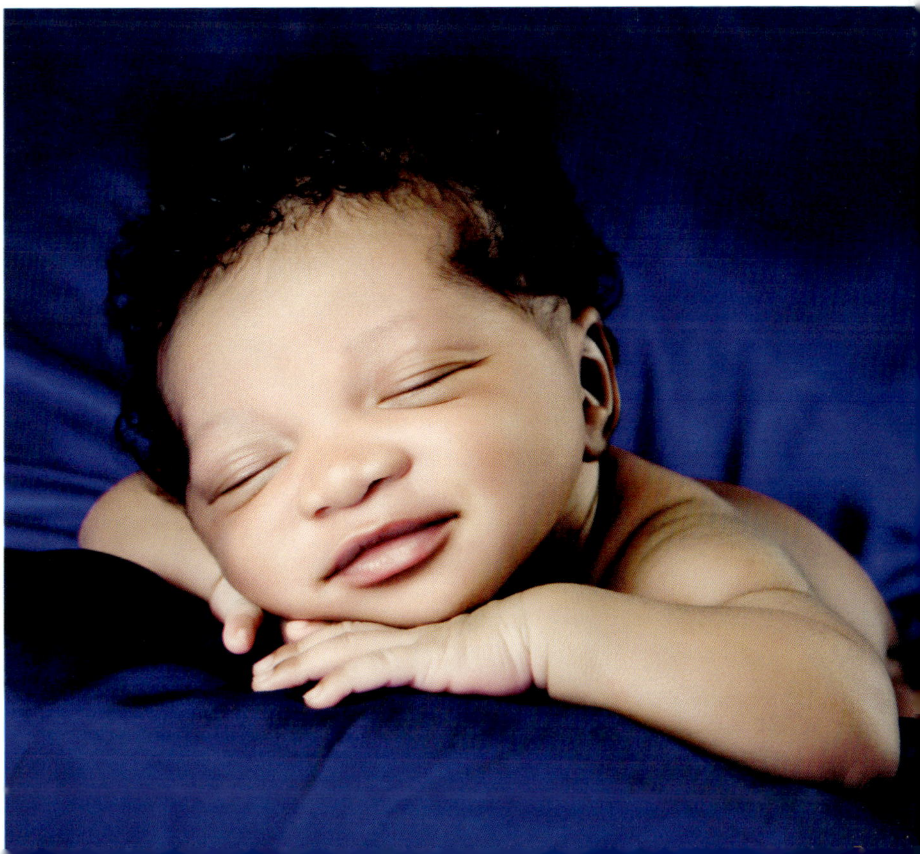

➤ Become the best you can be in your area of expertise.

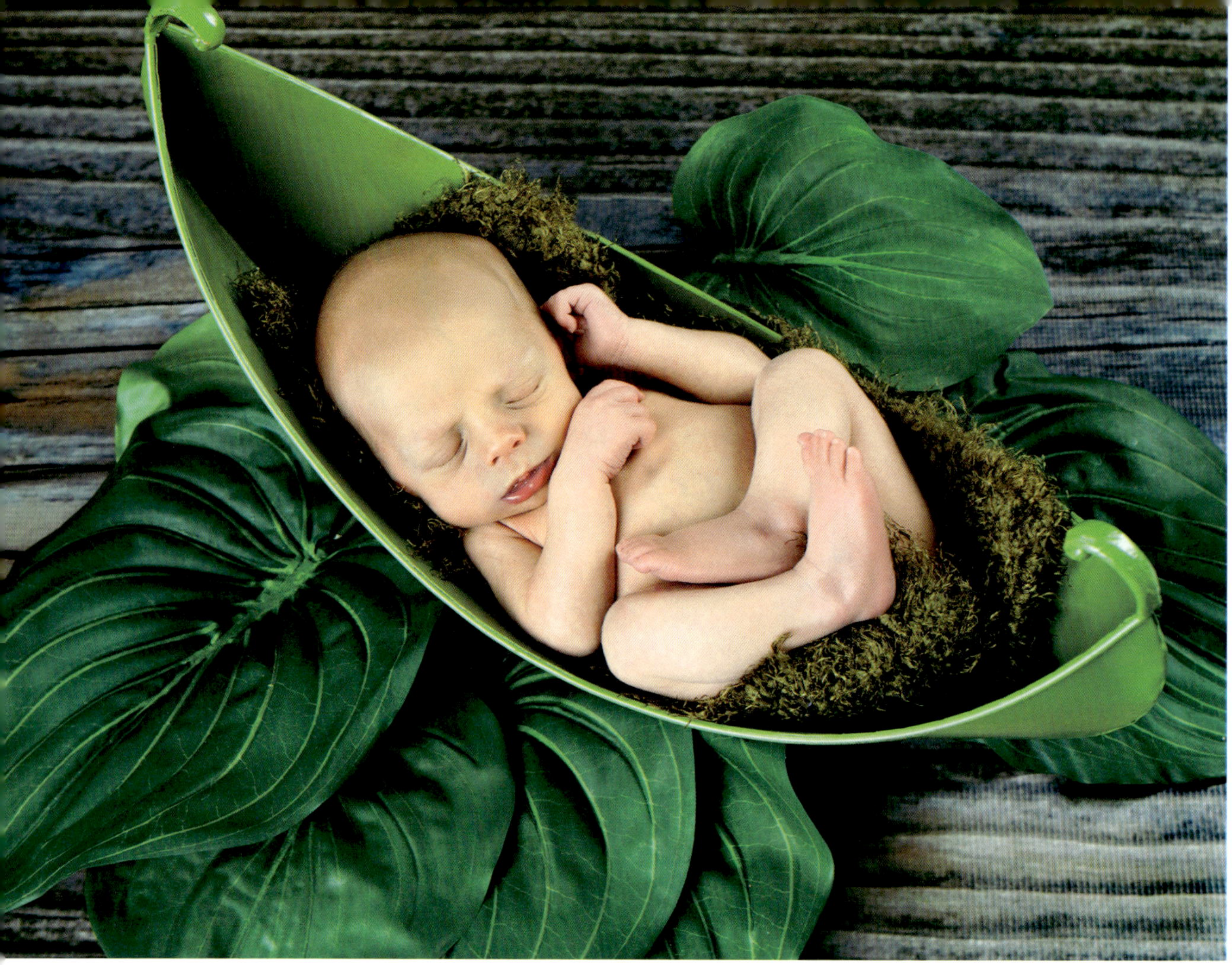

some excellent-quality DSLR prosumer cameras. You can start there and invest your money in top-quality glass. It's generally the lens, not the camera, that provides you with better image results.

Once you've purchased your gear, read that little printed book called the manual. Yes, it's a tedious process, but it sure does teach you how things work.

Not too many years ago, people could find the money to buy the things they really wanted. The recent economic downturn has caused people to tighten their wallets and focus on quality and making value-driven purchasing decisions, much as people did thirty to fifty years ago. In the 1960s, the lady of the house bought a

▲ Sharpen your skills and adapt to a new way of thinking.

refrigerator, confident that the brand was built to last the years. Purchasing decisions were based on quality and longevity. Later, things changed. Manufacturers' focus turned to making things fast and cheap. The same trends can be seen in our industry. Twenty to thirty years ago, the skills of a professional photographer were revered. The general consumer wouldn't dream of competing with the professional whose expertise and equipment were out of their reach. Today, cameras have become more and more affordable. Most middle-class families can afford a decent camera that produces

"Rejection is a zero-cost failure. And since the risk of rejection only offers an upside, you might as well go out and risk as much rejection as you can."—Lewis Schiff

acceptable images and have opted to take their family portraits themselves. To get a piece of the pie in this environment, professional photographers must sharpen their skills, adapt to the new way of thinking, and be creative in attracting clients. Only time provides experience, but you can have the confidence now in your passion, talents, and abilities to make your business work!

We've all heard it before, but there really is no way around this one. Only time and patience will eventually get you to where you want to be. There is no easy method, template, address, or mailing list that will catapult your business into the stratosphere. It's a collection of many things. You must painstakingly lay one brick at a time to create a castle worthy of royalty. When you've applied that kind of attention to the details of your business, you'll find that you're in store for great things.

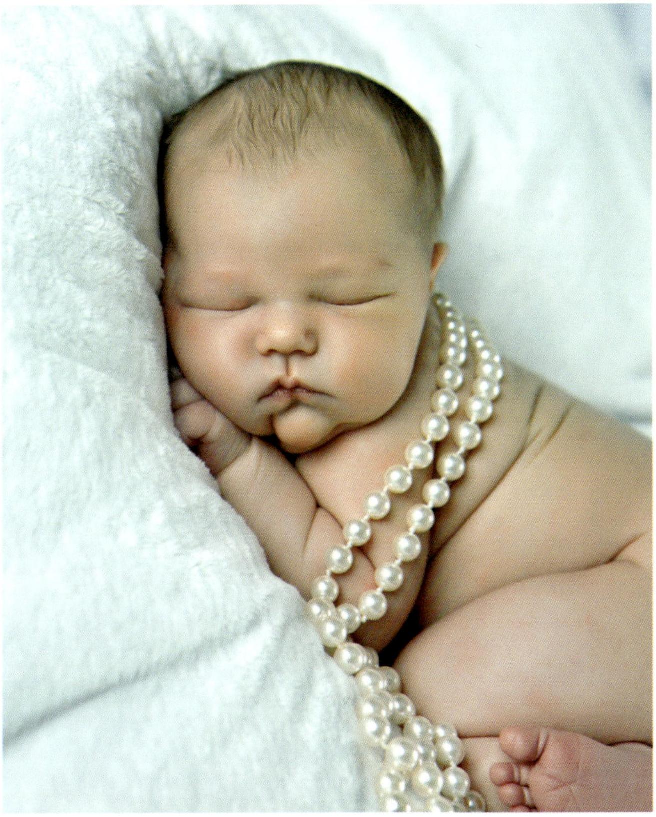

The Success of Failure

Failure is inevitable. We all attempt things and fail. But do you know that failure is a good thing? Many of us see failure as something we don't want to talk about and don't want anyone to know about. We put on a brave face and pretend everything is a-okay.

After reading the book *Business Brilliant*, by Lewis Schiff (HarperBusiness, 2013), I embrace failure. Bring it on, baby!

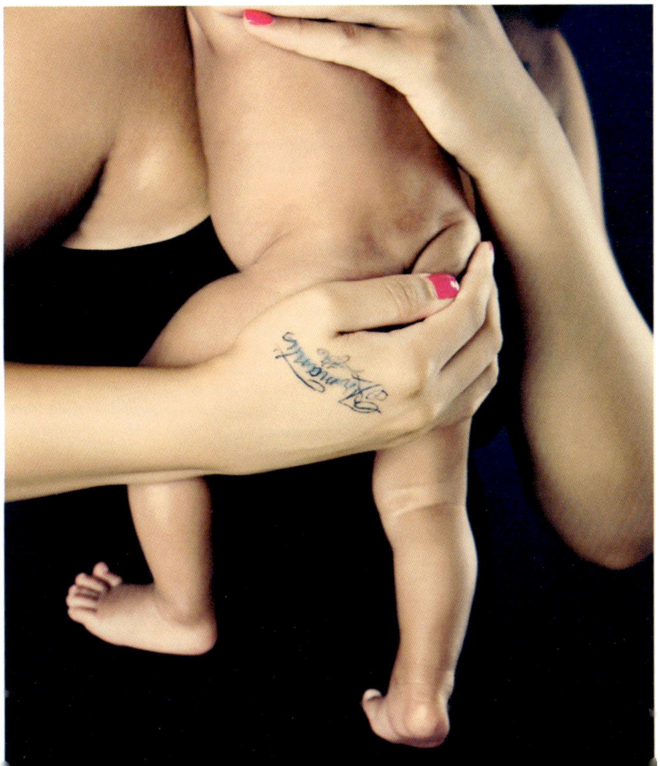

➤ Failure teaches us what we are good at.

In the book, Schiff discusses a national survey he conducted that revealed the eye-opening findings between middle-class workers and self-made millionaires. His research revealed the truth about how the wealthy get rich. It also dispelled some myths and conventional wisdoms about the definition of success. What I found fascinating is that the self-made millionaires felt that setbacks and failures taught them what they are good at, while fewer than two out of ten middle-class survey participants agreed. What this tells me is that when we fall off the horse, the millionaire's mind-set is to get back on. For the general populace, the instinct is to nurse our wounds and walk away. Why? All of the people profiled in the book faced serious setbacks, but their experience of failure turned out to be a key ingredient in developing business brilliance.

"The millionaire's mind-set is to get back on. For the general populace, the instinct is to nurse our wounds and walk away."

So how does this relate to us as photographers? I believe it means we need to embrace the "failure faith" mentality if we are to achieve ultimate success—we must believe that when you stretch and achieve something special, failure yields unforeseen

▼ Take the LEAP approach to daily activity and reach your artistic and financial goals.

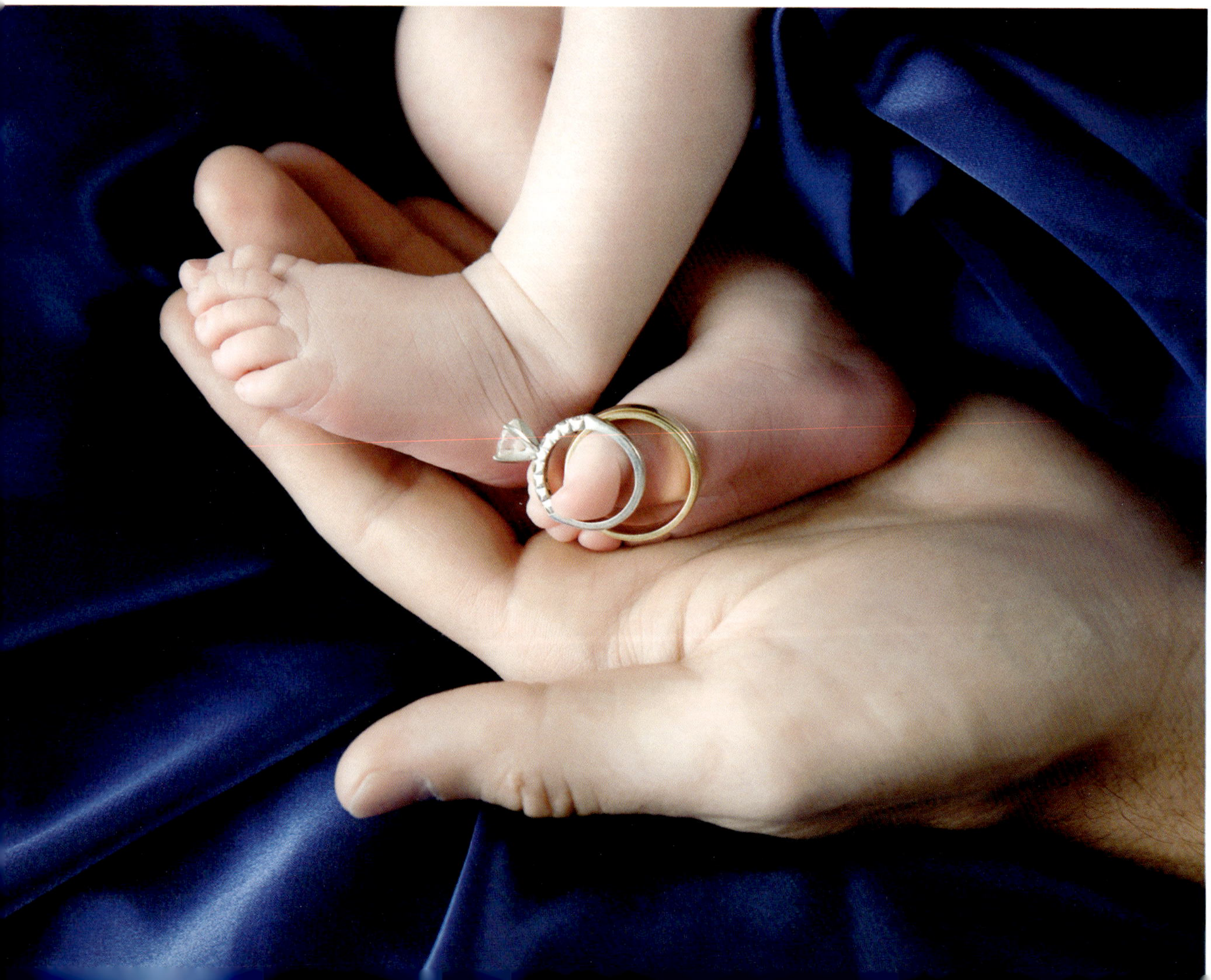

"Failure is not really about what happens to you. It's how you deal with it, and what you make of it."—David Neeleman, founder of JetBlue Airlines

lessons and benefits. This means that even though you don't get the job, win the client, or land a big opportunity, you should consider it a practice run for the next attempt.

Many successful companies are not keen to let the public know of their failures. They tend to cover things up and put on a brave face. However, we now live in the age of transparency; there is a tremendous amount of information available to the layman. If there is a problem, it will be uncovered, so it's in our best interest to embrace it and learn from it.

In the book, Schiff talks about the four broad areas of daily activity that successful self-made entrepreneurs do consistently. He calls it LEAP (see sidebar).

LEAP

- *Learning:* Millionaires spend more time and effort discovering what they do best and pursue opportunities related to their best attributes.
- *Earning:* They take on projects that maximize the dollar potential while limiting their downside risks.
- *Assistance:* They actively cultivate networks so they can get help and advice beyond their own capabilities.
- *Persistence:* They take an authentic interest in their failures and see them as necessary aspects of their eventual success.

Here are my tips for overcoming failure:

1. See rejection as a benefit. When you don't get the wedding job or session with a client, think of it as being one step closer to your next success.
2. Cultivate the "failure faith" mentality. Embrace failure as a necessary step in adjusting your path. Now you know to stop wasting your efforts on the wrong things.
3. Use your failure to correct your course and move yourself in the right direction.
4. Learn what you do best and do more of it.
5. Pursue opportunities to use what you do best by following the money. Just because you love to shoot a particular genre doesn't mean you should become the best at it if there is no money in it. Find the need and fill it.
6. Ask for assistance, learn from others, and cultivate a network.
7. Be persistent and never give up!

2. Branding

"We are all born for love. It is the principle of existence and its only end."—Benjamin Disraeli

Is Your Baby Ugly?

How ugly is your baby? Every mom thinks her baby is the most beautiful in the world, and rightly so. We carried and birthed our baby, and no matter what anyone thinks, we love our baby.

I'm the mom of three gorgeous kids (I know, I'm biased), but today I'm not talking about my children. Have you considered that even though you love your business and your photography, that perhaps you're biased?

▼ Getting feedback on your images will help you grow and reach new artistic heights.

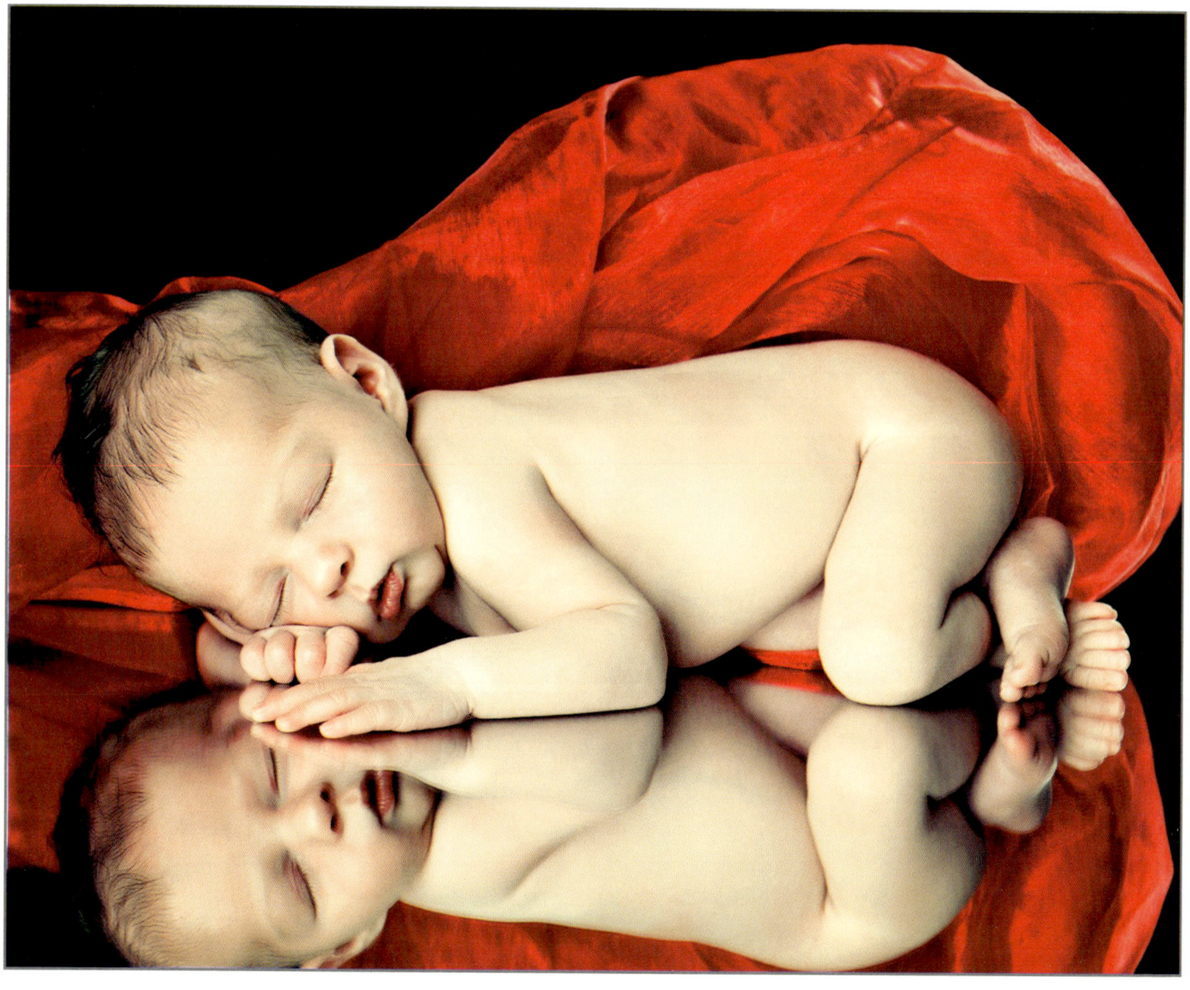

➤ Ask yourself, "What makes clients buy from me?"

Sometimes it helps to look at things from another person's point of view to really understand a buyer's behavior. Have you asked yourself "What makes my clients buy from me?" What I love about traveling to photography conventions is the honest and truthful responses I get. Entering print competitions results in feedback needed to push you to do better and create the best art you can create. What's the point of your friends and family telling you how wonderful your photography is if it isn't really true (they're biased, right?), and all the while you can't figure out why business isn't booming and you simply can't seem to get ahead of your competition.

When I went to London in early 2013 to teach two photography workshops, I made sure to make time to sit in on classes. One of my favorites was with renowned British fashion and portrait photographer Damian McGillicuddy, who is known for speaking his mind. With a direct approach and something of a potty mouth (be prepared for lots of F bombs), his approach is to ignite a reaction. Of course, his work is totally fabulous and his use of lighting is superb. It's no wonder that he is in high demand.

During Damian's class, I listened attentively as he explained some basic truths: "Understanding the basics makes all the shiny things easier to use." Simple, but so true. If you don't know proper lighting or haven't figured out how to use your fancy camera (because you don't want to read the manual), don't complain if your work is just "blah." It's not the economy, people! We have got to stop making excuses for sub-par work and blaming everyone and everything else. It's time to take the bull by the horns and take responsibility.

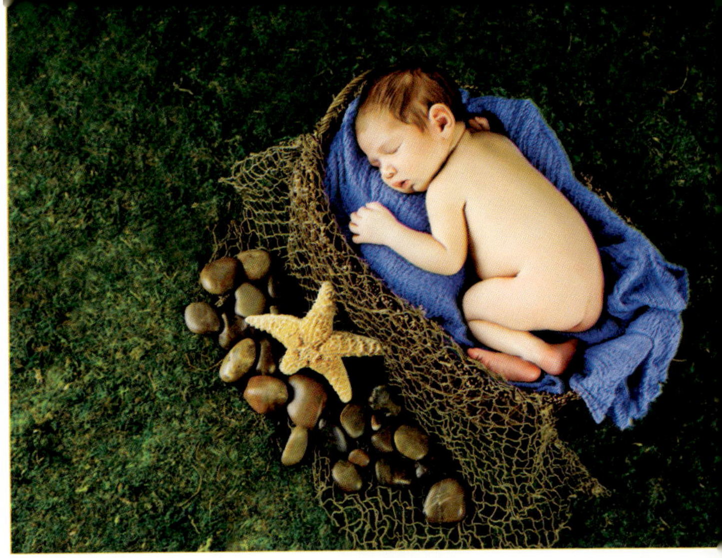

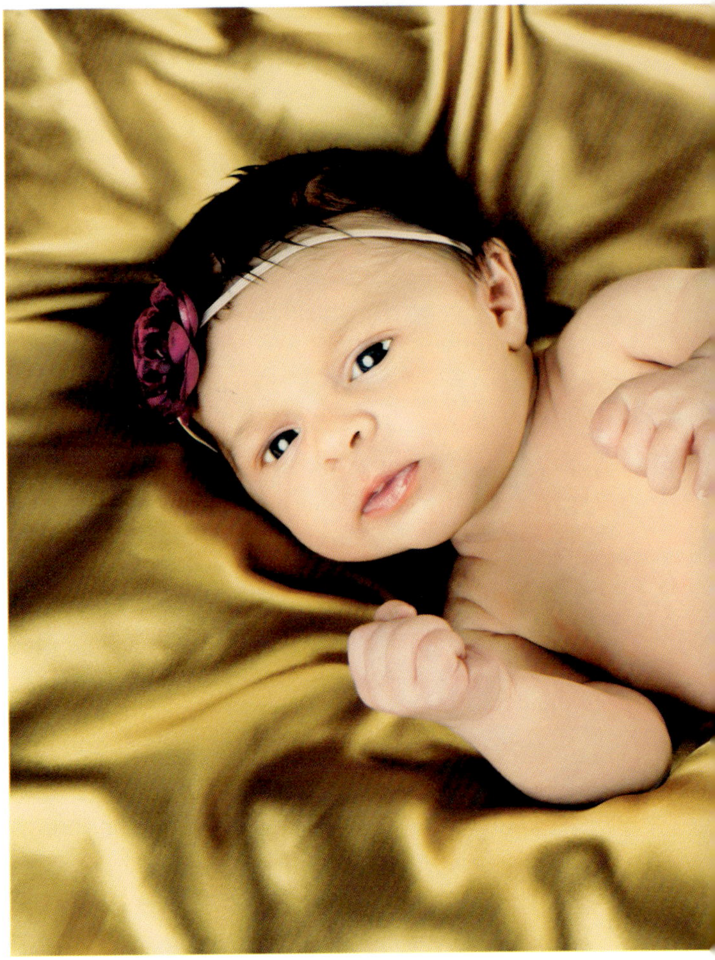

With so much competition these days, it's now a prerequisite to be unique and provide a service that is above and beyond what used to be considered the norm. We no longer live in

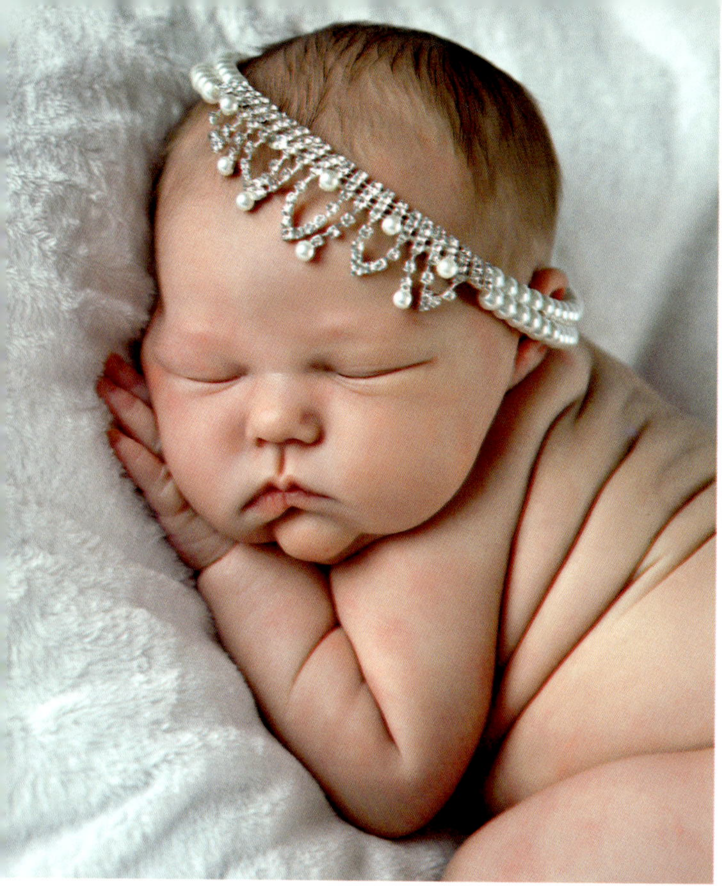

◀ Don't underestimate the power of the experience. The session and the resulting portraits will win client loyalty.

the commodity economy where people were happy to pay for a faceless service because they didn't know any better (goodbye second-hand salesman). We now live in the "connection economy" (to quote Seth Godin), which means people want to do business with people they like. Think about it . . . when is the last time you bought a high-ticket item? How did making the purchase make you feel? Did you make the decision to empty your wallet because the shiny features made a whole lot more sense, or did you feel excited about your final choice?

Damian McGillicuddy agrees with me too. At his photography lighting class, he also said, "What are you trying to say? What must the viewer think or feel? Make them look good—not short, fat, and dumpy!"

I love that last part, but hey, it's true! Your clients want to look good and feel great too. Don't underestimate the power of the experience.

So what this means is this: you need to have a plan in place to elevate your worth in order to become successful.

1. Become the expert. Start by learning as much as you can about really good lighting and the craft of photography. Read a book, take a course, and practice, practice, practice. Learn how to see the light, how to manipulate it, and shoot in manual mode for ultimate control. Enter print competitions and seek honest feedback (constructive criticism will push you to do better).
2. Design systems. Create a client workflow that takes your prospects down a system that turns them into paying customers. You repeat the same steps over and over, so instead of wasting time, how about systemizing it? Make notes on what you want your customers to know about you and how you do business. Do you want them to know that you expect session fees to be paid up front, and do they need to come back for an ordering appointment, etc.? Eliminate misconceptions and misunderstandings.
3. Underpromise and overdeliver. Break away from being a commodity by offering your clients a really fabulous experience. Think about what services you can offer to make them fall in love with your brand. Providing what you promised isn't enough anymore—you have to go above and beyond to impress. Think about the small details like offering what-to-wear guides, hand-written thank-you notes, birthday cards with a gift with purchase, pretty packaging, and fast turnaround service.

Do whatever floats your boat and suits your style, and be prepared for a change in your bottom line. When you totally wow your clients, they can't help but gush about you, and the river of prosperity will start to flow!

What Does Your Brand Say About You?

Finding your unique voice can be difficult when the world shouts so much noise. Geez Louise, all of that racket can give you a headache. But there are brands out there that have managed to clamor through the masses and become "sticky," and I always think of them.

"Do whatever floats your boat and suits your style, and be prepared for a change in your bottom line."

For example, whenever I see the colors red and white and curly fonts, I think of Coke. The simple swoosh of Nike reminds me to "Just Do It." A simple "O" brings the queen of branding, Oprah, straight to mind. So what does your brand say about you? What feelings do your business's name, logo, and tagline conjure up? A brand is more than a name; it's how people feel about you. We've heard it before, but it really is true, ask any politician—

▼ A brand is more than a name—it's how people feel about you.

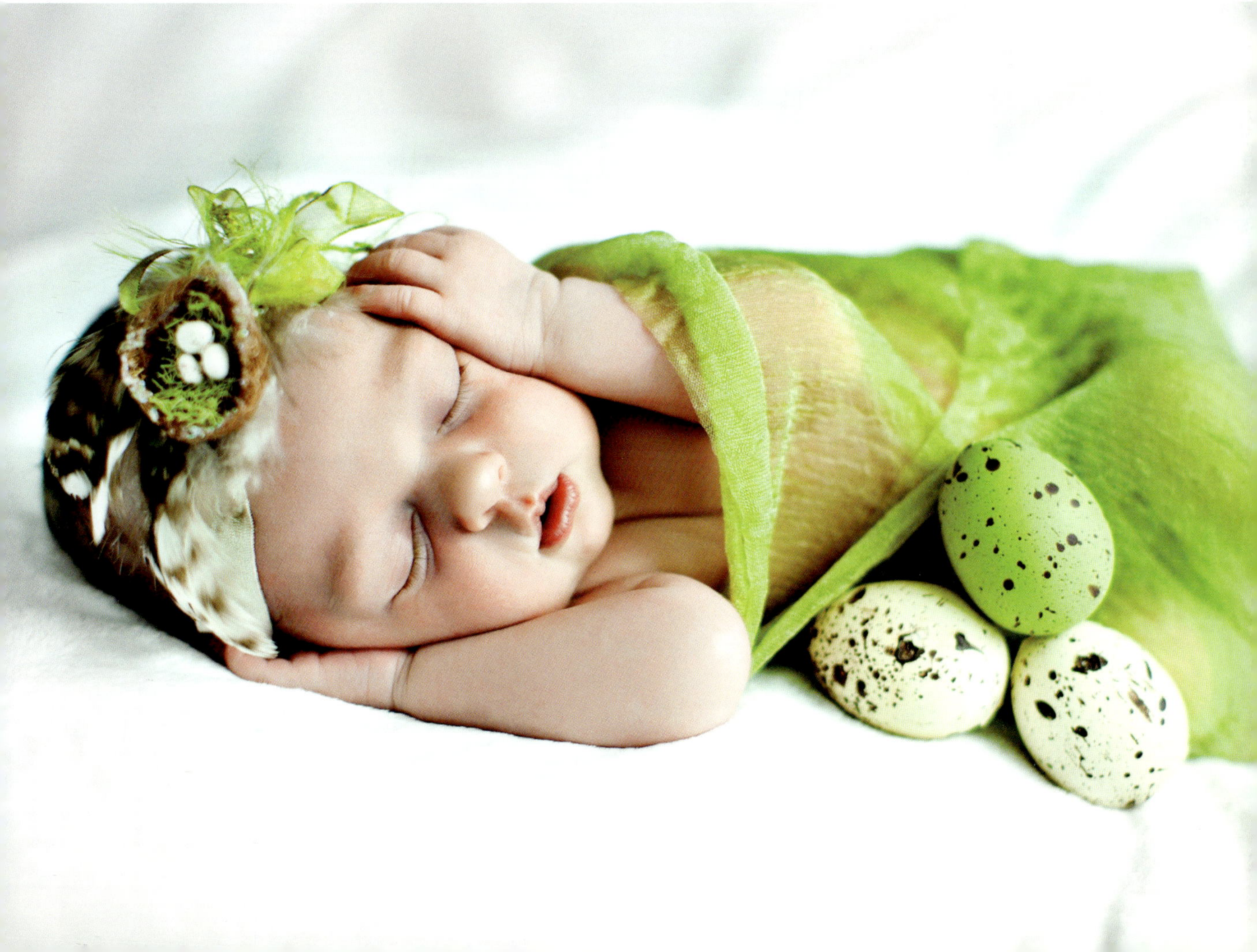

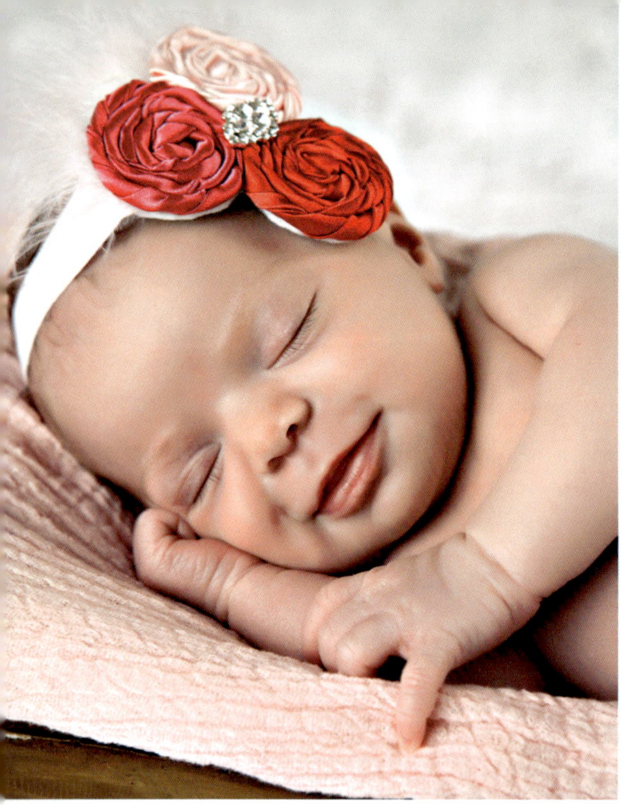
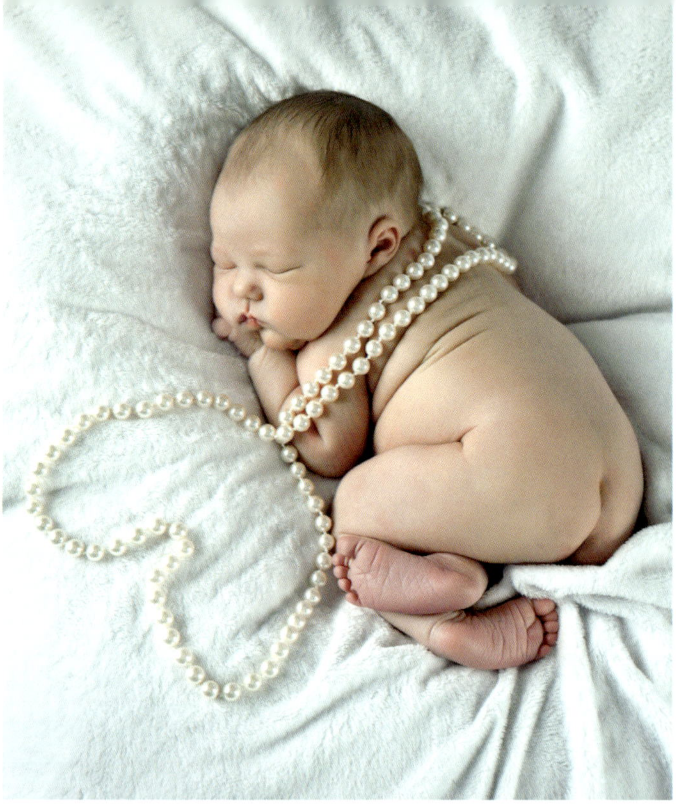
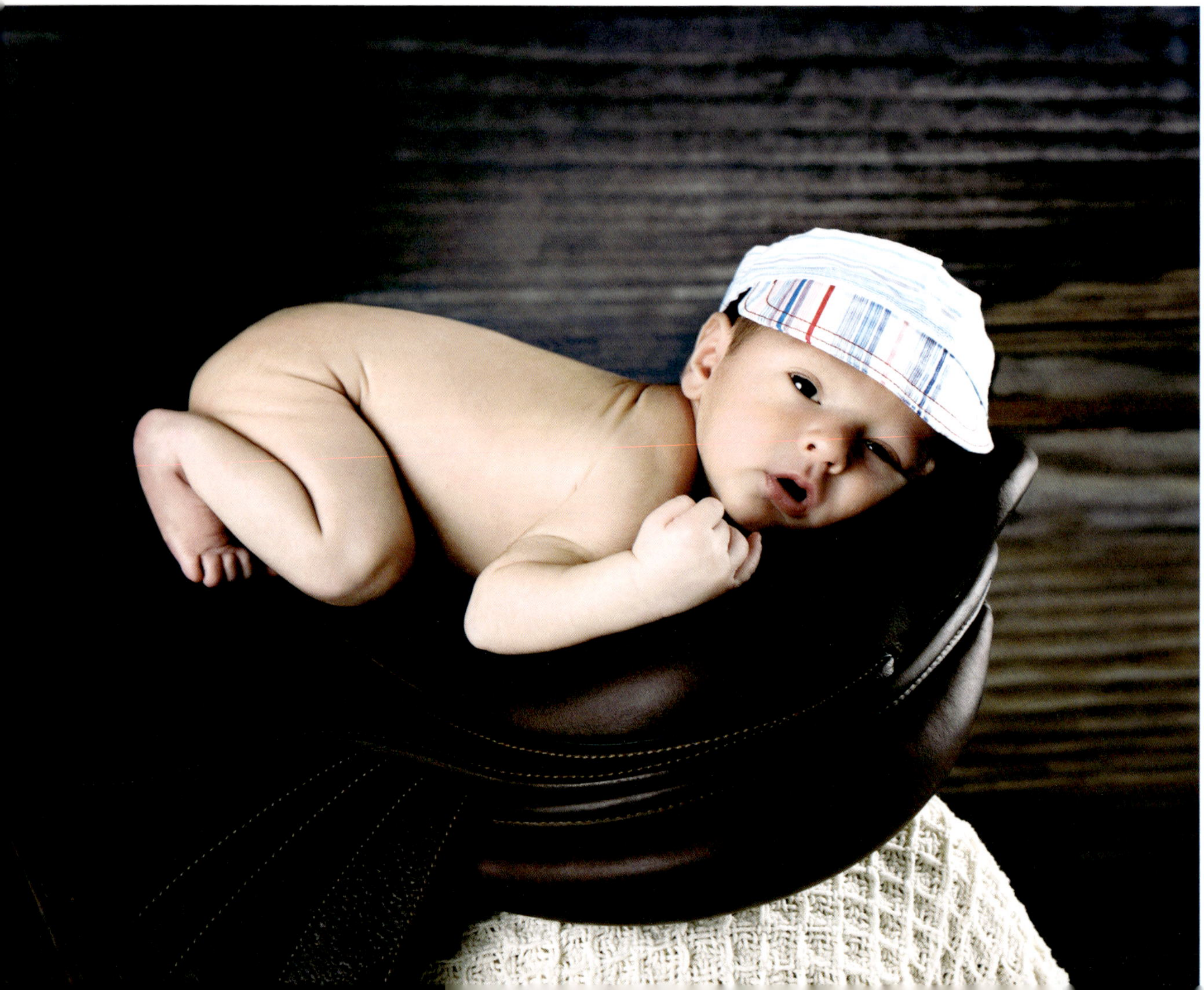

people buy from people they like. Yes, it still feels like the playground at school. We all vie for people's affections and want to be popular. We can't win them all, but our unique voice will appeal to the right kinds of people.

Think about how you are speaking to your target client. What three things do you want people to see, feel, and know about you? Here is a simple yet effective exercise.

1. Ask your family and friends what three words come to mind when they think of you.
2. Create a Pinterest board of your likes, loves, favorites, and dreams. Check out mine at http://pinterest.com/mimikacooney/mystyledefined/. Creating it has been an eye-opening exercise.
3. Pick out three elements that stand out from your board. Think of emotive, descriptive words like beautiful, edgy, peaceful, dark, etc.
4. Collate the words from friends and the words from your board and circle the ones that match or are similar. You should have a pretty good idea of your style and how people feel about you.

From your master list, you can start to define your core values. These will help you stay within the parameters of your brand and help you define and refine your voice. I learned that even though I like moody photos, they are not my personal brand. My brand is beautiful, emotional, light, airy, colorful, and fun.

From here on, you can use your style board to direct your website designer, graphic designer, and yourself so you keep "speaking" in your one true voice—the one that only you have to give to the world.

◄ Your unique voice will appeal to the right kids of people.

How to Build Your Love Brand

Keeping a client costs less than attracting a new one. It makes sense to keep your existing clients happy by giving them a reason to keep doing business with you, or in the case of newborn photography, to refer their friends to you.

Competition nowadays is fierce, and there are new photographers entering the market all the time who are willing to give their services away for next to nothing and charge pitiful prices just to get the deal. However, this negatively affects the photographic industry as a whole as it lowers the perceived value of photography in the minds of consumers. Photographers who charge a small fee just for their time and happily hand over the CD of digital negatives are, in my opinion, setting themselves up to work harder than they need to.

If we all want to keep ourselves self-employed doing what we love to do, then we need to work together to keep the standard of photography high. Consumers have become wise, and with the accessibility of the Internet, it is possible for the average consumer to get rock-bottom prices on goods and services. When it comes to photography, this is not necessarily a good thing. People have lost the appreciation for good quality and complain bitterly when things don't turn out as they expect. Competing based on price is a race to the bottom. Who wants to win that war?

For longevity purposes, we all need to provide a quality service with quality products and stop cutting corners just to grab a few bucks. The truth of the matter is that most start-up businesses won't make it past the first five years. If you want to be one of the survivors, then you need to put in more effort to create lasting relationships with your clients.

As we've mentioned before, people buy from those they like. To gain someone's trust, you must show them that you care. For example, sending hand-written notes is a personal way of thanking a client for placing their trust in you.

Boutique businesses charge more than the average vendor. As such, you need to keep them "in love" with you to avoid the dreaded buyer's remorse. Referring to each person by name goes a long way in showing you are paying attention. There are several suppliers on the market who offer custom-printed stationery, and many photo labs are now offering digital press-printed cards at a reasonable price. My favorite are the press-printed cards by White House Custom Color. Their paper range and quality make them a standout. Artsy Couture and Simply Color Lab also offer a great selection of different paper weights and finishes.

The second most important thing to remember about a person (after their name) is their birthday. No matter how old, each one of us likes to be appreciated on our birthday. As Dr. Seuss said, "A person's a person, no matter how small."

Keeping an accurate database of your clients will help you remember upcoming birthdays so that you can send out a card on time. You can include a voucher/coupon/gift certificate to give the individual an incentive to do business with you again, and including a current

As Dr. Seuss said, "A person's a person, no matter how small."

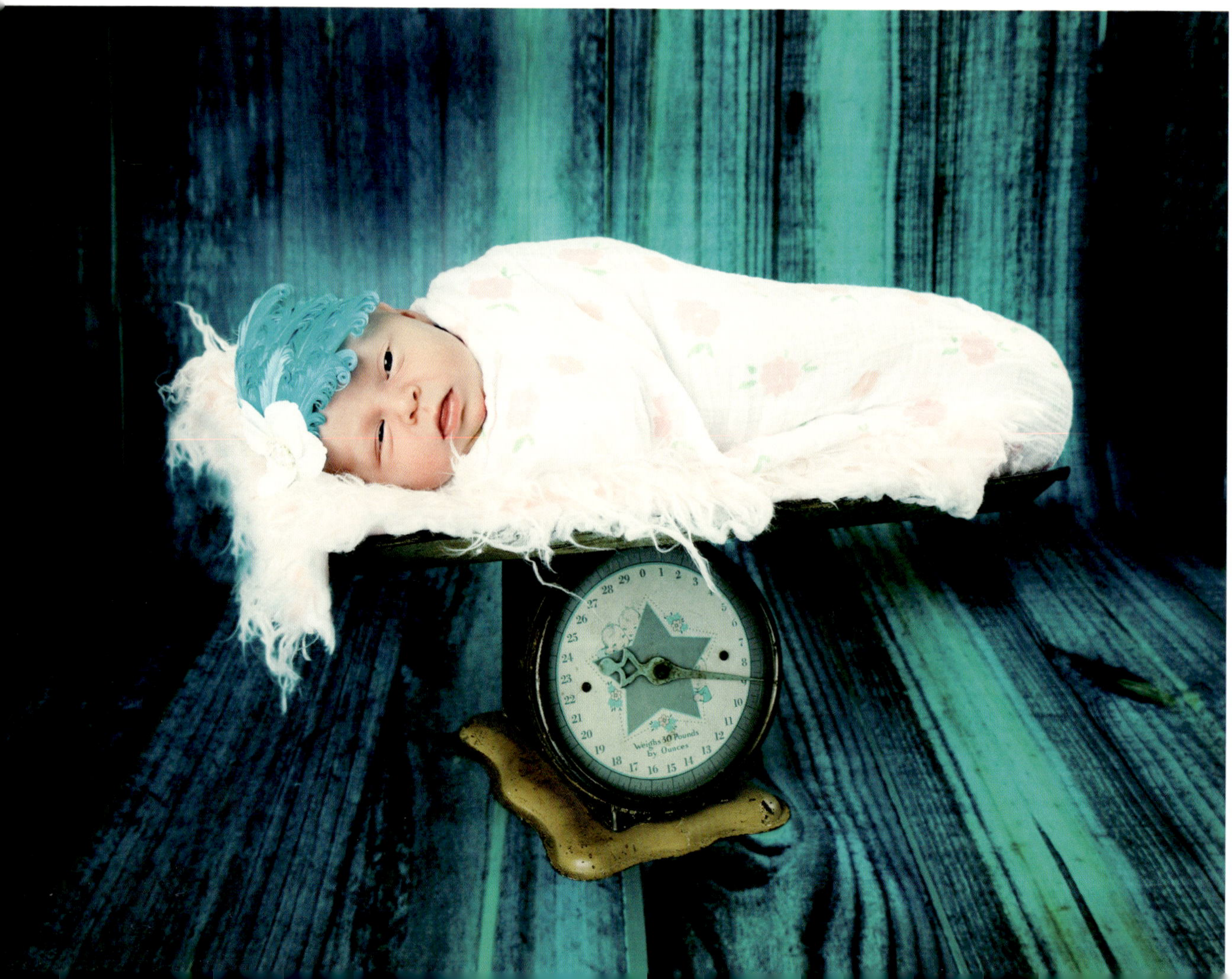

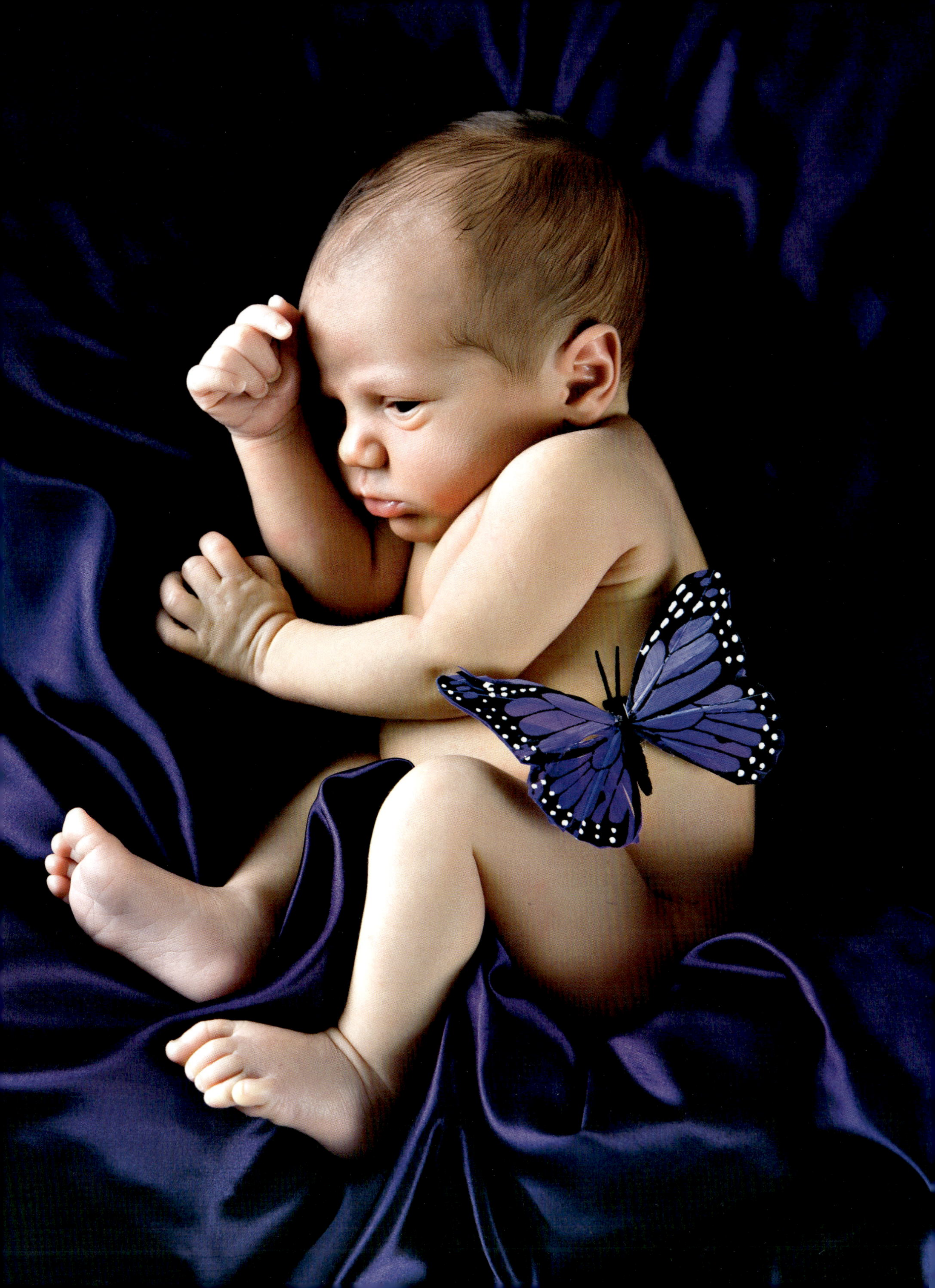

promotional idea or offer with a deadline will give them a reason to call. There are various methods to sending out birthday cards, from buying preprinted ones in bulk, to having custom ones printed through your lab.

A company called Send out Cards (www.sendoutcards.com/mimikacooney) offers a fantastic way to send an individualized card (you can add a photo too). All it takes is a little time to set up; you input the client's name and contact details and the system will automate the printing and mailing for you.

Surprising Mom with an extra gift also goes a long way in spreading the love. Busy moms with babies and young children have very little time to do things for themselves. Provide play-date cards with Mom's contact info or an extra set of wallets with your info on the back. You may want to include a special offer coupon (e.g., $25 off or free wallets) for both the referring mom and the new friend as an incentive that gets them talking.

Once you have a client, you need to do everything you can to keep them. One of the first questions people ask when inquiring about professional photography services is "How much is your session fee?" The session fee covers the time and talent of the photographer and most definitely needs to be valued; however, there are times when forgoing the session fee and building it into your prices works in your favor. Pick a list of your top-paying clients who love what you do and who are loyal to your brand. They are the ones who should receive your special treatment.

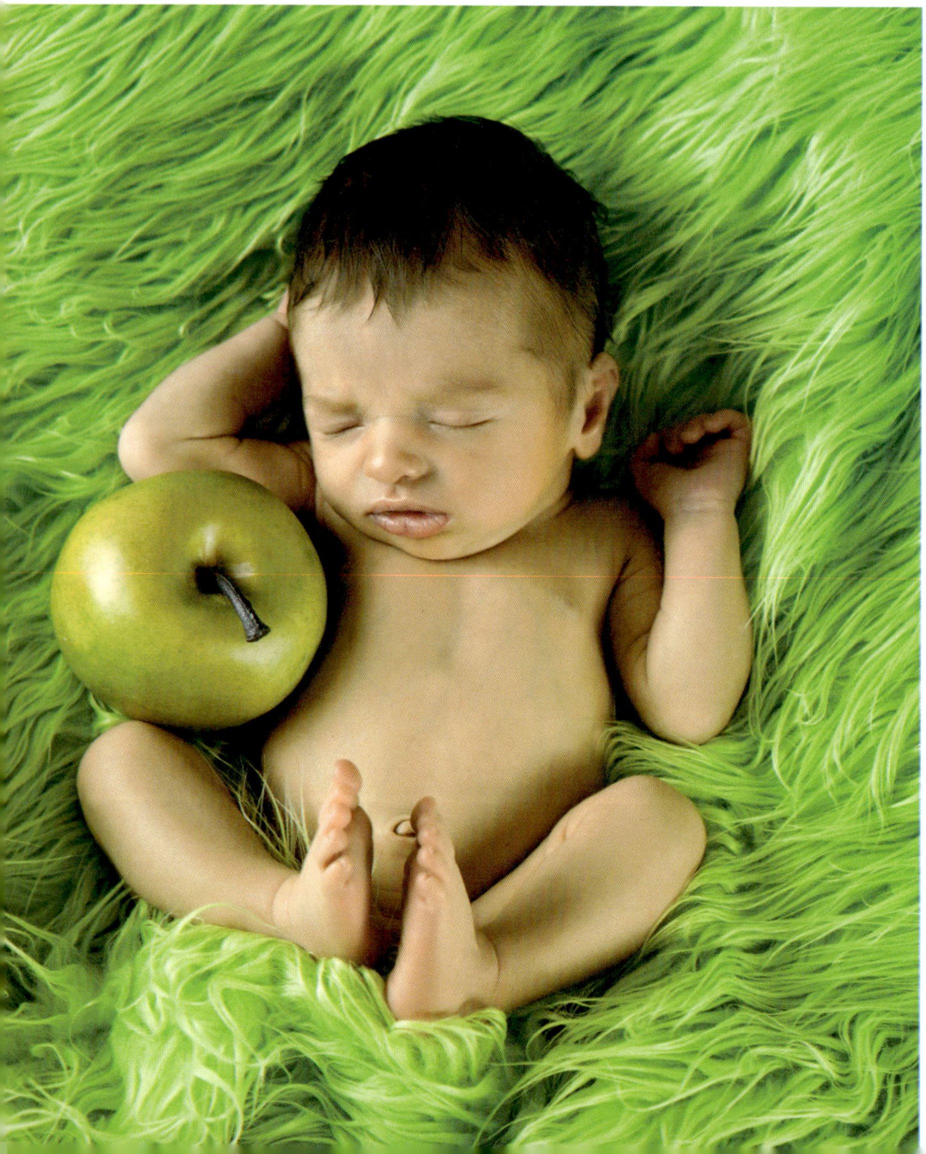

How Much Is Free?

When something is free, it has no value, right? Kind of like a McDonald's toy you get in the kids' meal, not worth a single pretty penny. Assuming that offering something for free is the best way to get your foot in the door is one of the biggest mistakes new business owners make. Allow me to explain.

Picture Sally. She got a DSLR for Christmas and she's excited to take photos of her kids, her dog, flowers, the sky,

◄ Your images have value. Don't give them away for free.

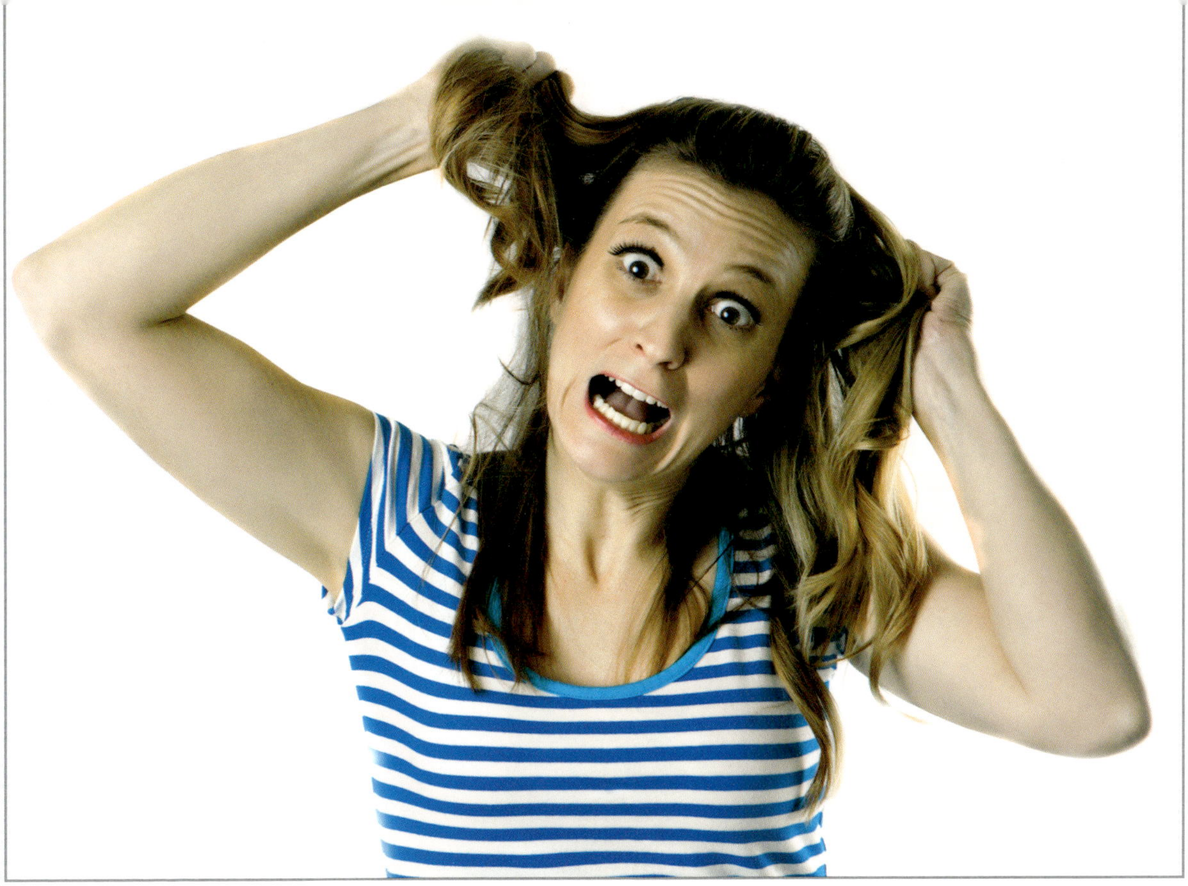

▲ Knowing your numbers will help you avoid unnecessary stress!

"I love taking pictures and it's so much fun. I should be charging for my time."

her pedicure, soccer games, kids having a water fight, her kids' birthday party, her friend's daughter, her friend's daughter's daughter, her son's karate class, her son's friend, her best friend's new baby, etc. Then all of a sudden, she gets noticed; someone says "Wow, your photos are great!" Her neighbor asks her to take photos of her kids. Soon the neighbor tells her friends about this great gal who has an awesome camera, loves photography, and takes great photos of babies and kids for nothing. Then Sally gets e-mails asking to take photos of people she doesn't know. The boost to her ego is awesome. She feels like a million bucks.

Sally goes on YouTube and starts watching all the how-to Photoshop videos, buys the software, and starts playing around. She buys twelve books on how to get started in photography, reads all the photography blogs she can find, spends hours on FlickR drooling over photos, and she starts getting really excited. All of a sudden, a light comes on: "I love taking pictures and it's so much fun. I should be charging for my time." She figures she loves photography, and there must be money in it. "Wow I get $50 just for 20 minutes of my time doing something I love? Awesome!"

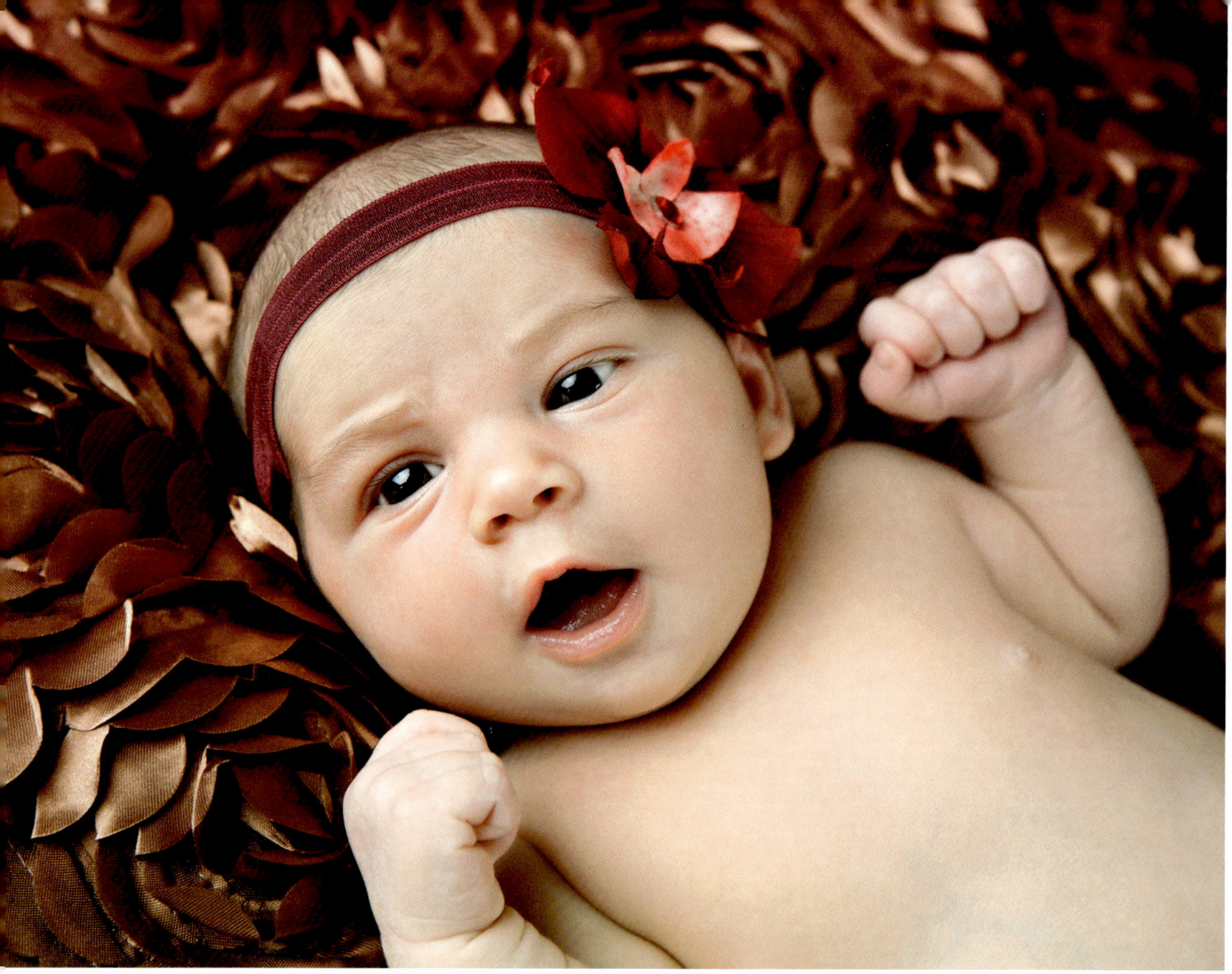

So Sally sets up a Facebook page, calls her business Photography by Sally, and invites her friends to "like" her page. The first post she adds is: "Free photo session. Bring your new baby, kids, family, and your dog. All images on CD $100." Sally waits for her e-mail to ping with the flood of inquiries. Then crickets. Nothing. She thinks,"Maybe it's too much. I should change it." So Sally changes the offer to "Free mini photo session. Bring your new baby, kids, family, and your dog. All images on CD $50." Slowly she gets an e-mail here, an e-mail there, then she starts to add another post, then another. All offering her magic formula of "free." That seems to work, right? Soon she has twelve sessions booked and has made a whopping $600.

Fast forward three months. Sally is sitting in front of her computer in her PJs, the house is a mess, the kids are hungry, the laundry is building up, and her hubby comes home from work and asks "What have you done all day?" Argh!

▲ Many of us undervalue our time when pricing our images.

"If you're serious about turning your photography passion into a fulfilling career, you have to charge for it."

Sally has been chained to her desk editing photo after photo to give all those clients the CD she promised with all of those wonderful images. Of course, she's still learning, so the lighting wasn't great and a bunch of images needed fixing in Photoshop.

After three months, she's spent over 60 hours on the editing alone. She's neglected her responsibilities. She's frazzled, she's fighting with her husband, her kids are running around like lunatics, and all she wants to do is scream and cry.

How much is free worth now? That "free" time she eagerly offered has cost her time, peace, and happiness. All of a sudden, the nostalgia of earning money from "her time" has faded and she's left feeling taken advantage of, overworked, and stressed out.

So, what now? What should Sally do to attract clients who will value her time so she can get paid her worth? It's simple. Although it seems like everyone is doing it, she should stop offering her time for free!

Many of us undervalue (or don't place a value on) our time. All the love in the world won't pay the bills, and if you're serious about turning your photography passion into a fulfilling career, you have to charge for it. My accountant, financial advisor, and business consultant all charge for their time. My expenses go well beyond a pencil and calculator. I have to charge enough to cover my costs.

If you are just photographing for fun, don't charge your subjects. Offer free services and enjoy the personal reward of building an awesome-looking portfolio. But, if you're serious about your business, here are three simple keys:

1. First, work out your cost of doing business. Include paying off your camera equipment, business insurance, gas, editing time (this is often forgotten), software, telephone, postage, photo printing costs, CD boxes, the babysitter, etc.
2. Consider offering a higher perceived value, such as a gift with purchase. When you buy cosmetics at a department store, they are never listed as 50 percent off or free. Instead, you often get a gift when you buy something bigger. When you have an offer like, "Buy one CD and get the second at $XX," "Buy a kid's spring session and get a fall family session for half price," or "Invest over $500 and we will 'gift' you the digital files," you can really increase your average sales without cutting into your profits.
3. Think about charging more and delegating the things you hate doing. Delegating your retouching to a student or online company will cost far less than doing it yourself. Think about it—you could be out shooting and earning another $500 per client instead of wasting your time on a $10-per-hour job.

"My expenses go well beyond a pencil and calculator. I have to charge enough to cover my costs."

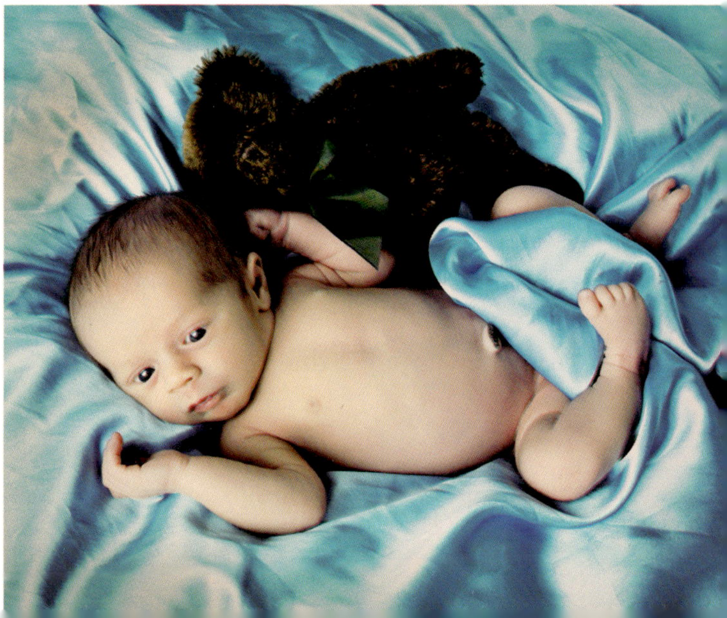

3. Marketing and Promotions

"Having a child is surely the most beautifully irrational act that two people in love can commit."—Bill Cosby

Why Marketing Won't Get You Clients

We've all heard it from the business books and marketing gurus, you have to do some marketing to bring in business. Marketing, marketing, marketing should equal clients, clients, clients, but it doesn't work that way.

Before you get your knickers in a knot, let me explain. This makes me think of Paris. I recently visited the city with my mom, and even though it was a cold, one-day whistle-stop tour, it left me wanting more. If New York is built for men, Paris is built for women!

Every street has gorgeous architecture with curvy lines and ornate details. It's a feast for the eyes. I love history; knowing that hundreds of years ago, people who shaped history walked the same streets makes me giddy. There is no need to drive; walking the streets is the best way to appreciate the city.

Of course, the street on which the designer shopping mall is situated is any woman's dream come true! My mom and I had to saunter into Cartier and Prada to feel what it's like to shop like a celebrity (okay, minus the budget, so it was more like window shopping).

When I saw the Eiffel Tower for the first time, I felt like I had dropped into an Audrey Hepburn movie. The sense of wonder and mystique is effervescent in Paris. I can't wait to go back when the flowers are in bloom. I'm sure it will be even more beautiful!

I've never seen a "Come visit Paris!" advertisement. When I mentioned to my friends that I was planning my visit, they immediately piped up with advice like, "Make sure you see the Eiffel Tower from the vantage point of the Trocadero—it's breathtaking! You have to drink cappuccino at one of those quaint coffee shops. Remember to wait until dark to see the Tower lit up." The advice and tips were free flowing. Everyone I talked to was enthusiastic about the city.

I know why it's called the "City of Love." You see lots of romantic couples walking hand in hand, but more than that, you fall in love with the city's essence. Everything from the architecture, to the scenery, to the art makes it a city worth visiting more than once. So why is it that Paris is not marketed as a must-see destination? Why don't we see huge billboards in New York's Times Square saying "Viva la France!" I think it's because Paris sells itself. People talk about it, they share their favorite experiences, and they are loyal to the "brand" that is Paris.

In my view, Paris didn't have to do a hard sell on me to visit because I really wanted to go. With all the good things I'd heard, do you

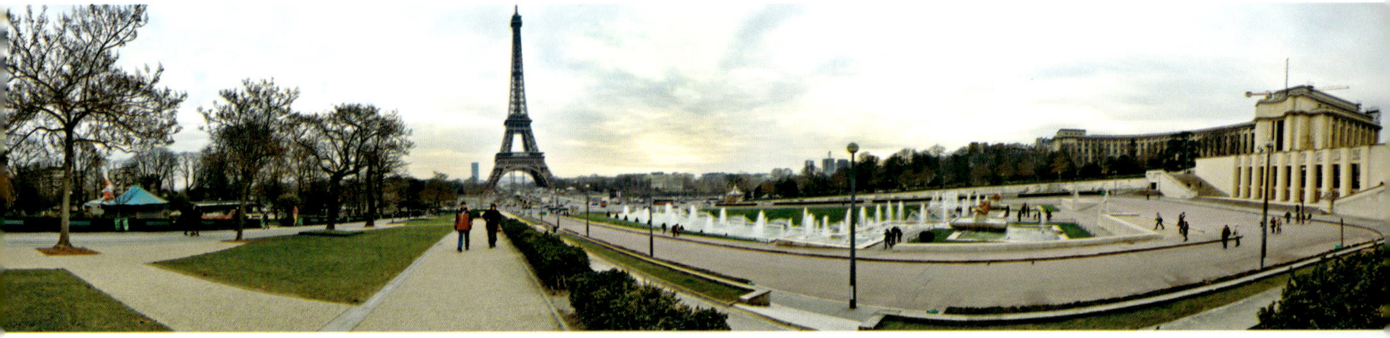

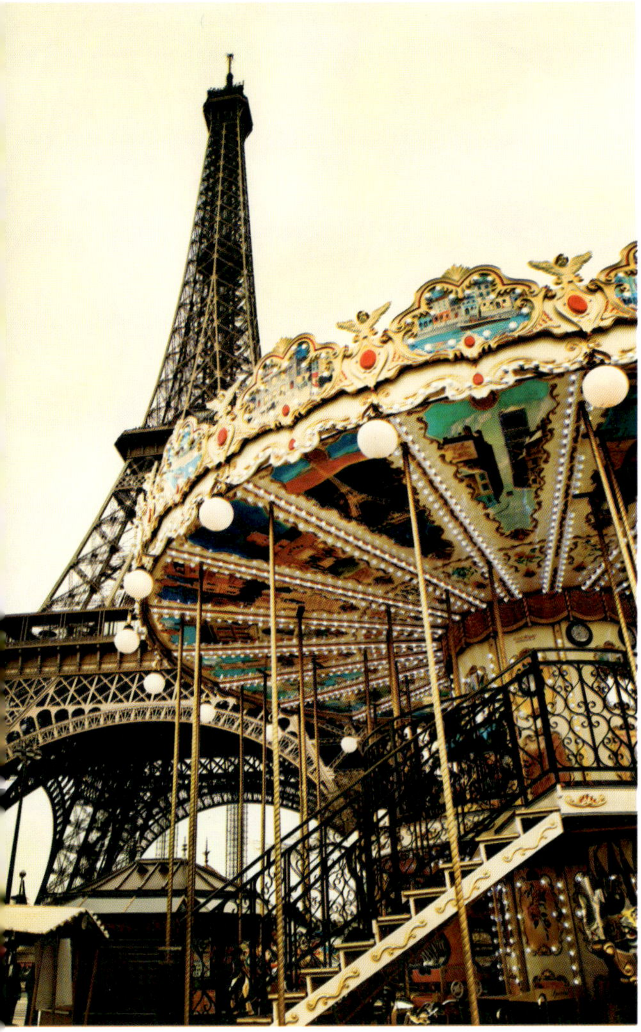

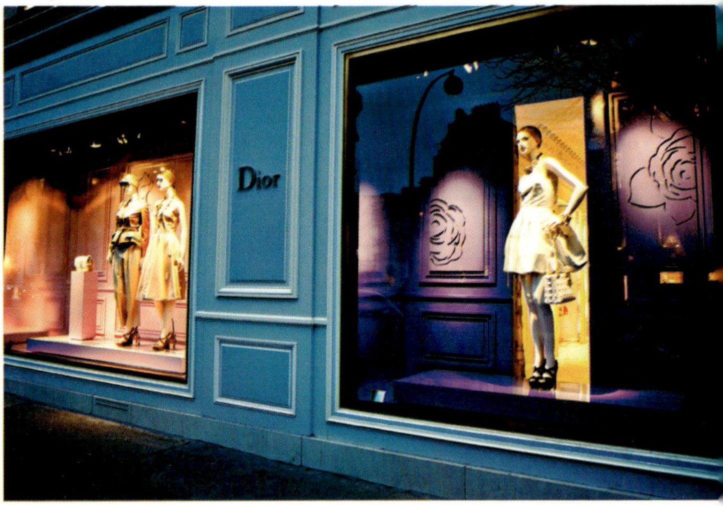

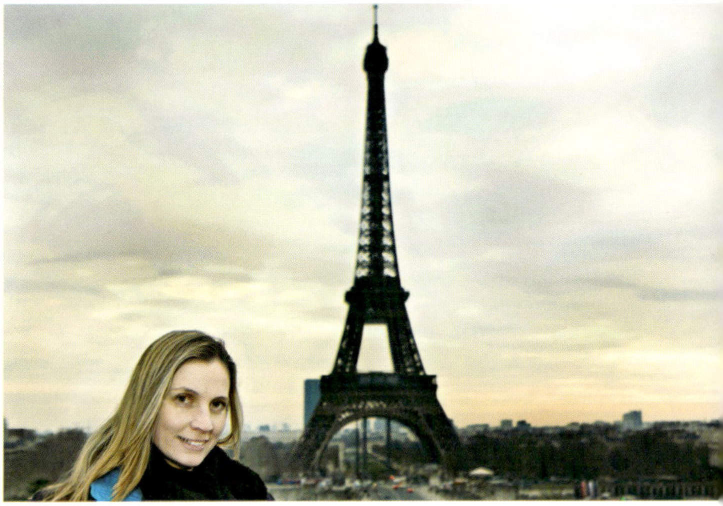

know what convinced me? It was the stories interwoven into the experiences that resonated with me the most.

My friend had told me about watching the sunrise over the Eiffel Tower while studying art for the semester. Once, I heard about a guy who proposed to his girlfriend on the Lover's Bridge and they "locked" their love with a painted

▲ My first visit to Paris was magical.

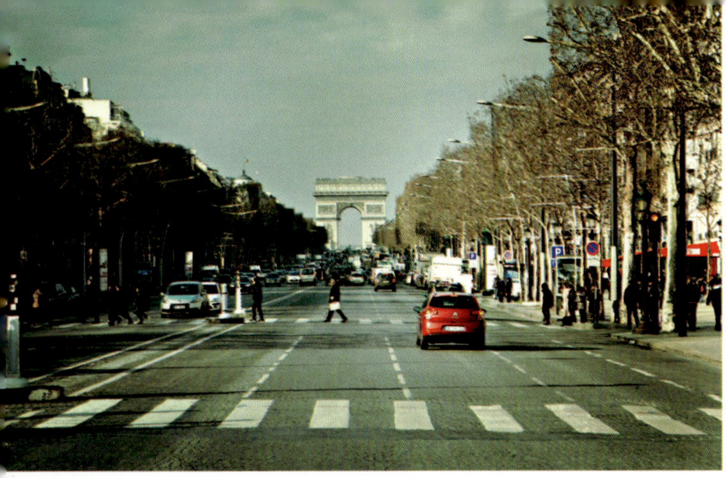

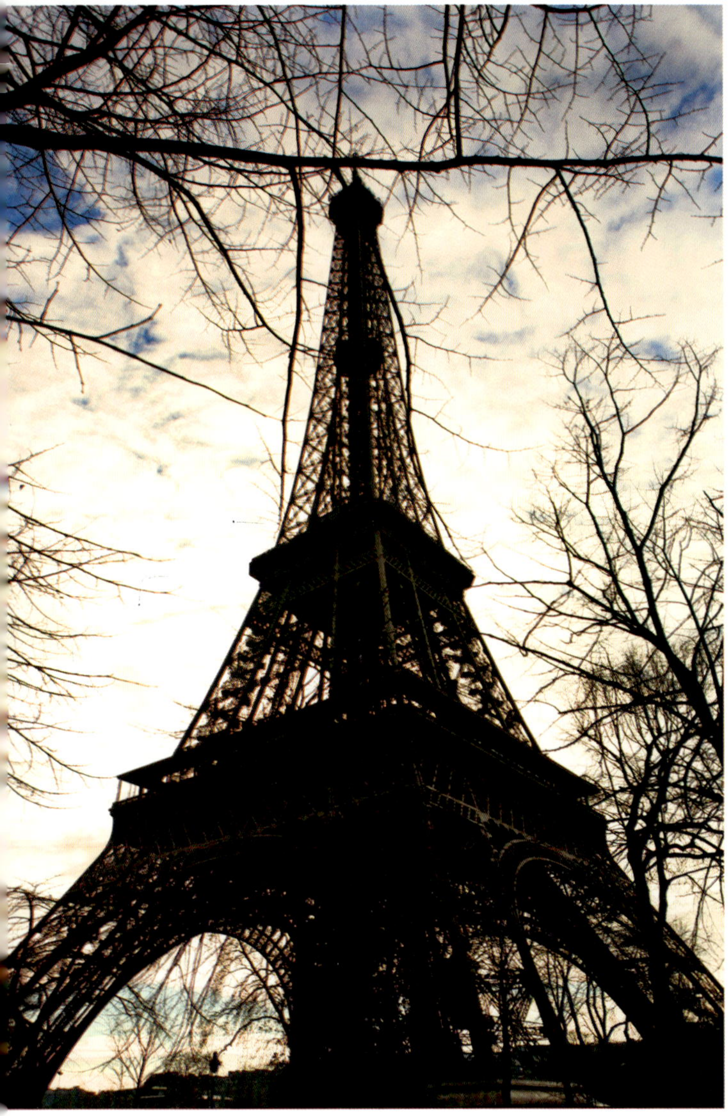

▲ Take your customers on a journey.

padlock on the fence—and then threw away the key. Another friend of mine stayed up all night to catch the train to Paris just to eat breakfast at this little cafe that "had *the best* omelettes." It's the story, the journey, and the experience that makes people remember and share the details of their journey.

Author Seth Godin has a book titled *All Marketers ~~Are Liars~~ Tell Stories* (Penguin LLC USA, 2012). When it was first published, it didn't sell well. People didn't respond to the title *All Marketers Are Liars.* Who wants to admit they've been hoodwinking customers? Only after the title was adapted to include "Tell Stories" did the general public "get it," and it went on to become a bestseller.

Michael Port, author of *Book Yourself Solid* (Wiley, 2010), says that marketing merely creates awareness and starts the conversation. It's what we do after they are aware of us that gets the business. Once we have a client's attention, they are giving us a chance to gain their trust to earn their business further down the road.

In my opinion, we need to approach our businesses like a Paris experience. We need to build the story and emphasize the feelings surrounding what we do so people can't help but talk about us. Just as we would with a romantic relationship, we need to go slow, then go steady, then pop the big question.

Tips for Effective Marketing

- Make the connection: Offer something of value that will make your customers' lives easier, happier, and more enjoyable. Only then do you have their permission to continue the conversation (e.g., offer a free download).
- Take them out for coffee: Provide more value by showing that you care. Offer tips, advice, and give them something to talk about

(e.g., give a new mom tips for caring for a newborn).

- Ask them on a date: Offer your services by helping to make it easy to take action (e.g., provide downloadable what-to-wear guides to help them prepare for the session).
- Ask them to get married: Make booking a session easy by removing any obstacles (e.g., offer a link to your online booking schedule).
- Make it a big wedding: Treat your customers with care and respect—they are not just a number or a check (e.g., give them a welcome kit with chocolate or a gift).
- Stay married: Keep in touch and keep the relationship going. Never assume that if they don't respond immediately they don't have a need. Timing is of the essence. Stay in touch by publishing a monthly newsletter—you

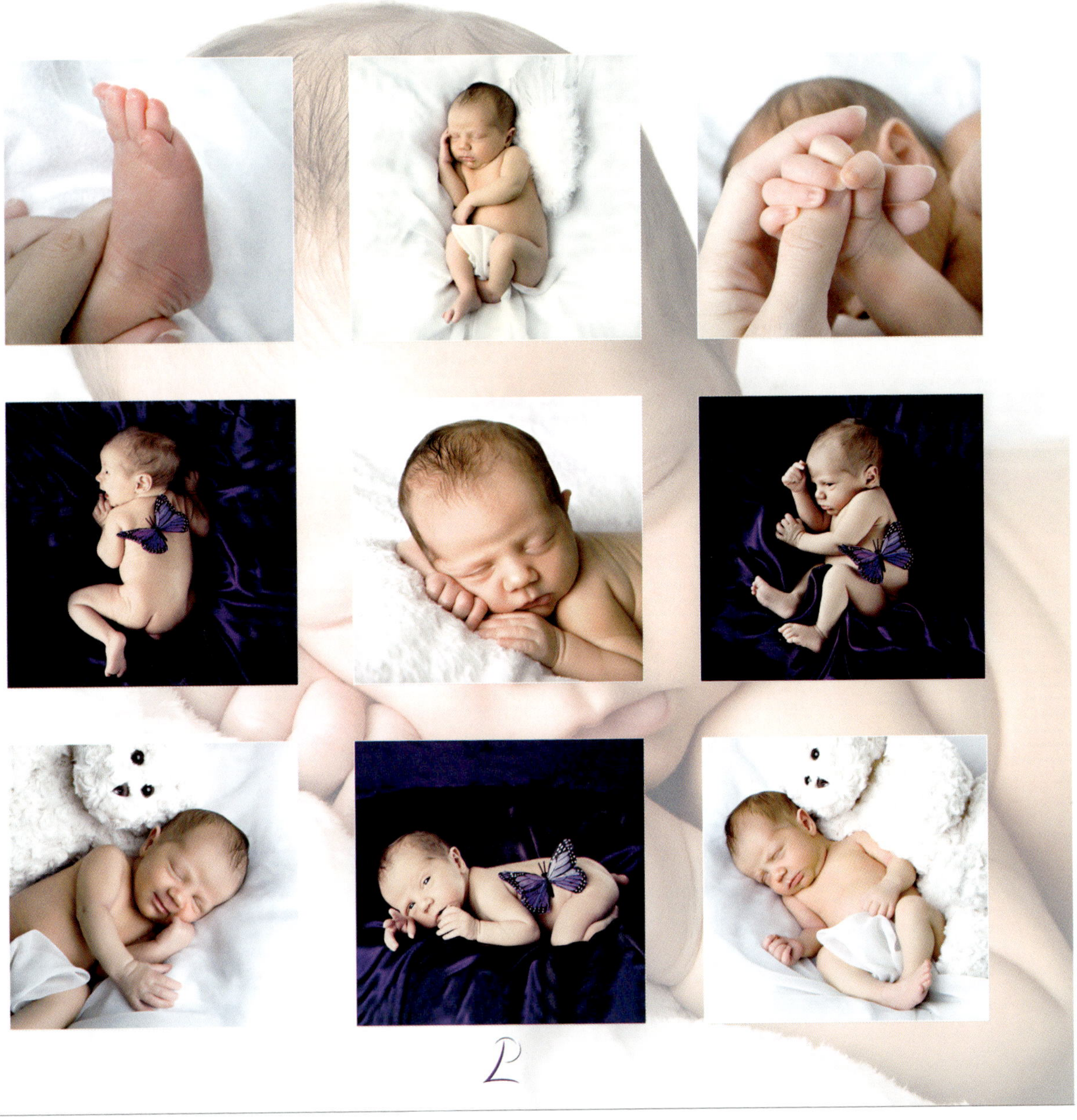

A good business leader identifies their market.

never know when the time is right for your customer.

So before your relationship with your customers goes south, weave in a story with everything you do and they will have no option but to stay in love and gush, gush, gush!

The Bell Curve and Buying Behavior

In marketing, there is a well-known sociological model of a buyer's behavior commonly referred to as the "bell curve." It's based on the technology-adoption life cycle, which was originally published in 1957 by Joe M. Bohlen, George M. Beal, and Everett M. Rogers at Iowa State University. Originally applicable to agriculture and home economics, it was designed to track the purchase patterns of hybrid seed corn by farmers.

According to Wikipedia, "The technology-adoption life cycle model describes the adoption or acceptance of a new product or innovation, according to the demographic and psychological characteristics of defined adopter groups. The process of adoption over time is typically illustrated as a classical normal distribution or bell curve."

The model classifies people into different groups based on their adoption and behavior toward making purchasing decisions. It defines the first group of people to use a new product as "innovators," followed by "early adopters," then "early" and "late majority," and finally, the "laggards."

How this relates to us as photographers is important, especially when you are starting out in business. Different people adapt to change differently, and a good business leader identifies each group quickly so that their business model is aimed toward working with early adopters. The remaining populace will follow, and the consensus is to simply ignore the rest who will never come along anyway.

What Does This Mean for Me? When building your photography business, you want to put all your promotional efforts into attracting a client who can see your vision, not one who demands that you create what they envision. If you go after everyone with a pulse and a credit card, you will end up trying to please everyone. This will result in pleasing no one, and you will burn out.

Even when you haven't got a long track record or a comprehensive portfolio to show off, thinking about where you want to go will help you stay on the right track. Early adopters are willing to take a risk (especially if you're new) if basic questions are answered satisfactorily. If you can show confidence, competence, and satisfy their inherent needs, the early adopters will become your champions and talk about you.

As soon as early adopters make a move and say "Hey, check these guys out—they are great," the early majority moves in right behind them like sheep following a shepherd. As soon as the early majority moves, the late majority follow—they won't want to miss the party.

Then we have the laggards. They're often powerful, opinionated, well prepared, and smart. Their major distinction is that they are stubborn and ask way too many questions, even after the early adopters have moved in. The laggards rarely enroll fully in something new and untested, or a major change. They drag their feet and often protest all the way. In my opinion, the laggards should be ignored because there is no pleasing them. Every hour invested in them is wasted.

Your business survival and the ability to attain your dreams depends on your ability to

➤ Show confidence and competence and satisfy your clients' needs.

"When starting out, or when changing direction or genre, you need to show potential clients what your vision is."

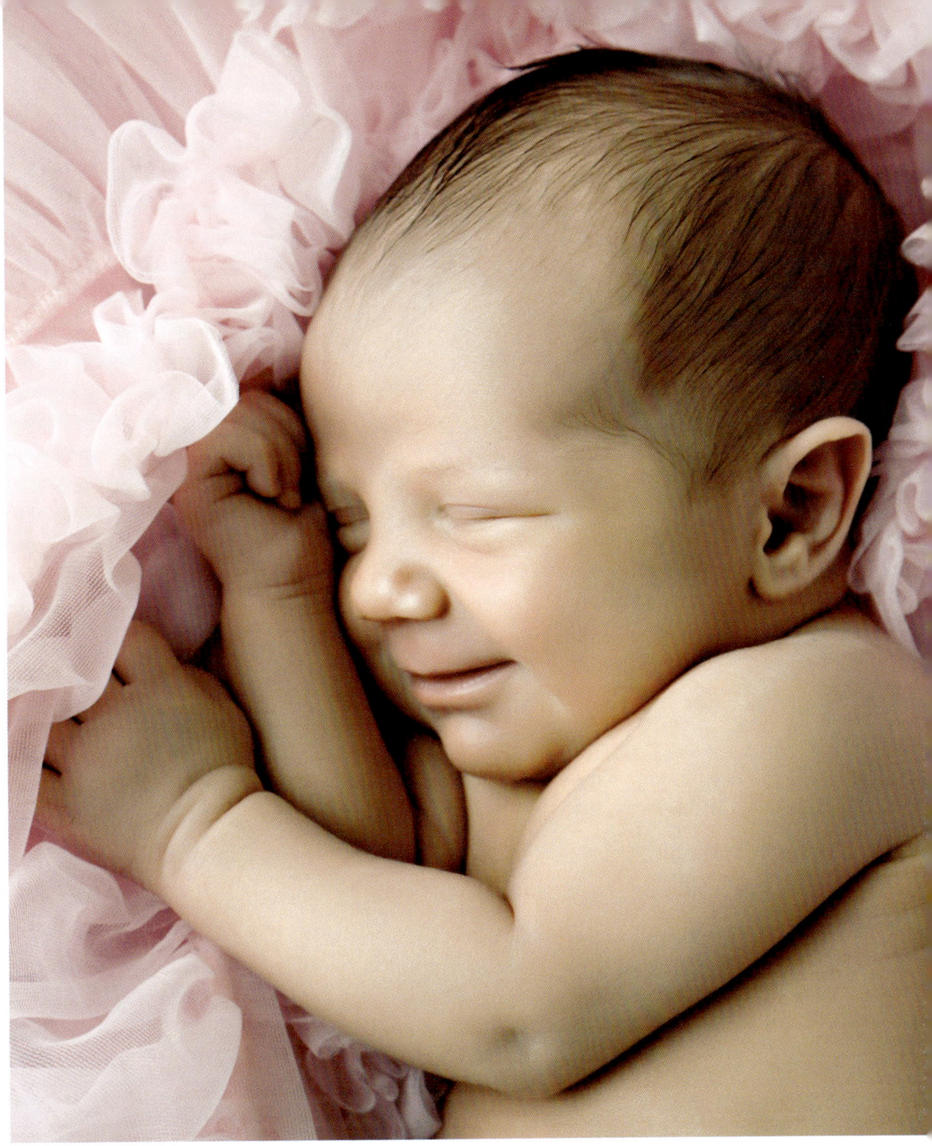

distinguish the laggards from the early adopters as quickly as possible. Once you've done so, you can pour all of your energy into finding the early adopters. When the early adopters move, everyone you need moves right behind them. Without them, your efforts are futile.

Portfolio Building

When starting out, or when changing direction or genre, you need to show potential clients what your vision is. Before the telephone starts ringing and the referrals begin racking up, you need to put your efforts into building a portfolio that will attract the right kind of clients.

Too often a new photographer who starts a business is taken up in the excitement of doing something they love. They start off

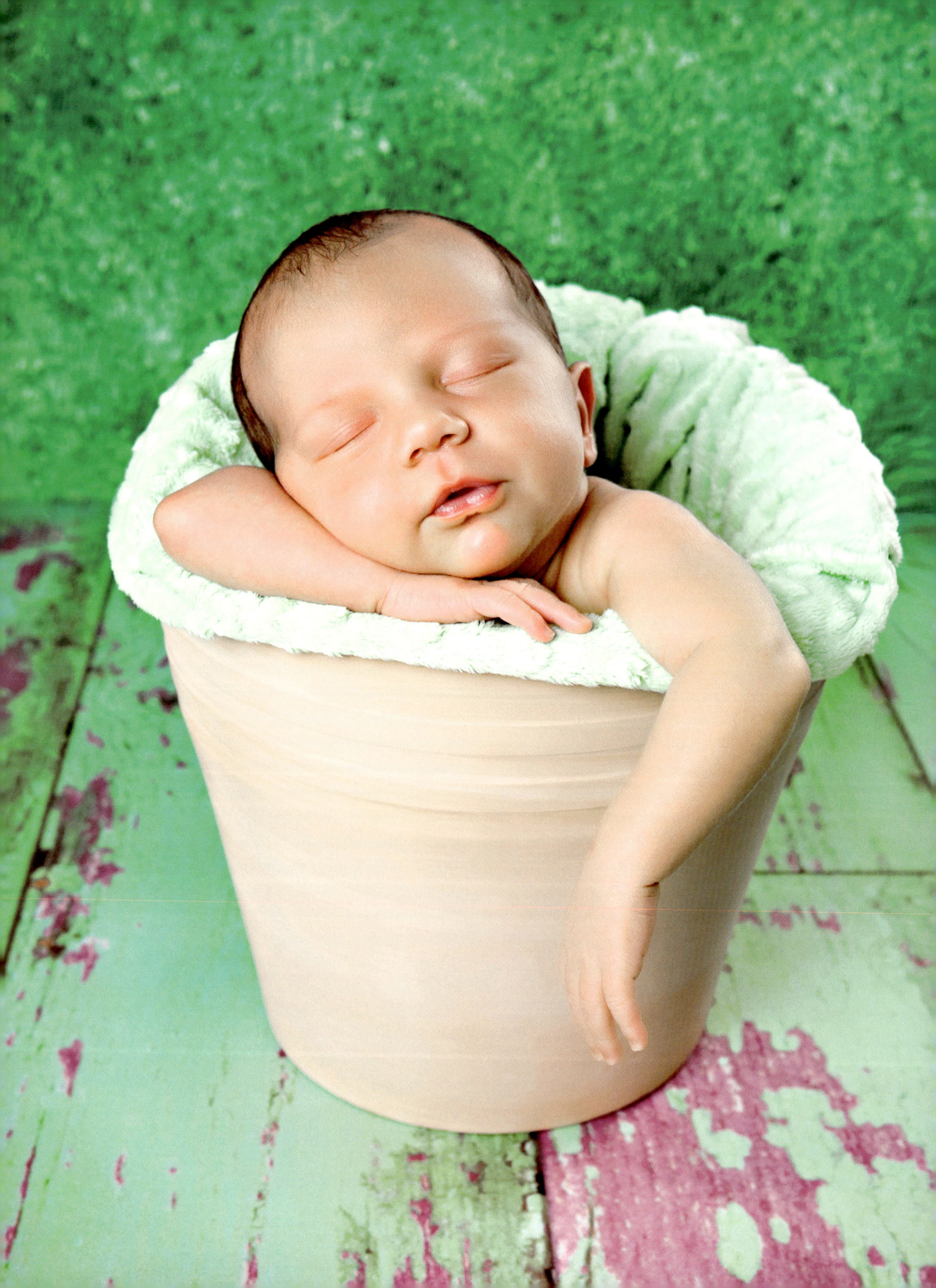

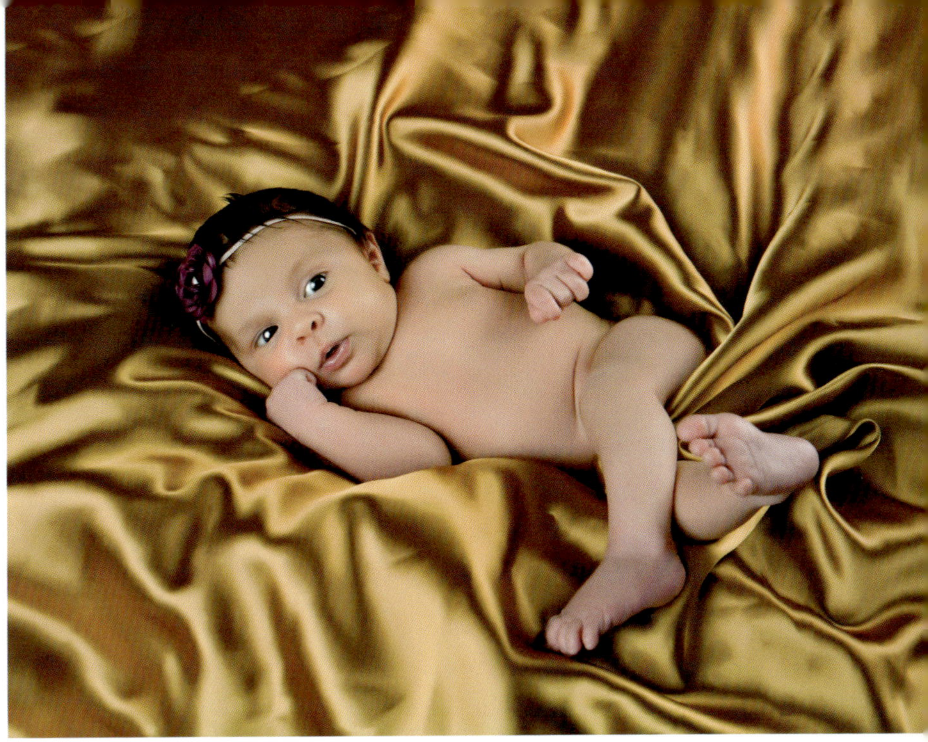

◀ ▶ Shoot for your own artistic vision, and your clients will love the results.

charging peanuts just to break into the market. It's only for fun, right? Well no—not if you're serious about your photography as a business.

Offering your services for free and offering them to build your portfolio are two different concepts, not to be confused. When you lack confidence in your work and want to attract any kind of client, you inevitably take anything that comes your way and charge little or nothing for your efforts. When you say "free" or "discounted," you tell your clients:

a. I'm cheap and not very good.
b. I'm cheap, not very good, and lack confidence.
c. I'm cheap, not very good, lack confidence, and I'm not to be taken seriously.

This makes it difficult for you to charge more for your services in the future without scaring off or losing clients. It also brings down the overall perceived value of professional photography, and who wants to compete on being the cheapest?

Instead, say to your potential clients, "I'm excited to start my photography business and I'm busy working on building my portfolio. When I'm up and running I will be charging $XYZ for my services. In the meantime, I would love it if I could photograph your baby as a model. I have some great ideas, lighting to test, and props I'm excited to try out. Would you be interested in modeling for me in exchange for a free print/gift voucher, etc.?" What this tells your potential client is:

a. I'm an artist with a vision.
b. I'm an artist with a vision and I'm serious about my business.
c. I'm an artist with a vision, I'm serious about my business, and I'm going to be successful.

Five Tips for Nursery Portraits

Here is an article I wrote for a baby magazine geared toward expectant parents. It's on my website now, and I offer it to parents to help them prepare for the session. When we educate our clients with the why, they will want to hire us for the how. Showing them examples of what their wall art can look like plants the seeds for higher sales. People buy what you show, so show big to sell big!

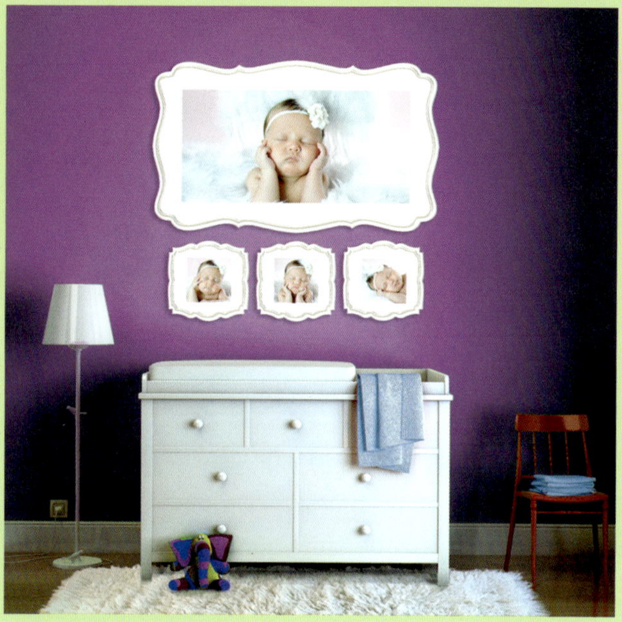

▲ Show, don't tell. Give customers guidance and products to fall in love with.

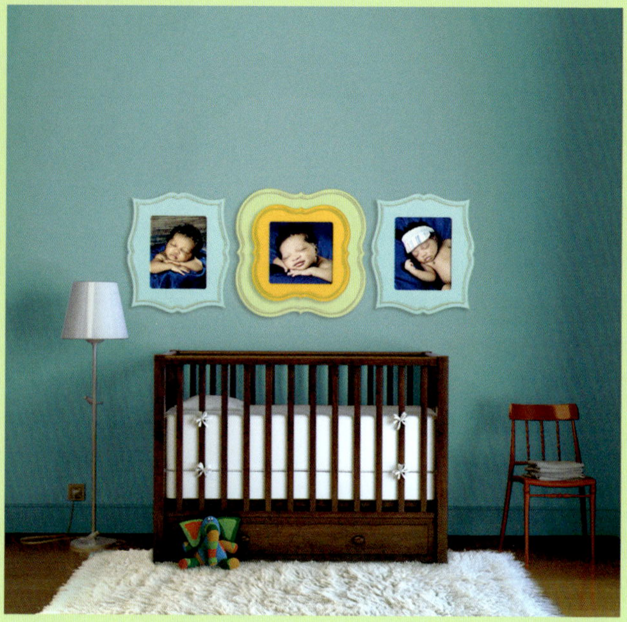

▲ Discover your inner designer.

Every first-time-pregnant mom knows the feelings of excitement and trepidation when waiting for her baby to arrive. The energy it takes just to get through the day with swollen feet and backache can be overwhelming. The thought of trawling the shopping mall to find pieces for a baby nursery that looks like it came straight from the pages of a catalog seems almost impossible!

The nursery layette list can seem overwhelming considering the sheer volume of options available. Crib styles and bedding, curtains, gliders, nursing accessories, diaper bags, safety equipment, baby clothing, the list goes on and on. When browsing, the options can be a little overwhelming. Fret not. With a little bit of thought and planning, you will be on your way to discovering your inner designer.

Consider your own family story as heirloom wall art that you will display to illustrate the story of your baby. Forget the impersonal poster or painting; making your wall space personal and meaningful will make Baby's nursery a place of warmth and give it a sense of serenity. With every diaper change and every rock on the glider, you can enjoy the memories of Baby's passing stages with portraits of Baby as they zoom through their first year. You will appreciate it even more as Baby starts to talk and point to "baby." Your heart will well with so much love you never thought possible!

Tip #1: Capture the Belly and the Baby

Treasure every stage in your parenting journey. You may think you look and feel awful, but your pregnant form is beautiful. You've sacrificed a lot to bring your precious bundle into the world. You should celebrate your pregnancy by having professional maternity portraits taken. This is the first step in telling the story of your baby's beginning. The second important step is to book your newborn portrait session while you are still pregnant, as the most ideal time to capture your newborn is when he/she is still itty-bitty at 4 to 14 days old.

At this age, when Baby is snoozing, your photographer can position him/her safely in artistic poses.

Tip #2: Create Your Own Inspiration Board

The saying is "Men are from Google+, women are from Pinterest." I get so much inspiration from the Pinterest community. I've found ideas I would have never thought of before. Using Pinterest to compile magazine ads, newspaper clippings, fabric swatches, paper samples, candy wrappers, gift wrap, etc., will help you develop a style for the nursery, rather than a theme. You can create an eclectic mix of your own loves from elements that bring you joy. Tell your photographer your style choice so he/she can incorporate the same color tones during the photo session with accenting fabrics, props, and backdrops (e.g., laying Baby on a pink blanket will perfectly blend with the pink accents in her nursery).

Tip #3: Pick a Color Palette

Take a trip to your local hardware store and pick out paint swatches that make you smile! Whether you're getting dressed or designing your room, remember odd numbers are a treat. Color sets in three shades are complementary, any more looks messy. Think light, midtone, and dark for the best results. In art terms, choosing complementary colors from the color wheel help to blend the design of a room. Popular matches are pink and green, yellow and blue, green and yellow, blue and brown, pink and brown, chocolate with purple and pink, navy with light blue and brown, green with white and tan, two tones of pink with cream, turquoise with white and navy, etc.

Tip #4: Pick Your Style of Furniture

You may be surprised to know that custom furniture orders can take 8 to 16 weeks to arrive. Depending on the manufacturer and style, the availability may vary greatly, so order early to avoid having Baby arrive before his/her furniture. If you prefer a contemporary look, consider a plain white crib, dresser, and changing table. If you like something more traditional with darker tones, you may like espresso furniture. With either choice, you will have the basis to pick the finish of your framed wall art pieces. I advise my clients to consider their décor when choosing frame colors and styles so that their wall art will complement the overall style of their room. Dark-wood frames look gorgeous hung above a

▼ Matching color schemes creates a complete look.

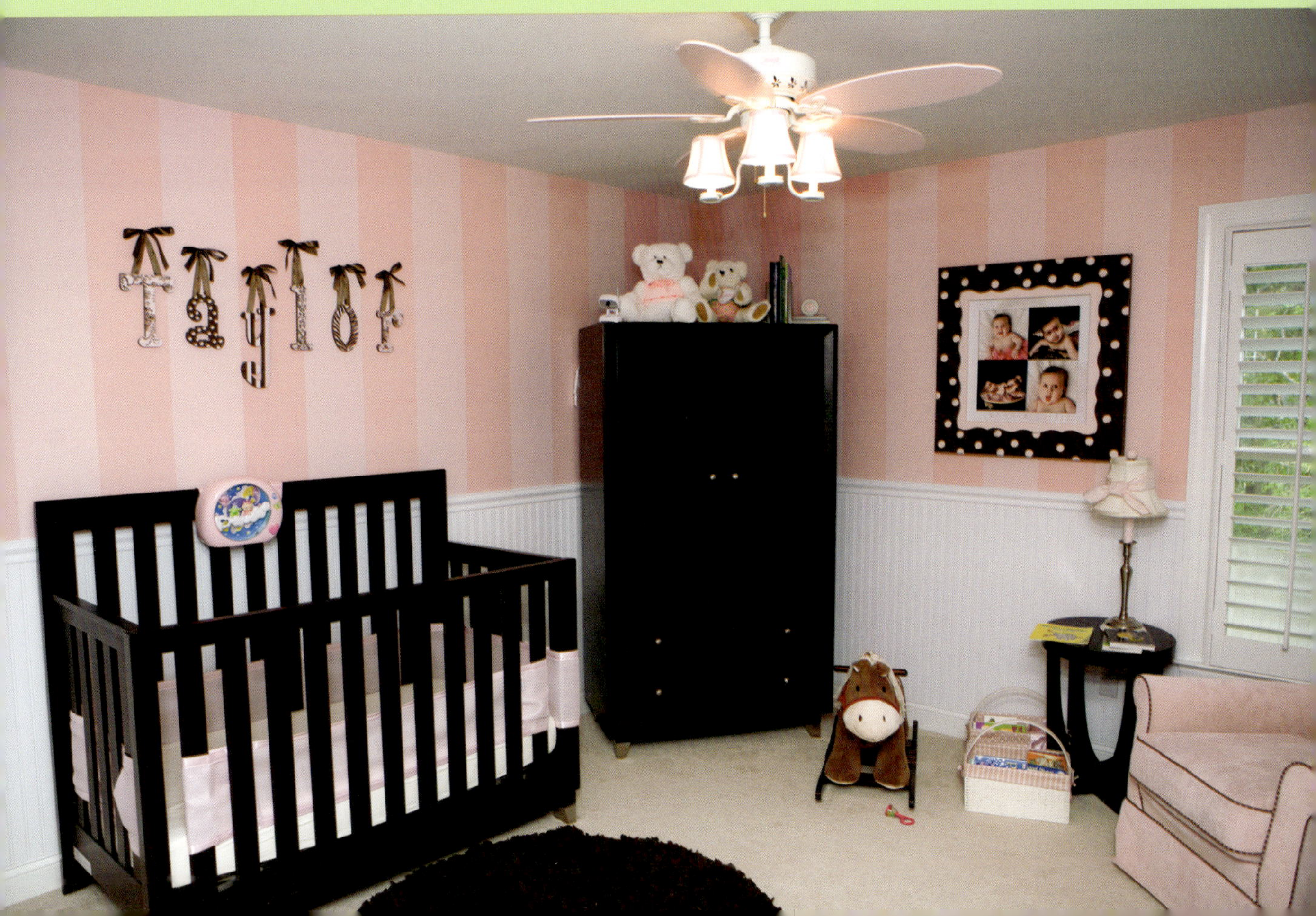

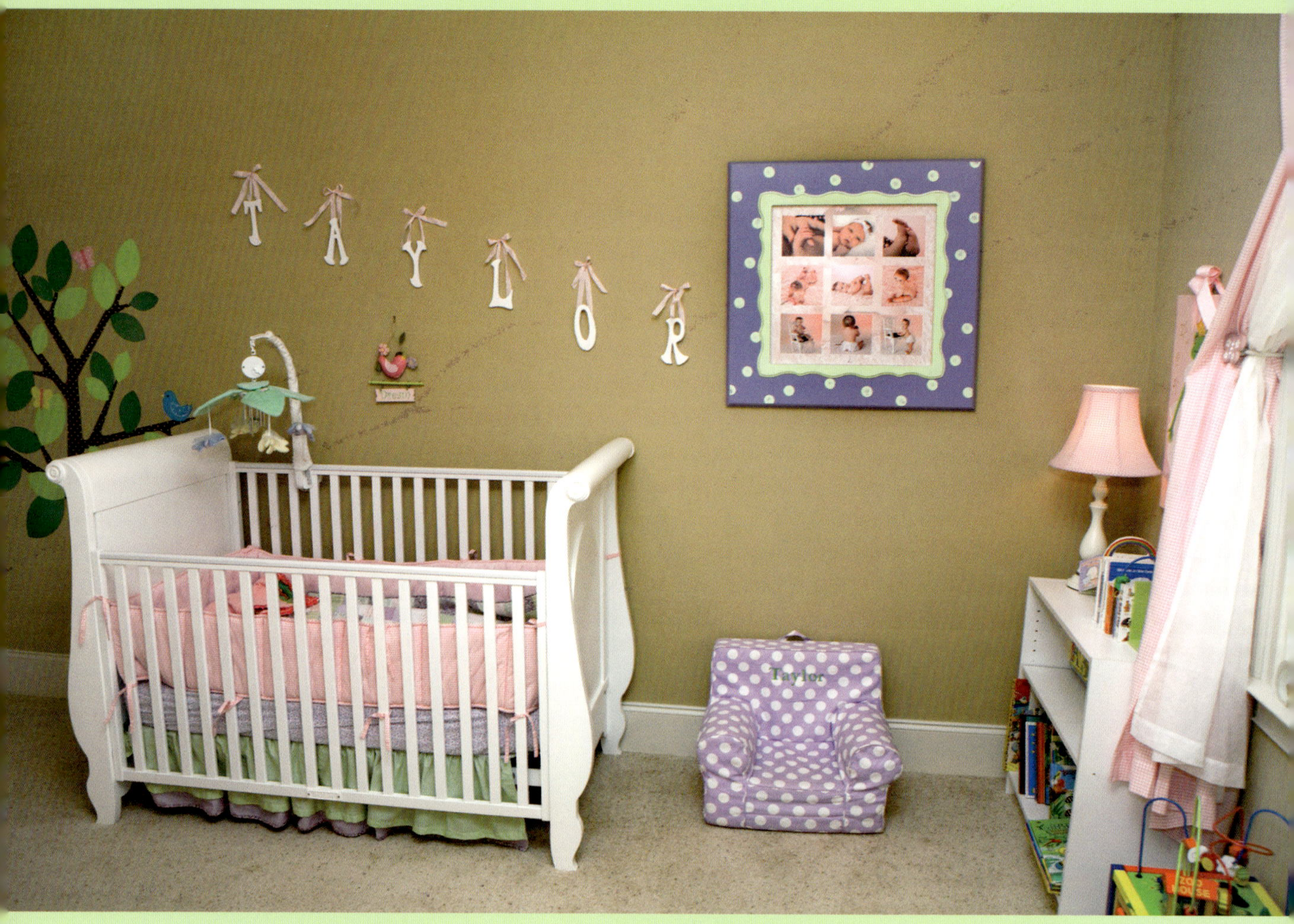

Match frames with the furniture for a harmonious look.

dark-wood crib, just like a stained-white frame looks beautiful hung above a whitewashed changing table. An even better option is to have their frames painted to match their color scheme.

Tip #5: Why Size Matters

In design terms, your wall is considered a negative space that "swallows" a portrait. An 8x10-inch image looks big up close, but when you hang it on the wall and take three steps back, it loses its impact. If you can't see the color of your subject's eyes, it's too small! This is why a larger-sized wall portrait is needed to create a wow factor. Measure your empty wall from left to right and take down the measurements. Make sure that the portrait size you choose will cover at least $^2/_3$ of the wall space. Also, avoid using a frame that is too thick for the size of the portrait, as the frame, not the image, will take center stage. A good rule of thumb is your frame should be $^1/_5$ of your overall portrait size.

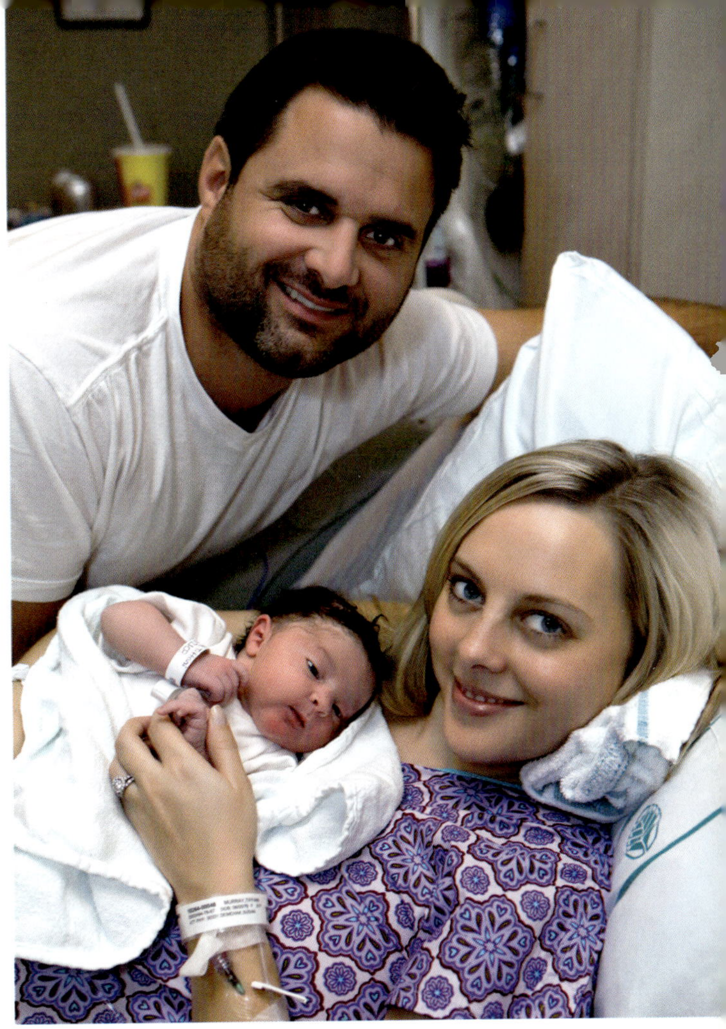

➤ In-hospital portraits capture the emotion of Baby's first hours of life.

Marketing and Promotional Ideas

In-Hospital Portraits. An in-hospital birth service is a collection of images of Baby's birth and their very first moments of life. Sometimes Mom asks us to photograph the birthing process, but more often I'm asked to document the first few hours of Baby's life. My goal is to capture fleeting moments so that the new parents can focus on their new arrival. I record the emotion, the happy tears and joyful laughter, the milestones of cutting the cord, the printing of Baby's first tiny footprints, Grandma and Grandpa's first glimpse of their grandchild—all the things Mom misses during her recovery directly after delivery.

I've been offering an in-hospital birth service for years, and I am often asked how I approach this type of service. Births are unpredictable by nature; therefore, planning is almost impossible. I work closely with the parents and keep my cell phone at hand for a last-minute rush to the hospital. It's up to you to determine your availability and the number of these bookings you're willing to commit to. I prefer one per month so I that I do not overcommit myself.

It's imperative that you plan ahead and have the parents sign a service contract and model release that gives you permission to post the image collection online. Also, make sure your clients notify their healthcare providers that you are being invited to attend the birth. Some hospitals have strict visitation policies, especially within the first few hours of recovery, so do your homework first.

Offering your services between 7:00AM and 7:00PM is reasonable if you have your own family to take care of. You're not required to

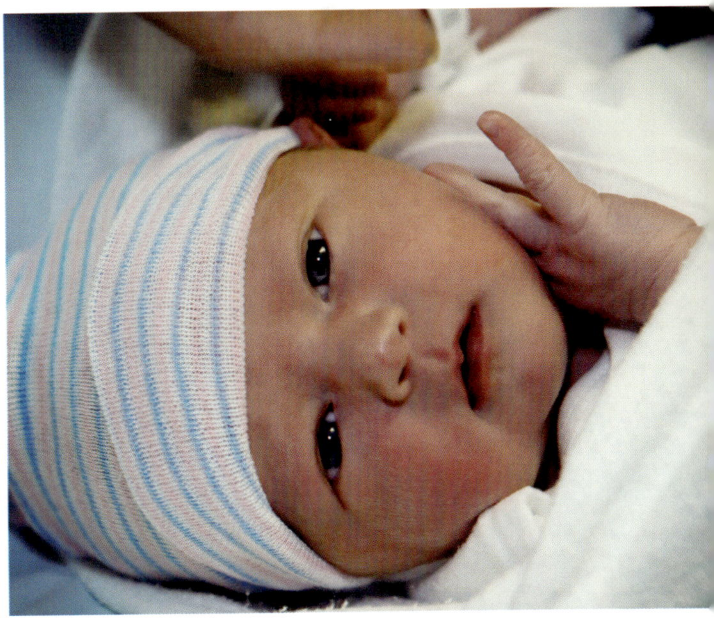

▲ Try to capture the first glimpse of baby.

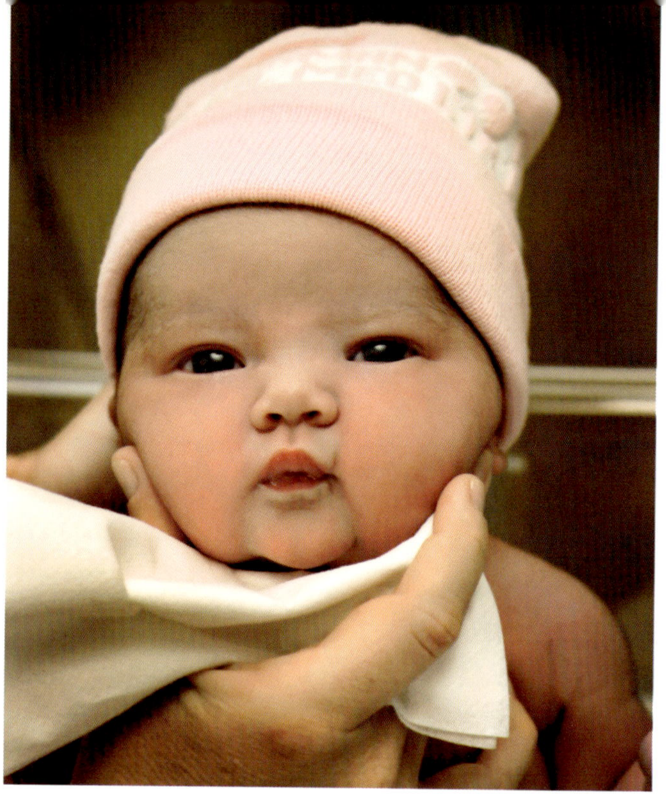

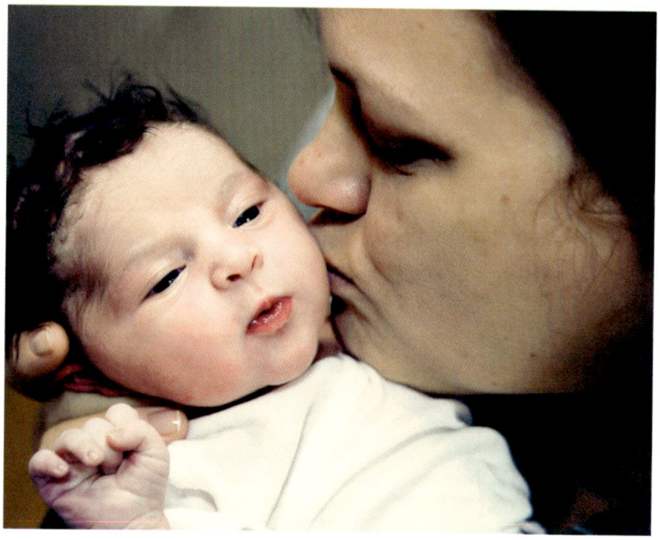

◄ (top) Make sure to get permission from the parents before taking photos.
◄ (bottom) Capture photos of a grandparent meeting their grandchild for the first time.

▼ (top) Make it a point to photograph the newborn within the first twenty-four hours.
▼ (bottom) Offer quick turnaround so that you can benefit from the excitement of Baby's birth.

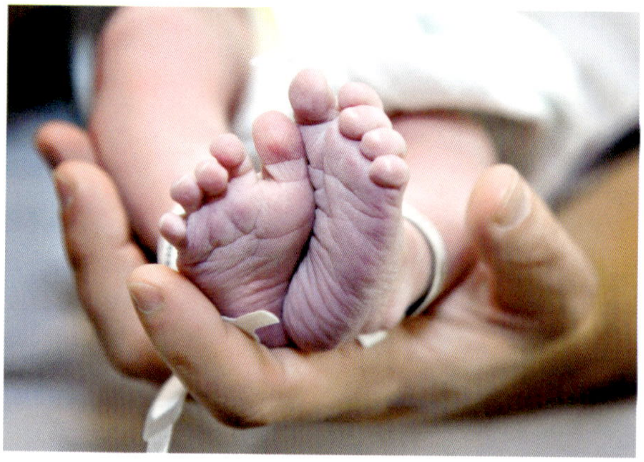

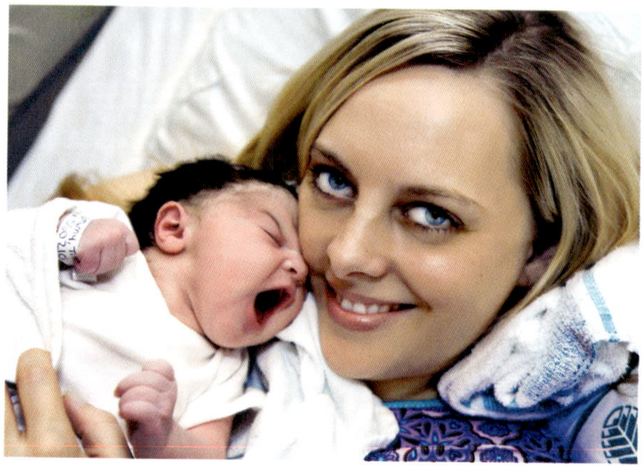

rush to the hospital at 4:00AM unless the parents specifically request it and are willing to pay for your time. I advise my clients to call me as soon as Baby has arrived. I commit to taking the photos within Baby's first twenty-four hours, so this gives me enough time to get to the hospital without a mad rush. I no longer provide full birth services because my mommy duties take precedence. However, it's a service you can certainly provide.

I also commit to producing an online birth announcement within twenty-four hours of taking the photographs. This is a online slide show set to music that features the baby's first portraits and birth statistics (weight, height, length, and date and time of birth). I distribute

"It's more difficult to get a new customer than to keep an existing customer happy, so why not give your clients a reason to come back?"

the announcement by e-mail to the clients' list of friends and family so that they receive the news within the baby's first forty-eight hours. If you have prior permission, you could post the announcement on social media, too.

Pricing for this service depends on the time that is allotted. Determine what your hourly rate will be, then multiply that figure by the number of hours you expect to spend. Consider (1) travel time to and from the hospital/home/birth center, (2) time capturing the photos, (3) time spent on the slide show compilation, (4) the cost of royalty-free music rights, and (5) the cost of hosting the image collection online.

Baby's First Year: The Milestone Bundle

It's more difficult to get a new customer than to keep an existing customer happy, so why not give your clients a reason to come back? A baby's growth in the first year is exponential, and every stage is fleeting. It's important to capture every milestone.

Ask any parent with a new baby how difficult it is to complete the simplest of tasks. Remembering to book photo sessions can

▼ The Milestone Bundle documents Baby's first year.

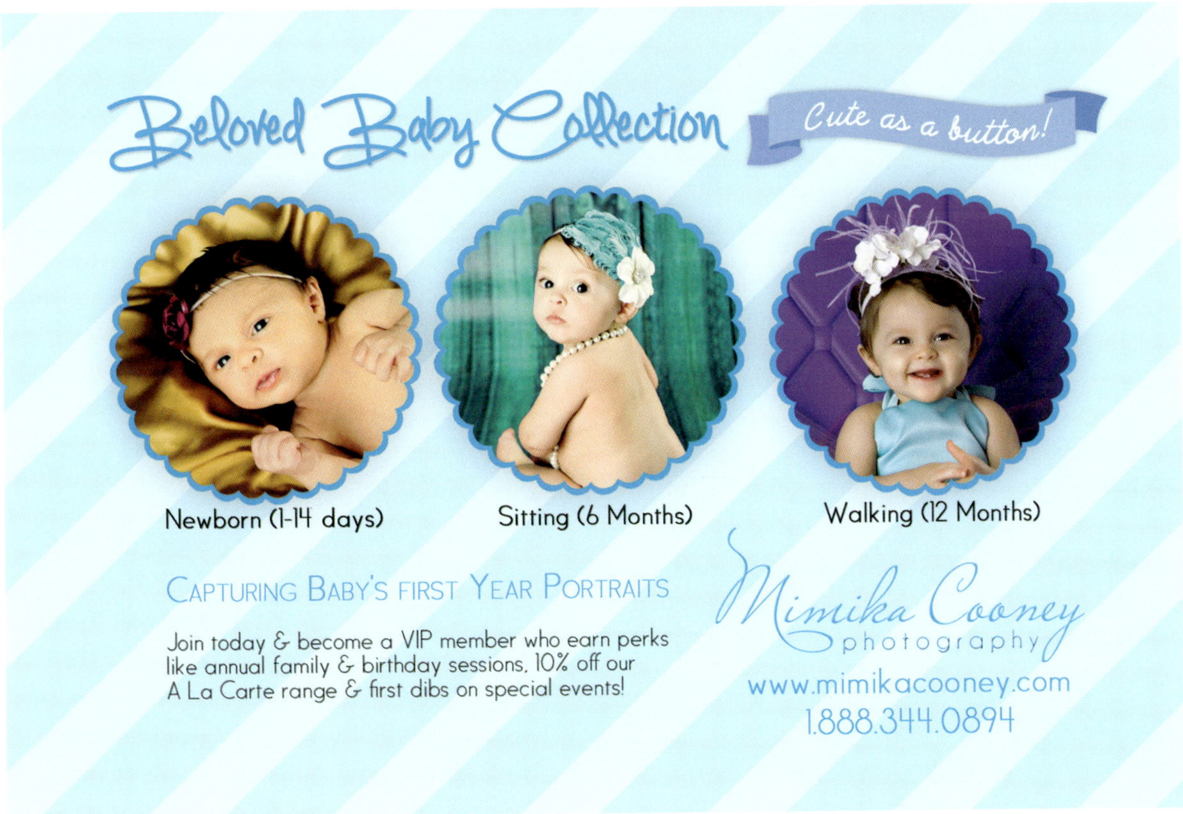

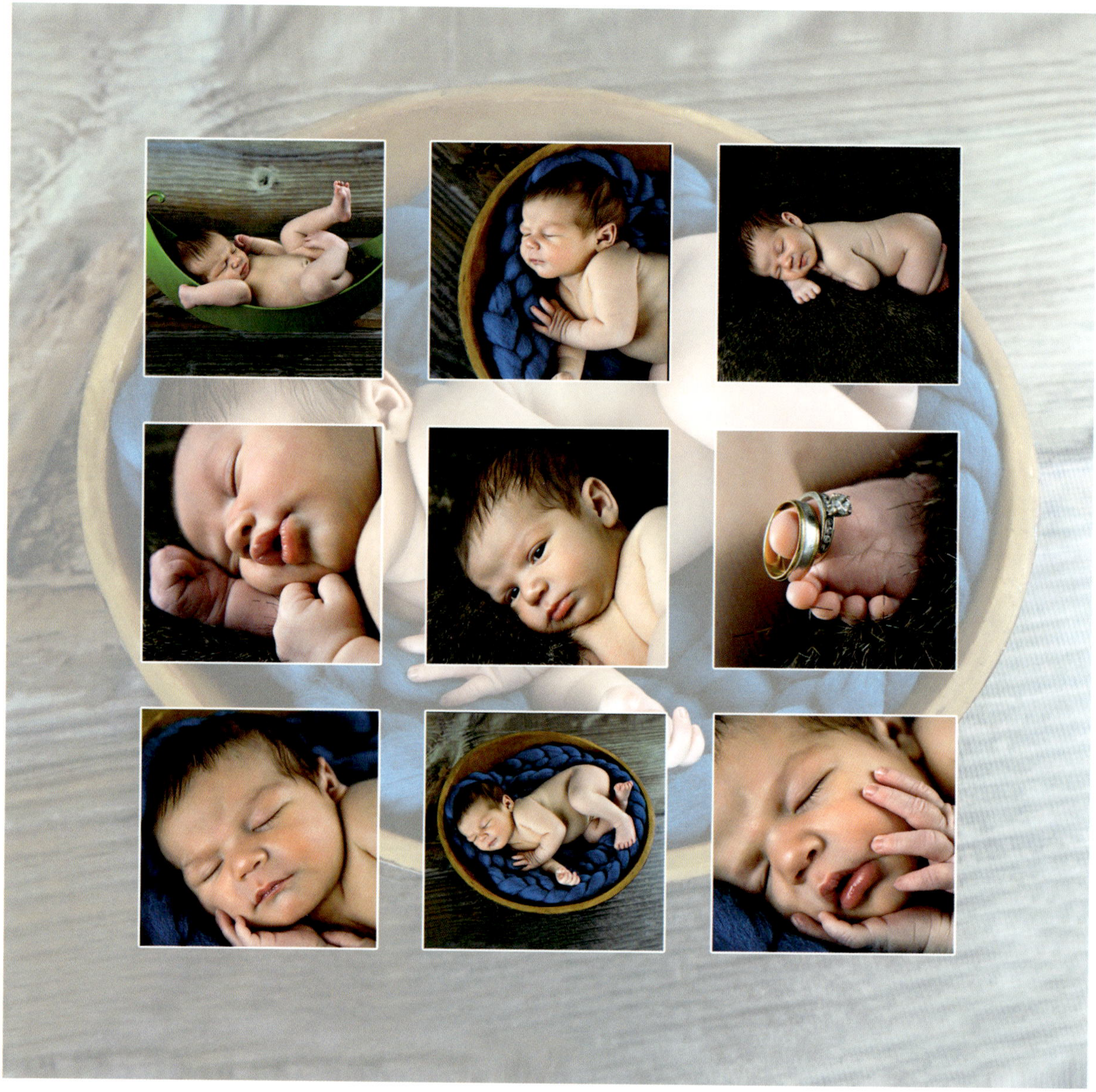

▲ A collection of Baby's kissable bits makes a great presentation.

be difficult, so we offer our Baby Milestone Bundle. At first, we conducted sessions at the newborn stage, six months, and twelve months, but I discovered that clients were taking their baby elsewhere to capture images between sessions. We now offer sessions at the newborn stage, three months when Baby is pushing up on their tummy, six months when they are sitting independently, nine months when they are crawling and pulling themselves up, a birthday session, and a session when they are walking. I don't charge for the extra sessions because each additional session results in greater sales than I initially expected, and I don't run the risk of having my competition steal my clients away.

It's a good idea to have the family commit to the bundle before the birth so that you can set a date for when Baby is four to seven days old. Once they've invested in you with the promise to return, you have won the toughest battle.

Newborns. The newborn session will be the longest shoot; it will likely last two to four hours. A newborn baby cannot be rushed and will need breaks to be fed and changed. It takes time,

"A newborn baby cannot be rushed and will need breaks to be fed and changed."

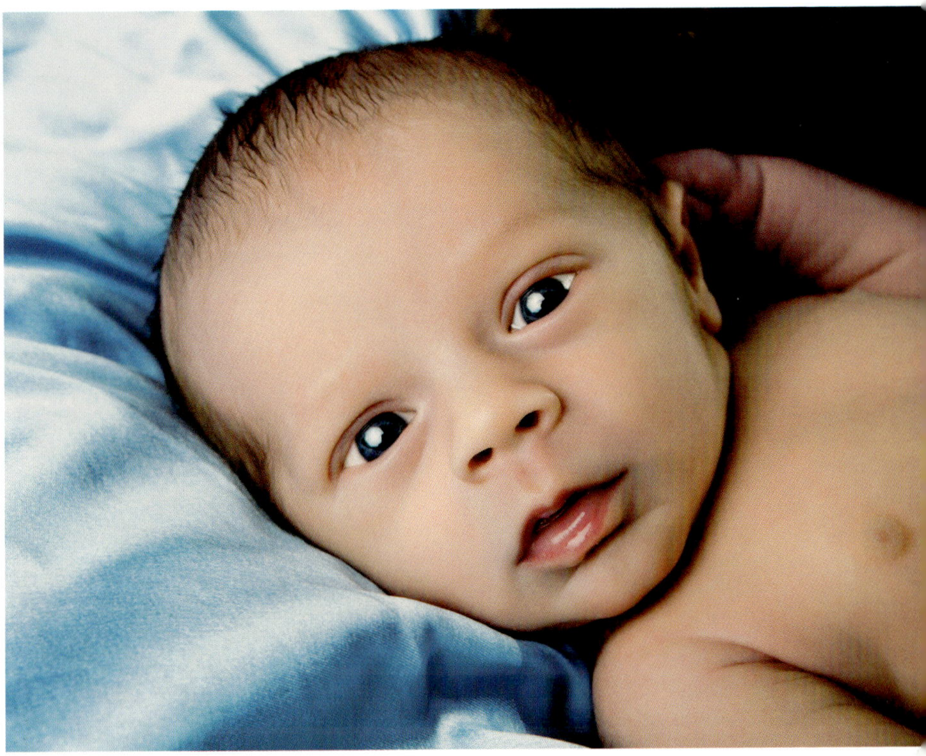

➤ Many babies are born alert. This gives us the opportunity to capture their eyes open. To get the sleepy baby shots, you need to take some extra time to rock, sing, and settle.

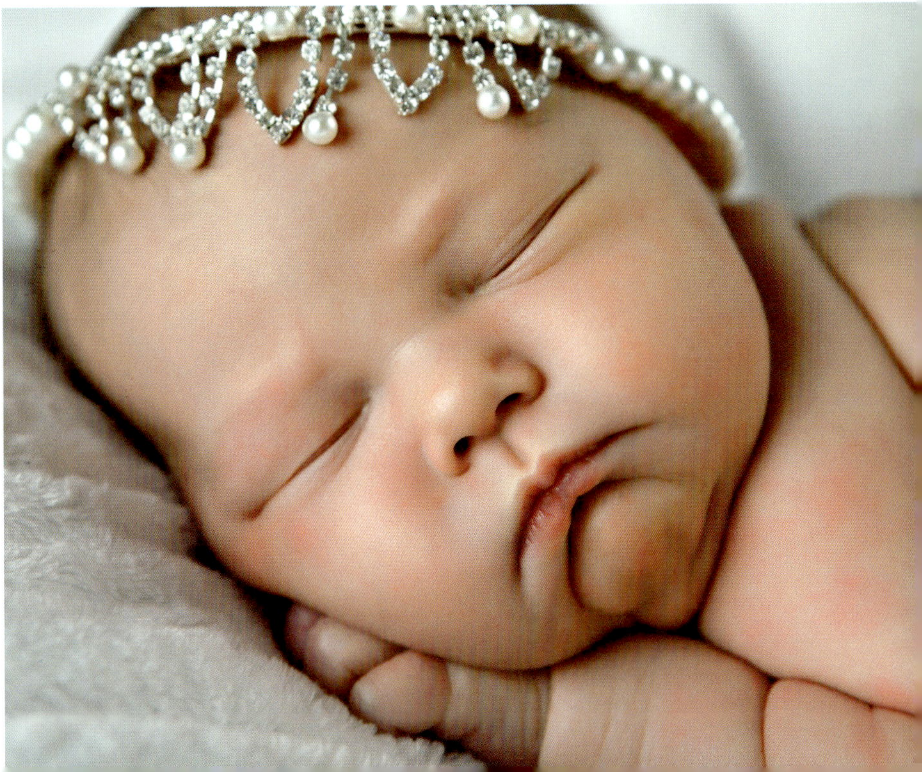

➤ Using props adds to the character of the portrait and depicts the family's style and preferences.

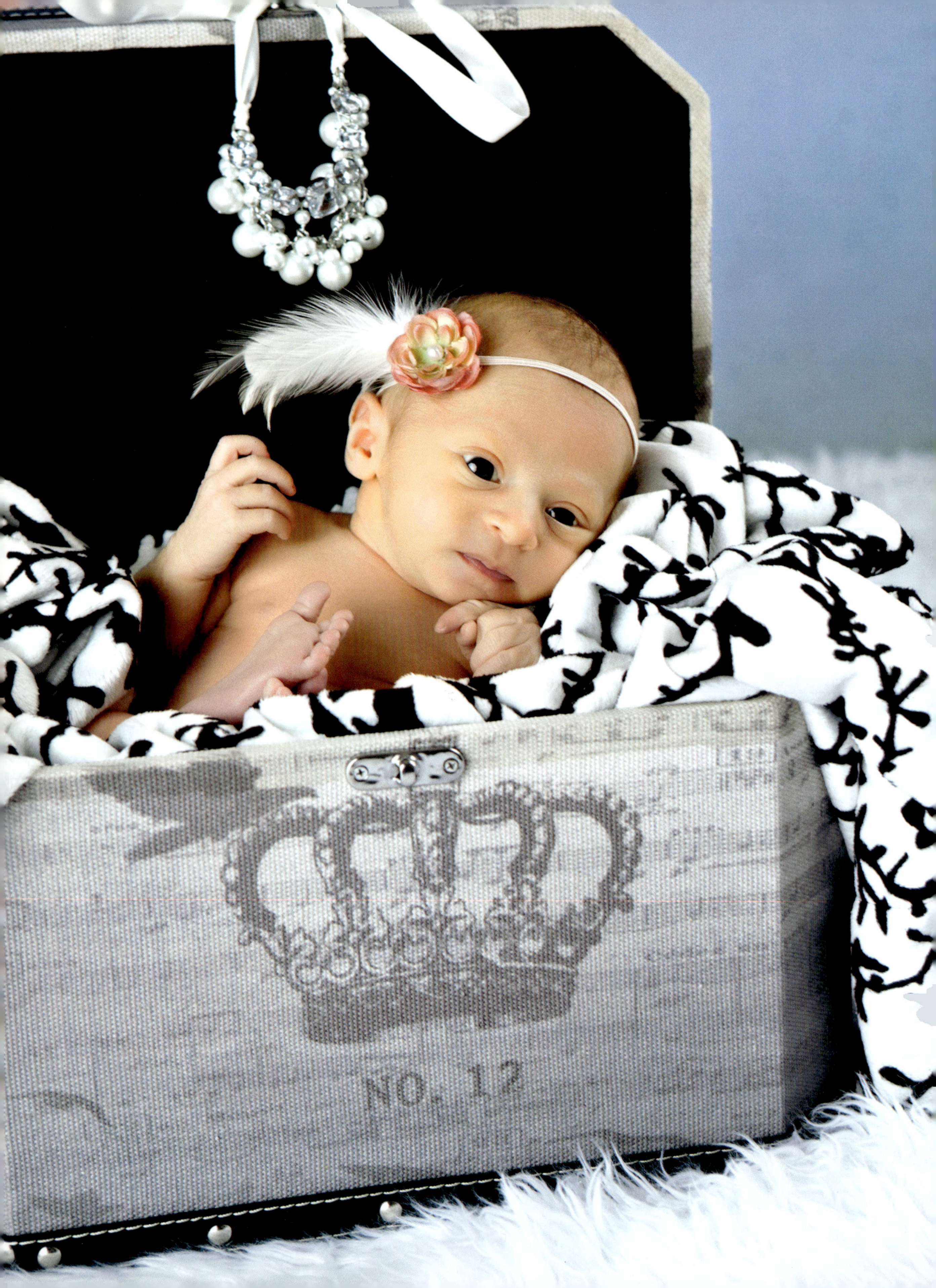
NO. 12

◄► Once Baby is asleep, it should be easy to pose him or her as you like. A heavy sleeper looks adorable gently placed in props and everyday items—and the size of those props can help viewers to gain perspective on the baby's size.

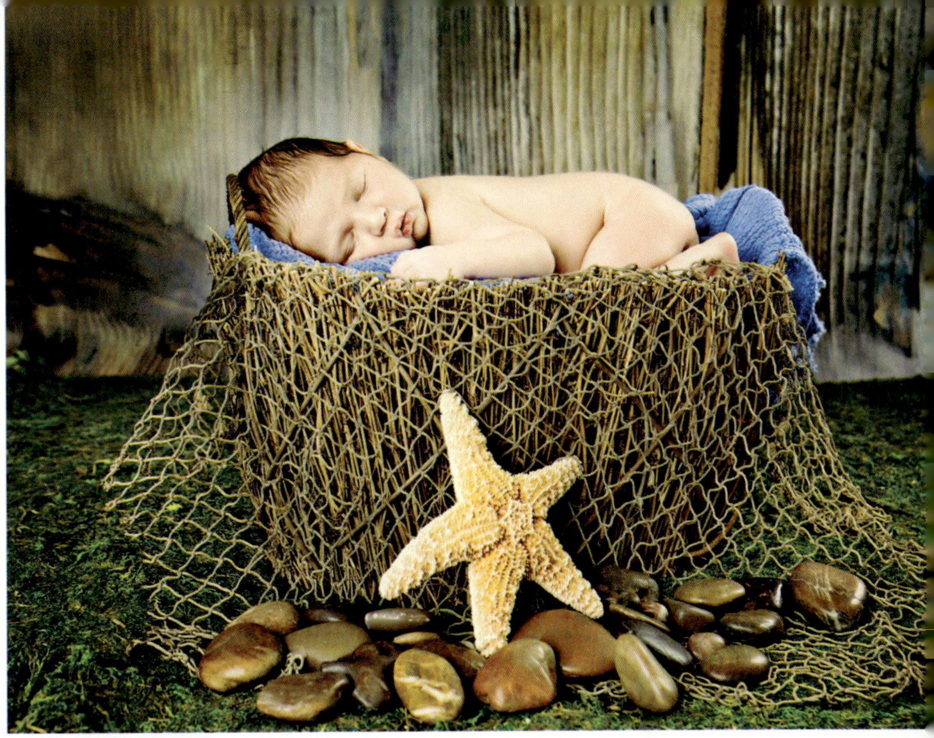

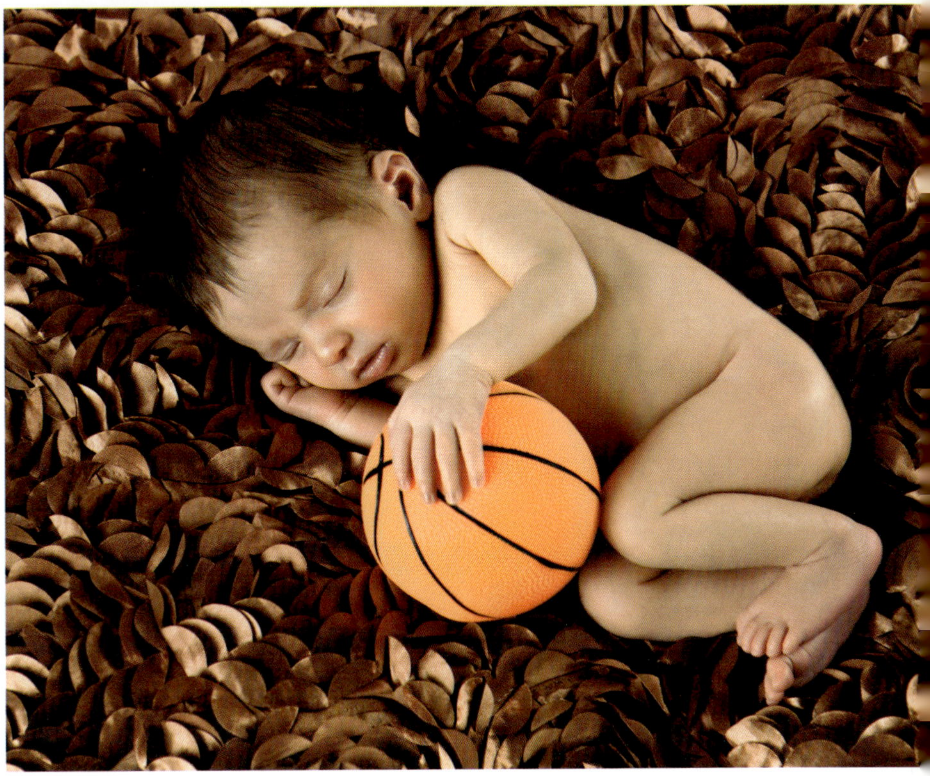

lots of patience, and an ability to endure some crying in order to get the baby to sleep. The parents will order baby announcement cards to send to friends and family, so be sure to get close-ups of the little one's face for this purpose.

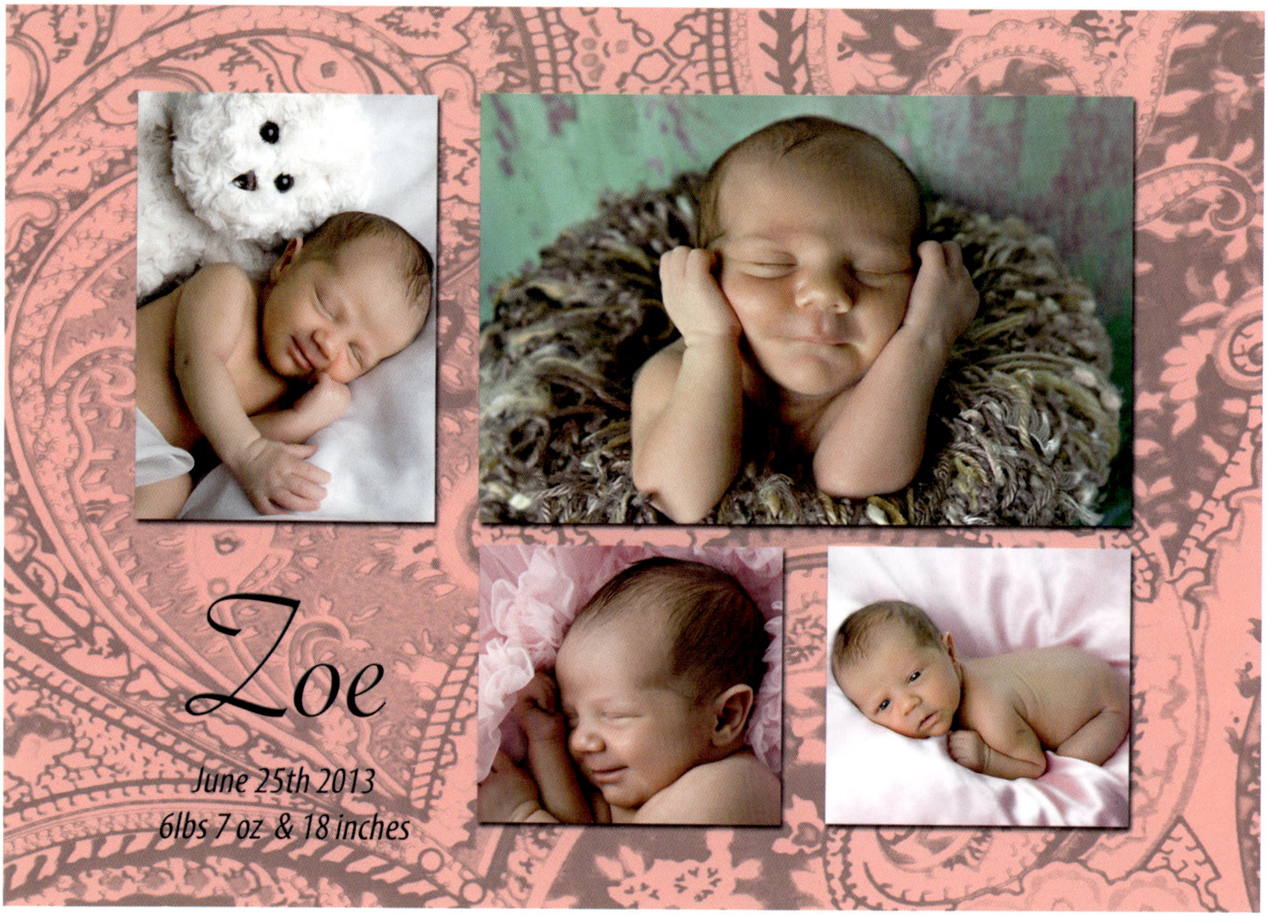

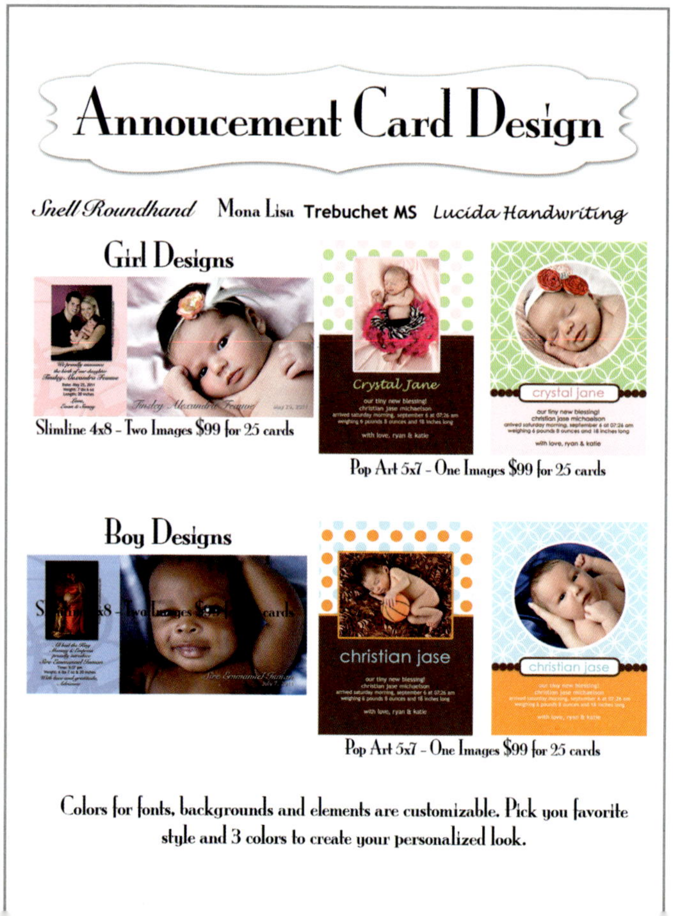

▲ ◄ Birth announcements can help spread the word about your work, so make sure your web address is on them. *Note:* Announcement cards are a common practice in the United States. In other countries, like England, sending out cards like this is sometimes viewed as bragging. Don't let that notion stop you from offering cards, though—you just may be surprised to find that your clients and their friends love them!

► Sleeping newborns can be readily posed. Here are some ideas.

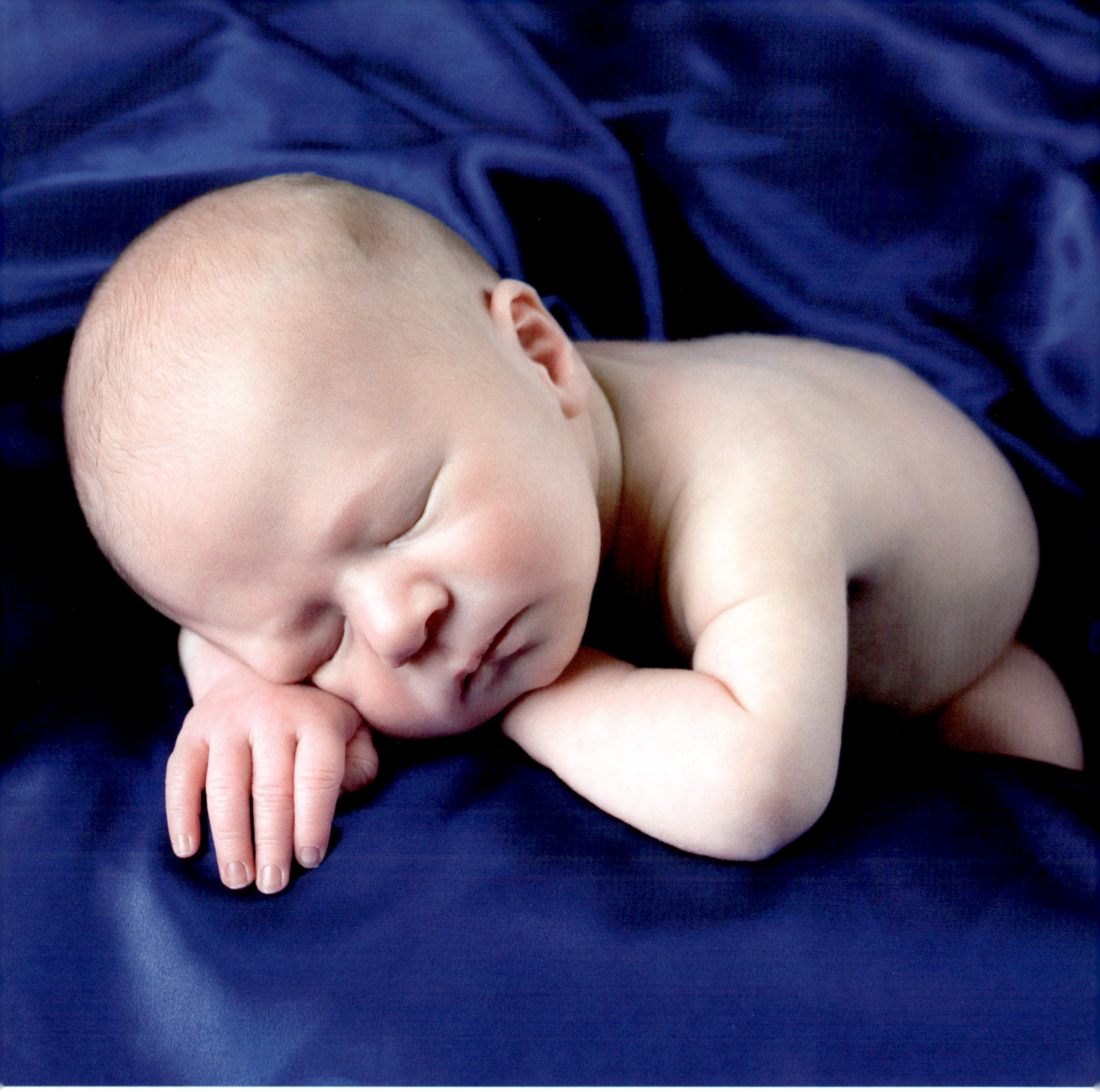
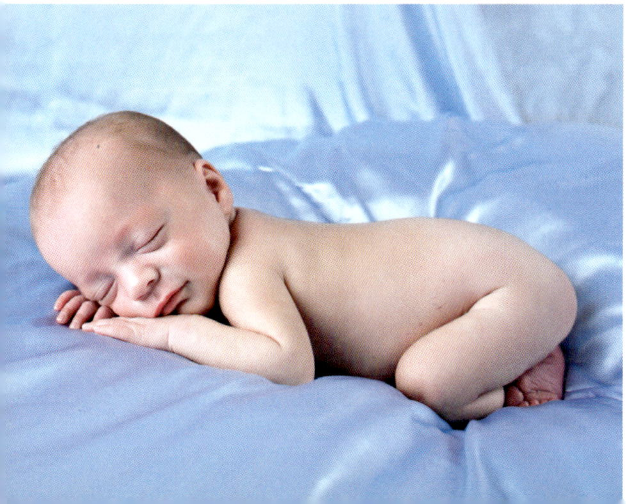
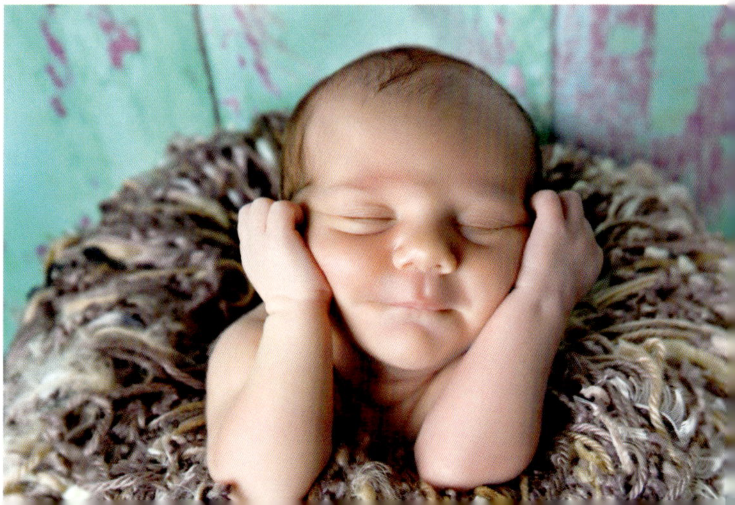

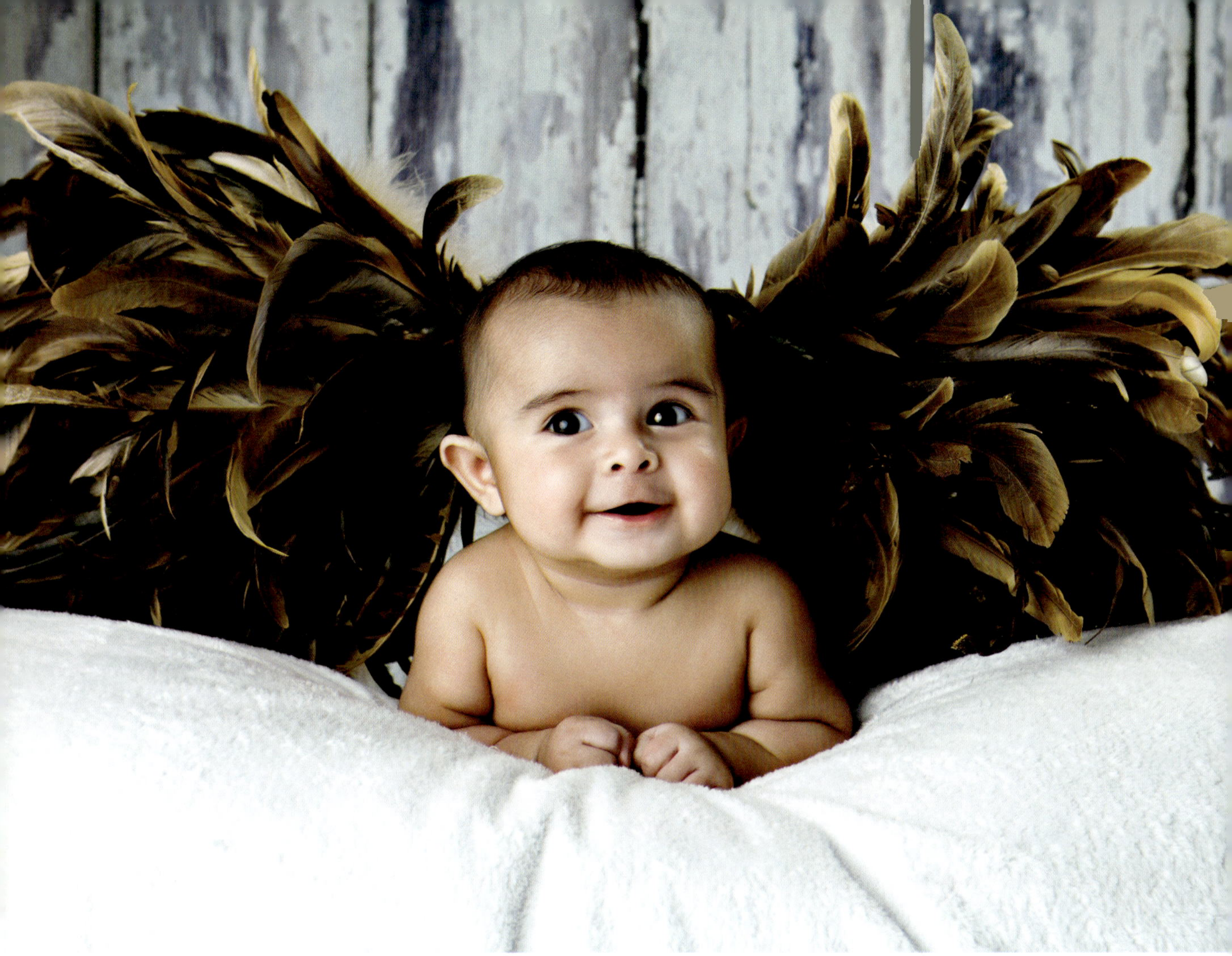

Three Months. A newborn is a floppy lump that sleeps, eats, and poops 24/7, but a three-month-old is alert and has gained control of his or her head and can hold it up for a few minutes. A three-month-old placed on his/her tummy will typically be able to push up on their elbows. Baby can also roll from back to belly and can manipulate their hands and grasp a toy. This is the session to capture that gorgeous big smile, so aim to get close-ups of Baby's face.

As Baby gets older, the session time will get shorter as their energy and attention span will wane, so keep things moving along. Depending on Baby's energy level, you could do two or three clothing changes. My favorite are the naked shots of Baby lying on his/her tummy looking up. Use pillows to prop Baby up so that their arms are hanging over the pillow for a more upright position.

▲ At three months, capture wide eyes and big grins.

"Use pillows to prop Baby up so that their arms are hanging over the pillow for a more upright position."

Including siblings and grandparents in these portraits only works if they can hold Baby up to face the camera. It's best to wait until the baby reaches the six-month mark and is able to sit independently to capture images with a sibling aged one to four.

Six Months. At six months, Baby has undergone significant changes. They are eating solid foods so their tummies are full longer, and they can sit in the tripod position (hands forward) or sit without propping. At six months, Baby can also hold toys and props, and their expressions are animated. Including young siblings in the portraits at this stage works better now that Baby won't be dropped or left to fall over.

Nine Months. At nine months, baby is more curious and has figured out cause and effect. Picking up and dropping things is a favorite activity, so consider using baskets, buckets, and small props to keep the baby engaged. A nine-month-old can experience separation anxiety, so ask Mom or Dad to sit close by to offer reassurance. Baby will be proud to show off their standing and cruising skills as they hold onto a prop, basket, furniture, table, or a pair of legs. Playing a game of peekaboo can prompt some cute giggles and laughs.

Twelve Months. Baby's first birthday brings lots of excitement and celebration. He or she has graduated from baby to toddler. At twelve

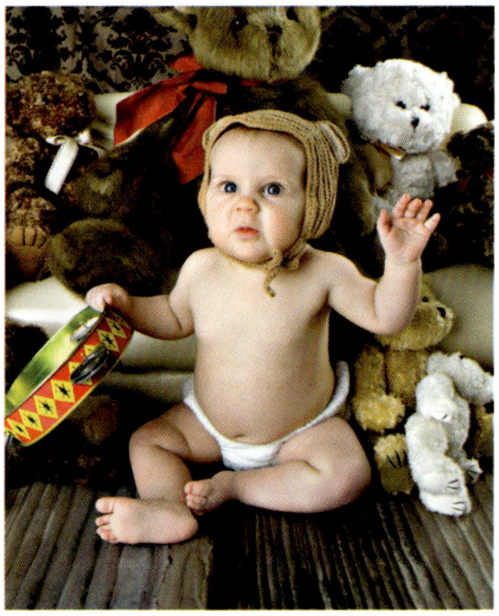

▲ At six months, Baby's personality comes out.

➤ At nine months, dress-up and holding props keeps the little one amused.

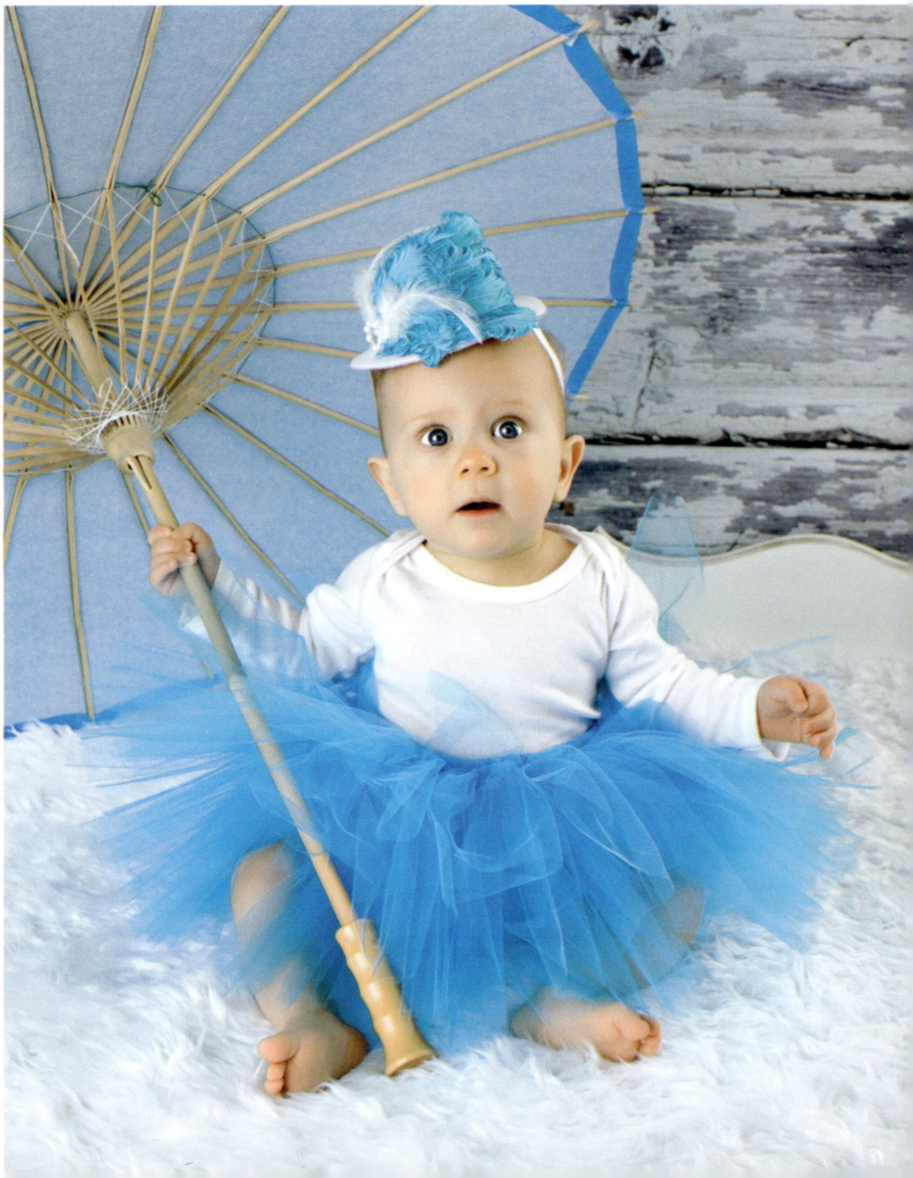

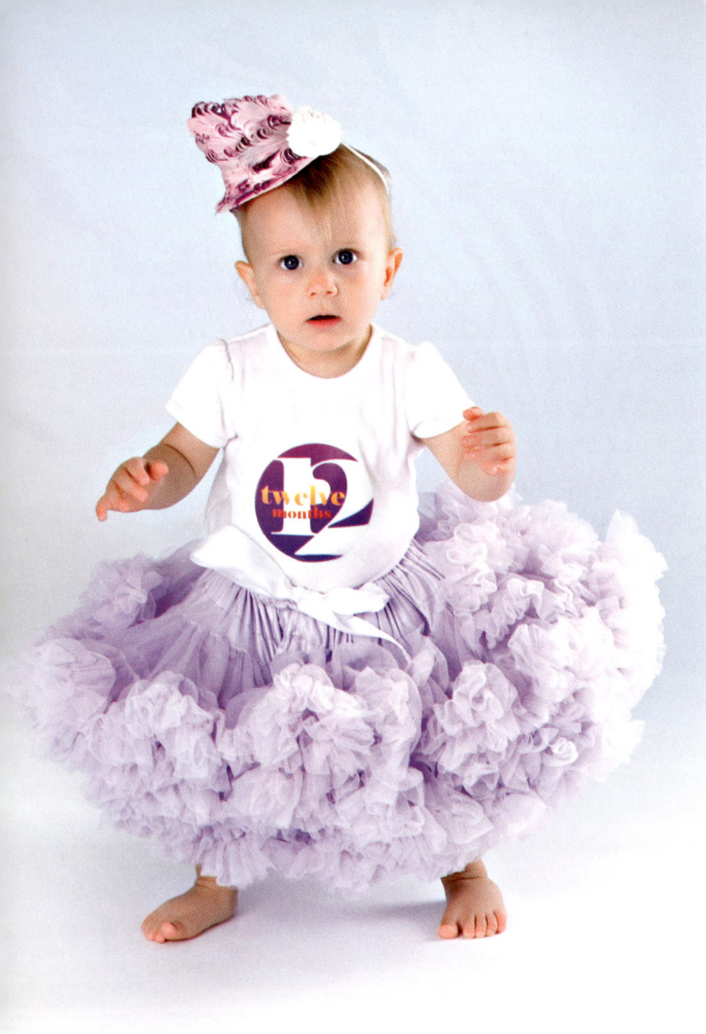

▲ Celebrate walking or standing at twelve months.

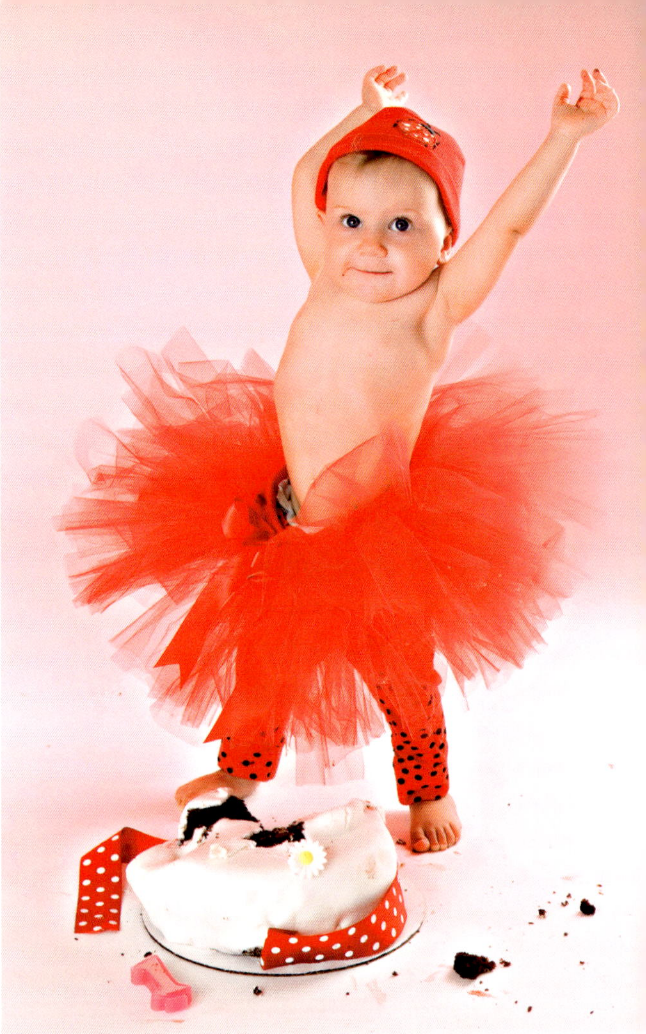

▲ The cake smash makes for great images.

months, these guys walk and run pretty quickly, so be prepared for a workout!

A toddler's attention span is short, so keep the session moving quickly and change your prompts often. Don't keep saying "Smile, look here!"—try different things.

I love to do our signature Pettiskirt Party for girls and our Trash the Cake session for both girls and boys during this session. Moms love to dress up their baby girl in pretty pettiskirts and tutus, and they help you create colorful portraits. I keep a selection of colors and styles of dresses, skirts, and tutus with matching hats and onesies. I advise parents to bring the outfits they want their child to wear. We photograph those first, then we proceed to the messy part of the session—destroying a birthday cake.

Trash the Cake. Not every child likes to get dirty—and I've found more boys than girls get completely into the experience—but for those that do, the resulting images are hilarious! The fun part is watching their expressions as they discover the texture and taste of yummy cake. Keep your camera ready because as soon as you put the cake in place, things will get messy.

Presenting a collection of images in the order they were taken makes for a great album, slide show, or card collection. We offer a press-printed birthday celebration card as a birthday party invitation or announcement. It's a product that Moms love. Remember to include your web address to generate business from those who receive the materials.

Albums. At the end of the first year, you will have a lovely collection of images that tells the story of Baby's development. Since the images were narrowed down to the client's favorites after every session, you should have fully retouched images that are ready to go. Offering parents a storybook album is another way of offering a complete turnkey service. Incorporating design elements and color schemes that suit their tastes make it even more special.

There are several ways you can create an album and there is no shortage of manufacturers to turn to, so do some research and decide on the style and price you'd like to offer. We offer upscale leather-bound albums from Finao Albums and press-printed books produced and bound by our lab, WHCC.

▼ This storybook album was made to document the baby's first year.

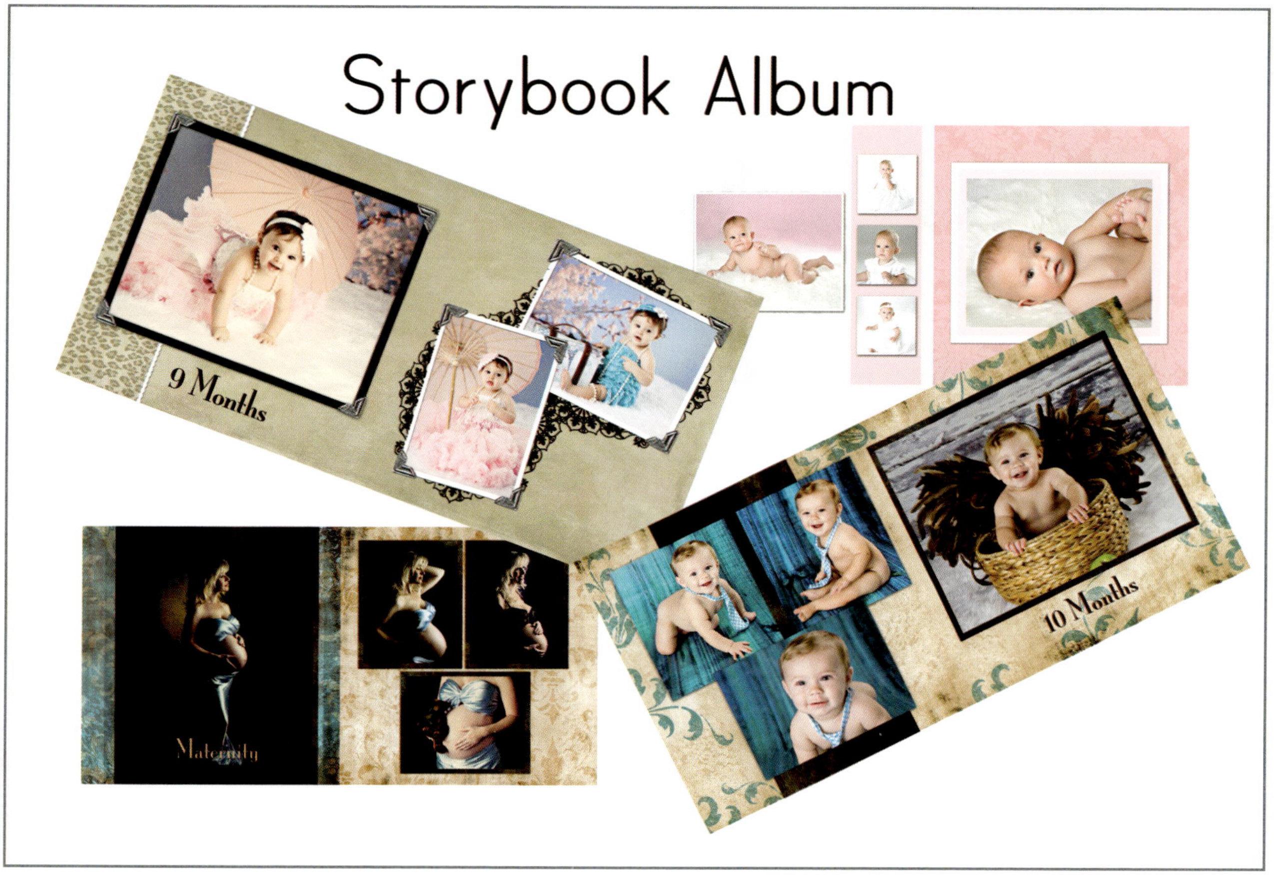

Working with OB/GYN Offices

Marketing to moms-to-be is ideal. At this stage, there is plenty of lead time to plan ahead for the session so that you capture Baby within the first four to seven days of life.

Approaching local OB/GYN offices can be tricky, as there is a chain of command involved. If you are a patient yourself or know of a patient who can vouch for your services, it will be easier

▼ Here is an example of the custom-designed cards I include in new mothers' gift bags.

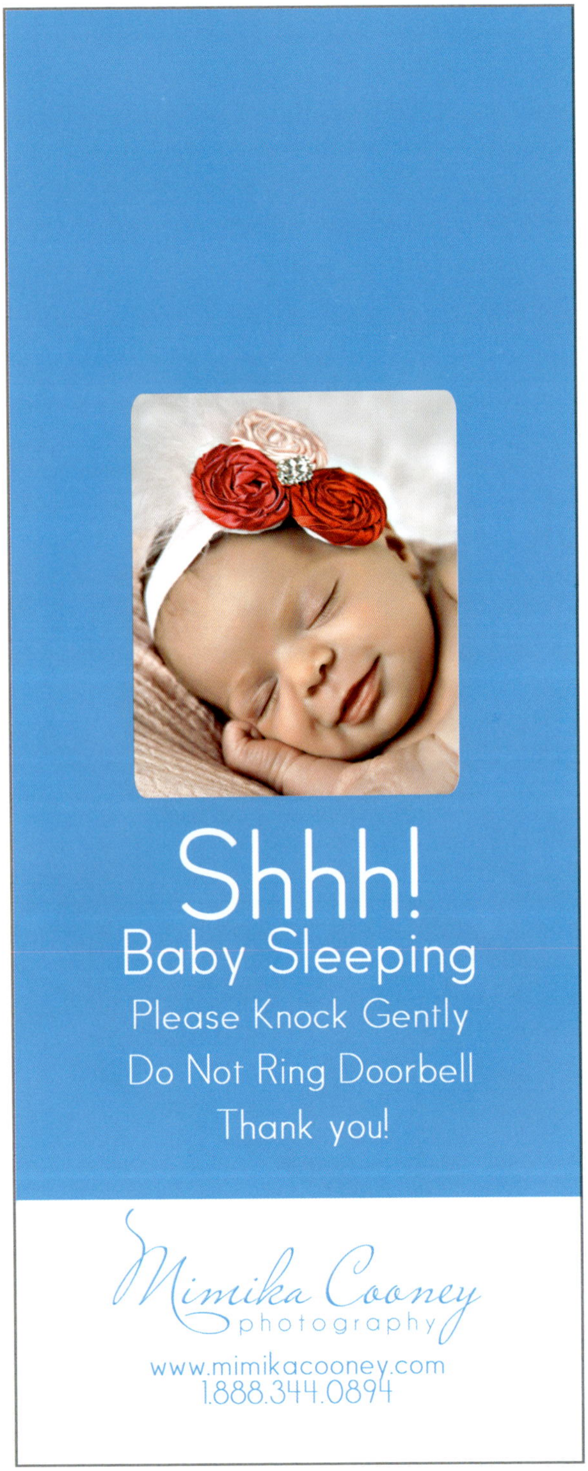

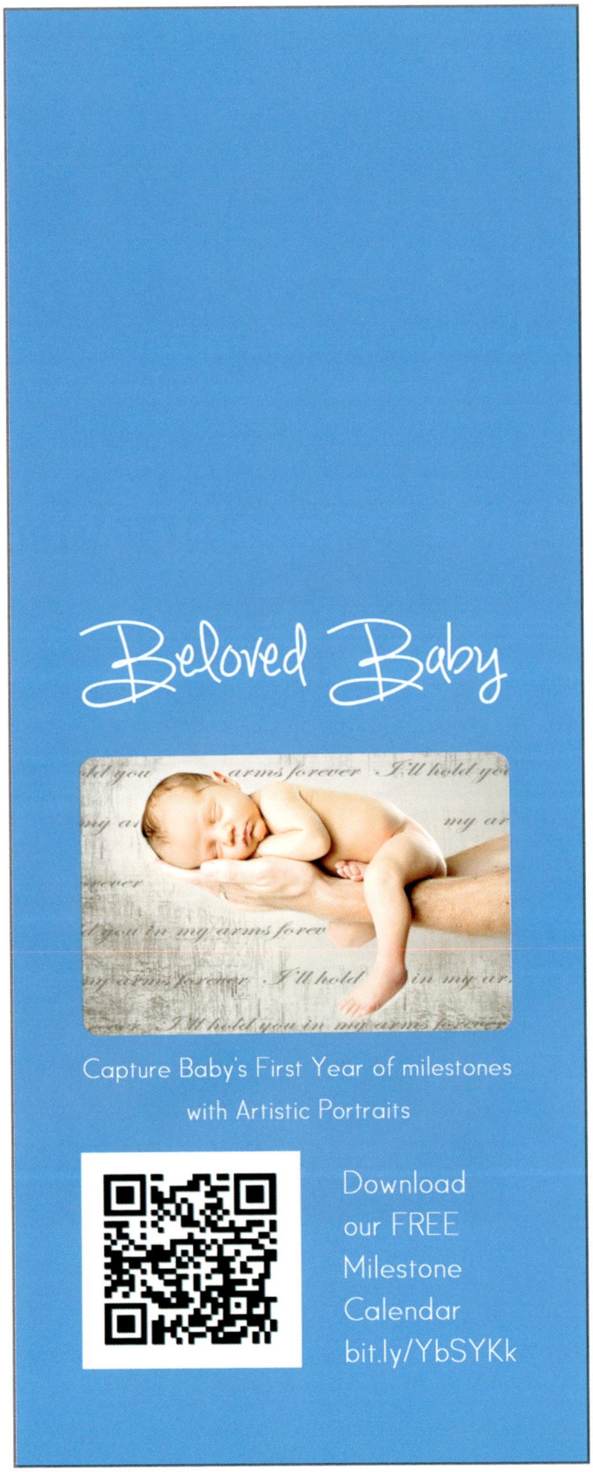

to get your foot in the door. I've offered my past clients the incentive of a free framed wall portrait if they can negotiate on my behalf to provide my services to the practice. Having a third party brag about you is far better than approaching the office cold.

Usually the person in charge is the office manager who will warm up to gifts of cookies, chocolates, and lunch.

Once you are in league with the medical providers, have work on display on the walls and your cards in the waiting area. If that cannot be arranged, at least have your cards placed in the gift bags that are given to women who learn they are expecting. The more places you can make your brand visible, the better.

In the past, I've offered to photograph the doctors and nursing staff for use on the practice's website, in exchange for exclusivity.

When approaching OB/GYN offices, remember that you will be investing time and products. Because the wall art on display in the doctor's office is donated, you can include your logo and contact information. Each office you contact will have unique wants and needs. Negotiating a win–win deal will be in everyone's best interests.

Partnership Marketing

Working with businesses that cater to your target market can double your marketing efforts. Donating your services to a worthy charity can create goodwill and give you access to many new contacts.

Organizing an event, like a baby shower, with other baby businesses that can donate their products/services can also help you build your client base. Sharing resources and combining energies can have a huge impact on the community, and you may find that you become the go-to photographer.

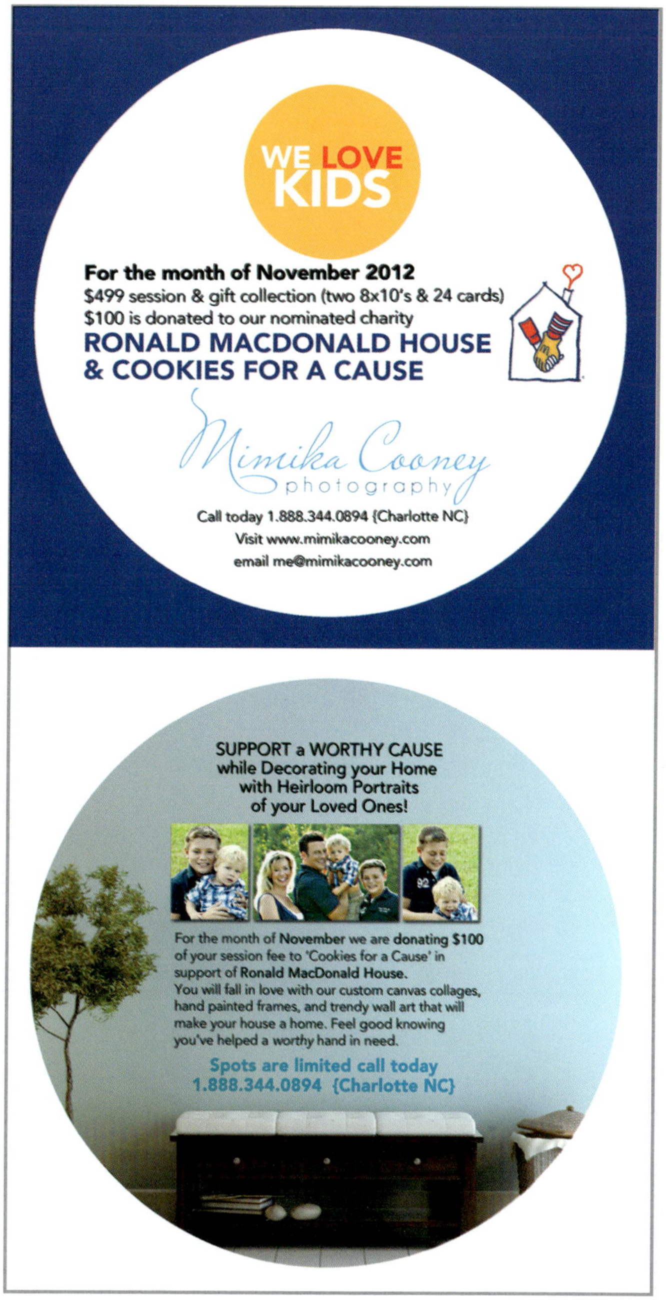

▲ This is a charity promotional piece.

Tips for Capturing Baby's First Year

Here is an article I wrote for Chic *magazine (Summer 2012) about helping photographers understand the importance of recurring income. As a newborn photographer, you have lots of opportunities to keep servicing your clients beyond the newborn stage. Consider this food for thought.*

Wouldn't you love the peace of mind that comes from having a reliable cash flow month after month? In today's tough economy, our schedule books must be full to keep our businesses afloat. However, there is a difference between being busy and being profitable.

There's an old adage that says, "It's easier to keep a client than to attract a new one." It's true—with the amount of effort that is required to market to a new client, we shouldn't short change ourselves by stopping at offering just one session. If a new mom likes your work enough to commission your newborn photography services, you've overcome the biggest obstacle—trust.

Lately I've noticed a flurry of new and veteran photographers branding themselves as "newborn only." Although I agree that it's important to specialize in an area you love and are good at, I feel it's just as important to hold onto your client beyond their newborn experience. I want my clients to fall in love with me so that they want to come back at every stage of their baby's first year. Once you've convinced the new parents how awesome you are and how wonderful your work is, you don't need to be a pushy salesperson because you're 80 percent there!

Why Should Parents Bring Their Baby Back?

The developmental changes in a baby's first twelve months are so drastic that it's important to show Mom and Dad the value in having them return to document each milestone. My preference is to show them a Baby's First Year album so that they can see the changes their baby will experience. I like to talk about how they will feel and how much they are going to appreciate the album later in life. Here is an example of how I paint the picture for them by explaining the benefits of capturing each stage:

> "A newborn is adorable when he or she is all curled up and sleeping soundly—and we can get some creative poses. At three months, their personality comes out, they can hold their head up, and they are smiling. At that age, we can capture gorgeous close-ups of their eyes and their gummy grins! At six or seven months, the change is remarkable; they are very animated, they can usually sit independently, hold a toy, and interact with an audience. At nine months, they reach their curious stage; they've developed the ability to crawl, cruise along furniture, and pull themselves up to a standing position. Of course, at twelve months, it's their birthday, which is always a great reason to throw a party and celebrate! They are probably standing, walking, and moving about. Every stage is precious and worthy of being captured. The album will be so meaningful to you once the moments have gone."

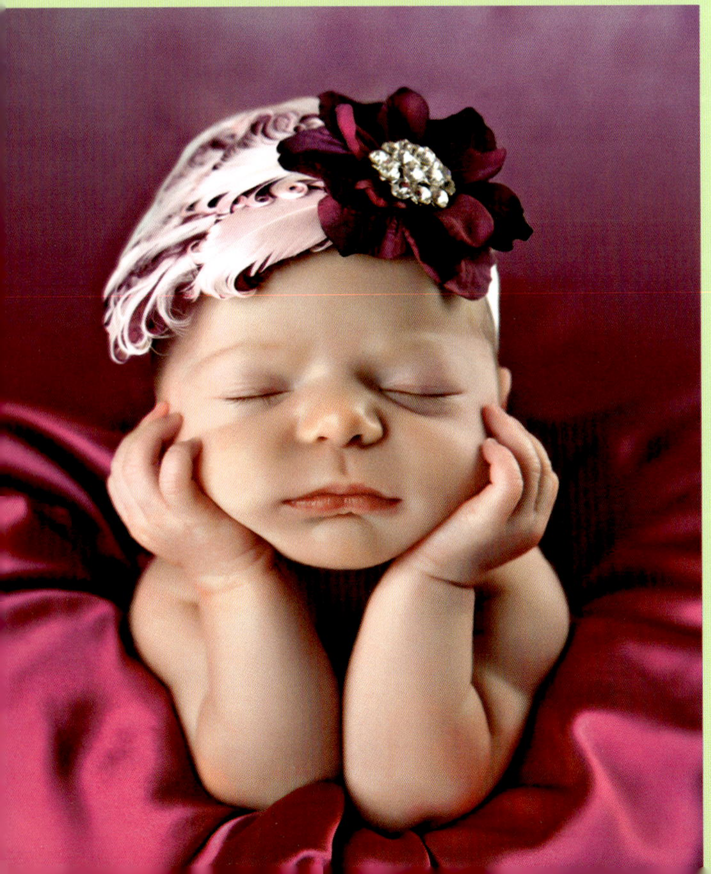

You don't have to be a pushy salesperson once you've gained your clients' trust.

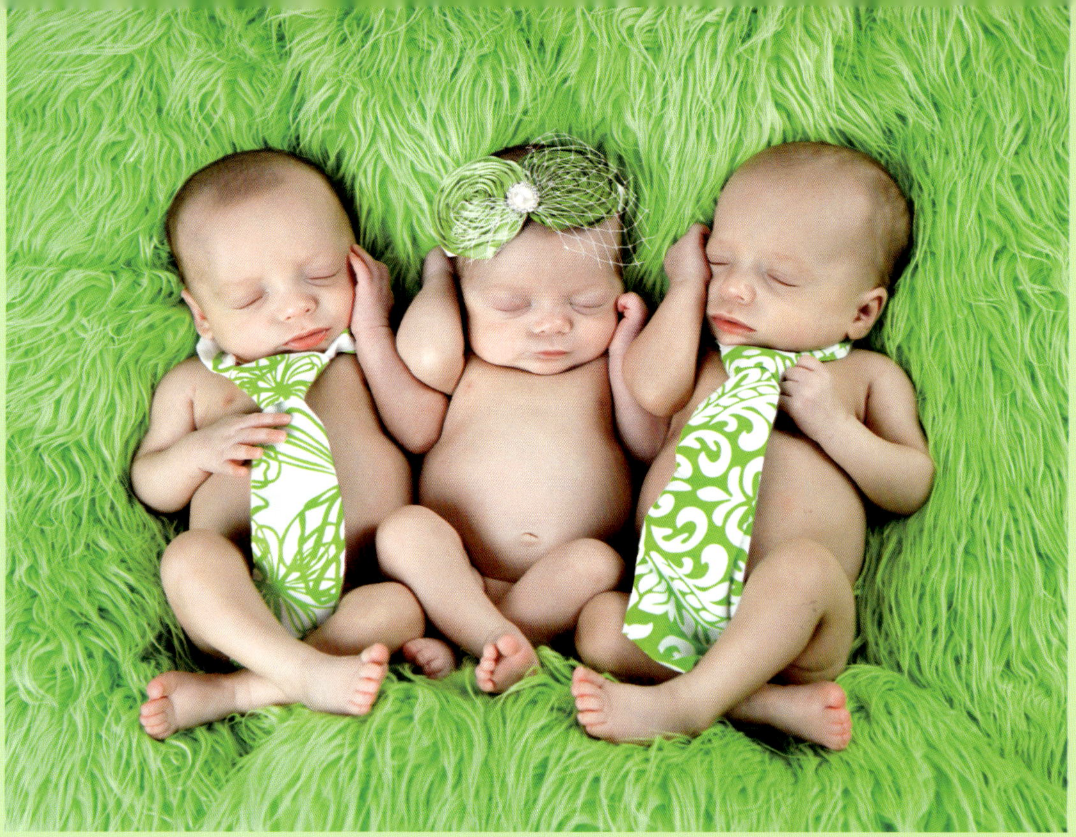

➤ Money spent is money forgotten.

How Do I Create a Package that Makes Me Money?

Selling the value of your service rather than the price will secure your business's future. I've built a package that includes all five developmental stages (newborn, three months, six months, nine months, and twelve months). When clients purchase this package, I discount my standard session fee. This way, they feel they are getting more value for their money. I also include a few bonus 8x10-inch prints. This makes them feel that they are getting a tangible product in addition to my time, and the cost is minimal.

If I've done my job right, my clients will find it hard to choose just one favorite image. The package includes a single 8x10-inch matted print at each session, but 95 percent of the time the parents buy more. It's important to upsell your services so you never create a ceiling. You want to encourage your client to invest more. In the long run, you will be making more money from the same client over the year because money spent is money forgotten.

How Do We Build a System that Works?

The trick is to hold the client's hand throughout the process. Treat them like gold and you'll give them a reason to come back. At my studio, our primary focus (besides producing great work) is client retention and working smarter. Having had my third baby in 2010, I don't have a lot of time on my hands. I have to fit a five-day work week into four mornings while my toddler is at preschool. I need to make sure that every minute spent produces results. I've developed a system that walks new parents from one milestone to the next so that they don't have to think about what to do next. I use phrases like, "This image is going to look fabulous above the fireplace" or "This will look gorgeous above the crib." I have a home-based studio and I only sell by projection. I insist that my clients come back after their session for a separate ordering appointment so I can help guide them through the process. I'm the expert, and they look to me for guidance. Leaving the purchasing decisions for your client to make at home on a computer screen is lazy—and it's a surefire way to kill your sales. Clients want guidance, so offer it.

I don't post any "sneak peeks" online until after they've come for their ordering session. Once they've seen the images online, it's hard to build the excitement up again. Photography is an emotional purchase, so we need to muster all of the excitement we can to keep the client invested in our services by creating the experience when they see their images for the first time.

For more help with developing a photography business around Baby's first year and beyond, read my book, *Boutique Baby Photography: A Digital Photographer's Guide to Success in Maternity and Baby Portraiture* (Amherst Media, 2011).

4. Lighting and Equipment

"A baby is born with a need to be loved . . . and never outgrows it."—Frank A. Clark

Keep the Lighting Simple

Sticking to a simple lighting setup helps to produce consistent results and saves you from making time-consuming adjustments during the session. The main light source should be large and soft to flatter skin tones and hide the tiredness that new parents will be feeling. I love my Elinchrom hexagon softbox for this purpose, and the catchlights in the eyes are just gorgeous.

Zoro Lighting

I like to refer to my preferred lighting setup as "Zoro" lighting (like the masked TV character Zoro who marks everything with a Z). My studio is small—it's 6x8 feet, as it's meant to be my dining room. I use track lighting on the ceiling to give me more floor space and to avoid busy toddlers knocking down my light stands.

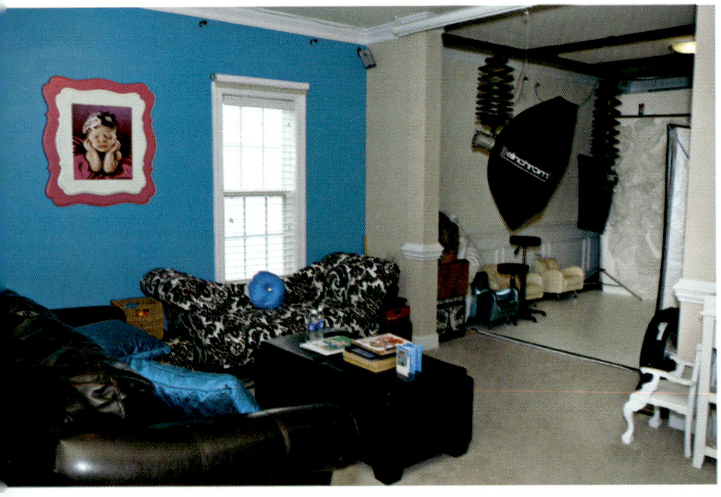

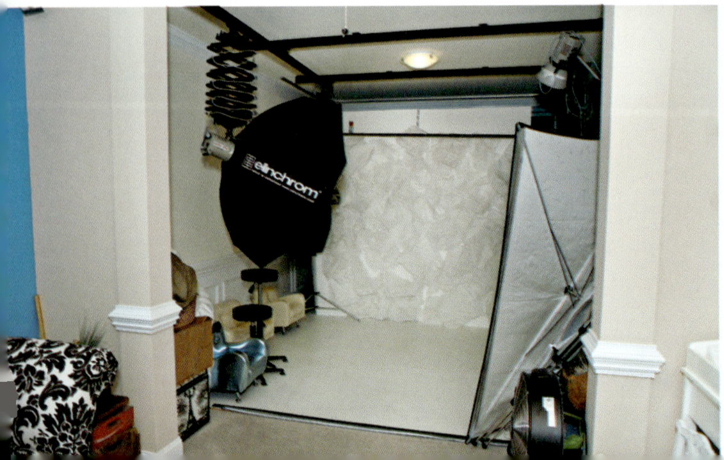

◄ (top left) My home studio.
◄ (bottom left) My shooting area.
▼ (below) When using the Zoro setup, my exposure settings are ISO 100, f/5.6, at $^{1}/_{100}$ second.

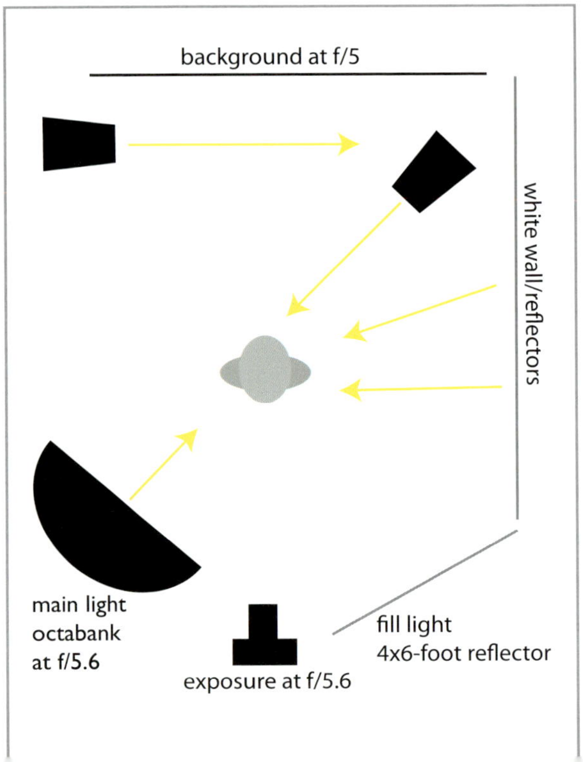

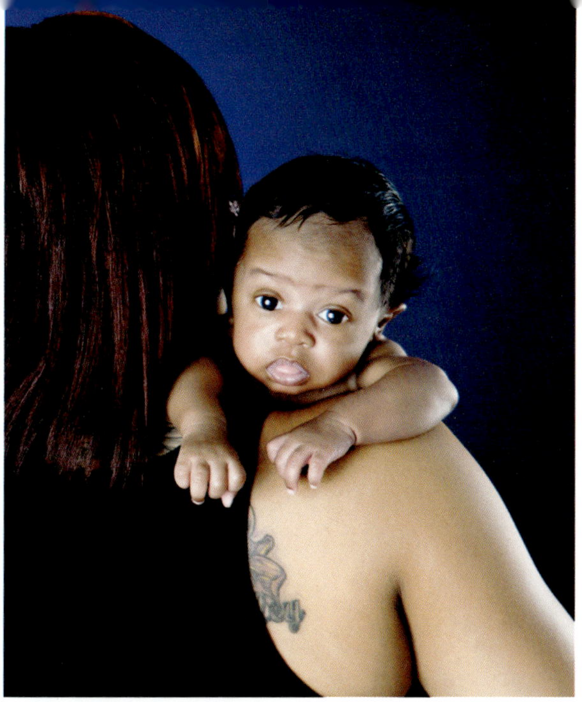

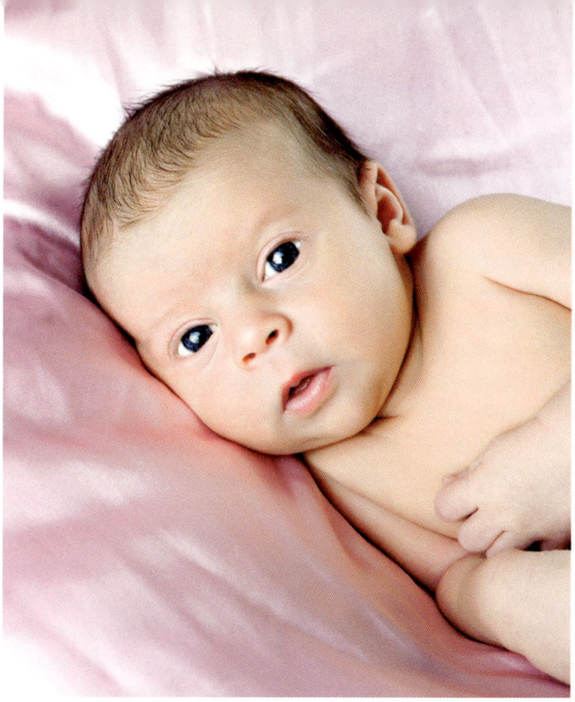

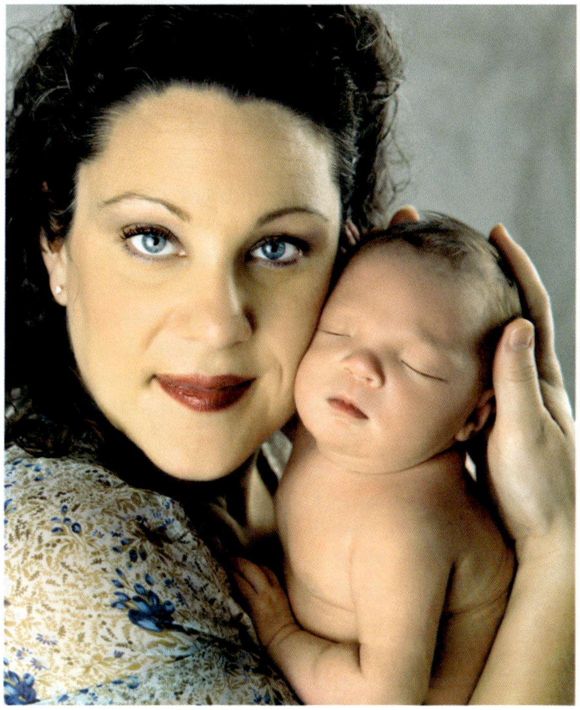

▲ (top left) Rembrandt lighting.
▲ (top right) The background light creates separation.
◄ (left) Snap, crackle, pop lighting highlights the eyes, creates separation, and shows depth.

Snap, Crackle, Pop Lighting

The words "snap, crackle, pop" remind me to create portrait lighting that creates the appearance of depth and dimension.

Snap. To create snap in a portrait, you need a soft and flattering main light source. I love my Elinchrom hexagon and strip softboxes for the purity of the light they produce. Placing your main light in the correct position is important to creating the right mood. I prefer my main light at a 45 degree angle to the subject's nose and elevated just above the subject's eyes. At this angle, the light creates a shadow on the side of the nose and helps to create a sculpted face. In photographic circles, this is known as Rembrandt lighting—a nod to the Dutch painter.

Crackle. Add some depth to your portraits by creating separation between the subject and background. This can easily be achieved by adding a background light to the mix. You can place the background light perpendicular to the background or point it at an angle for a spotlighting effect. Just remember to keep your subject at least three feet from the background to avoid light spill on the hair or face. You can place a hair light 45 degrees behind your

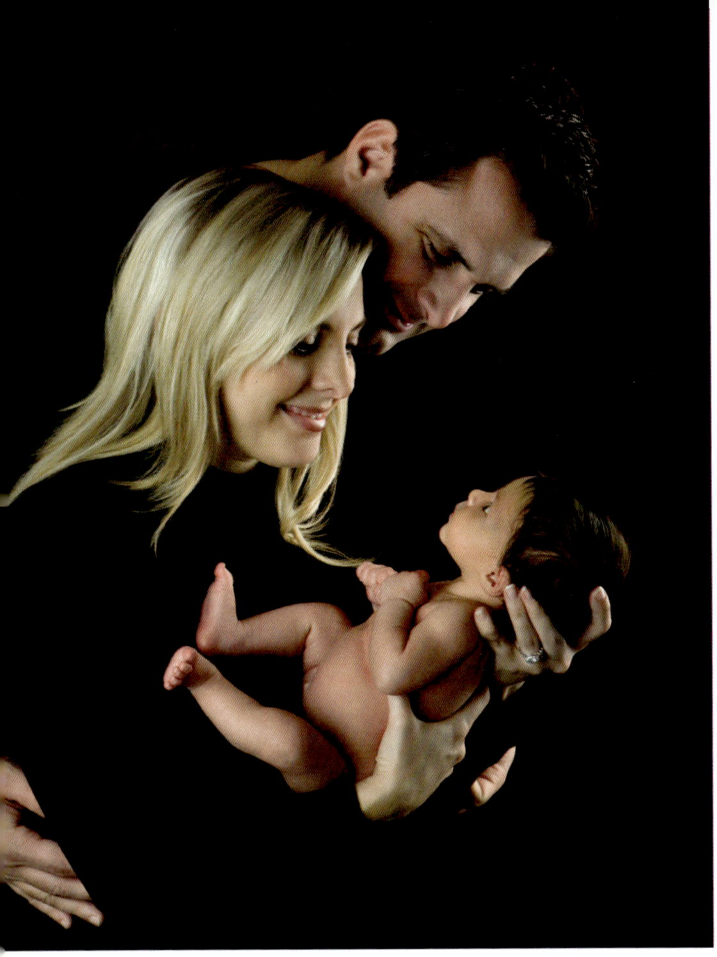

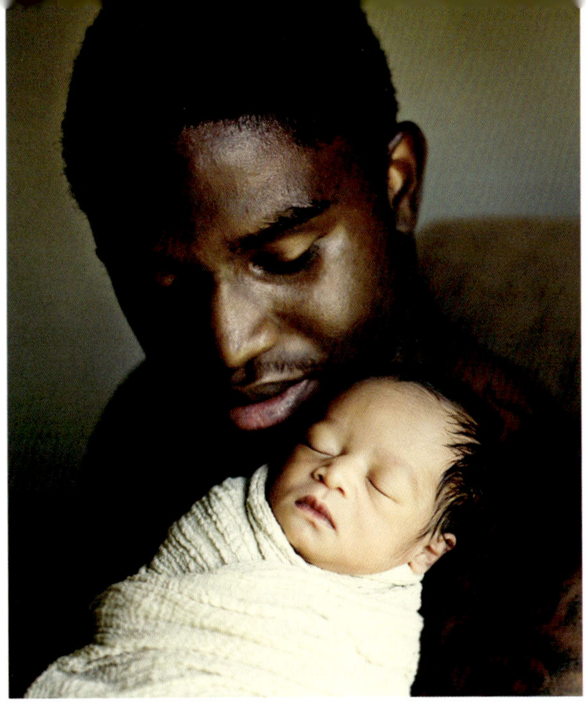

◄ Profile lighting is created when the subject faces the light source.

▲ Natural window light was used to photograph this dad and newborn in the client's home.

subject's shoulder, pointing toward the main light, to accent the hair and create separation.

Pop. The pop in a portrait comes from the eyes. The eyes are the most important part of the subject's face, and they must be clear and bright. To achieve "pop" in the eyes, you can use an additional light, but I prefer to create catchlights with a reflector. I use a 42x72-inch freestanding silver reflector at a 45-degree angle to the subject's nose, opposite the main light. It always does the trick.

Profile Lighting

Dramatic profile lighting can be achieved with one or two lights. This approach is deductive—you are hiding areas of the subject in shadow and highlighting areas you want to be prominent, such as when photographing a pregnant belly.

This lighting approach works well when you have Mom and Dad in position facing the light source so that you see their profiles and their hands holding Baby.

We use the same basic setup used for Zoro lighting, except we remove the large softbox and make the stripbox the main light. The background light and reflector remain in the same position, but you can use barn doors on the background light to direct illumination onto the subject's hair and avoid spill.

These are two staple lighting setups you can use in your bag of tricks that will always hold you in good stead. There are many more lighting variations you can use. For more information, turn to *Christopher Grey's Master Lighting Guide for Portrait Photographers* (2nd ed., Amherst Media, 2014). It's the best book I've read on the topic.

Natural Window Lighting

When working with window lighting you are relying on the sun as your main light source. This means that you should position your beanbag where Baby's face will be well lit by the window. I augment the light by placing a silver reflector directly opposite the window to pop some light into the shadows.

▼ This setup was used to create the image at the bottom of the page. The results are a soft light across the baby's face with very little gradation. My camera settings were ISO 100 and f/2 at $^{1}/_{250}$ second with an f/1.2 lens.

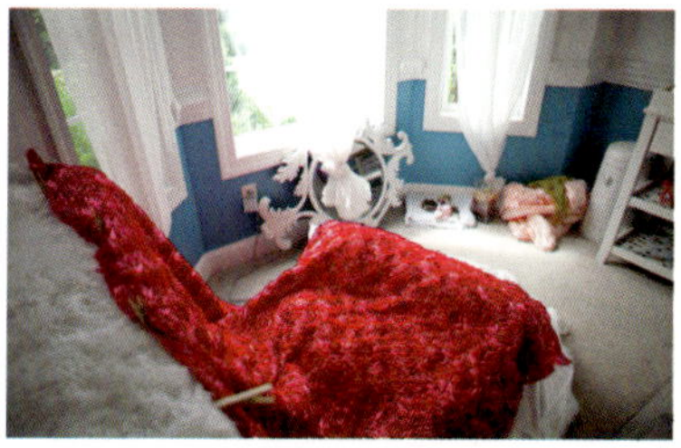

When working in a client's home, use the same concepts you employ in studio lighting. Look for large, diffuse light that creates a soft shadow to produce a sense of dimension. Having the window behind your shoulder at 45 degrees and using a reflector to pop light back in the eyes gives the best results.

The downside of using natural light is that the color temperature will change when the sun moves behind the clouds. If you are in a country where the light is erratic or dull (think Alaska, Scotland, or the Antarctic), you will be at the mercy of the weather. Perfect sunny conditions are readily available to those living in Florida, California, or Sydney, but not all of us have that

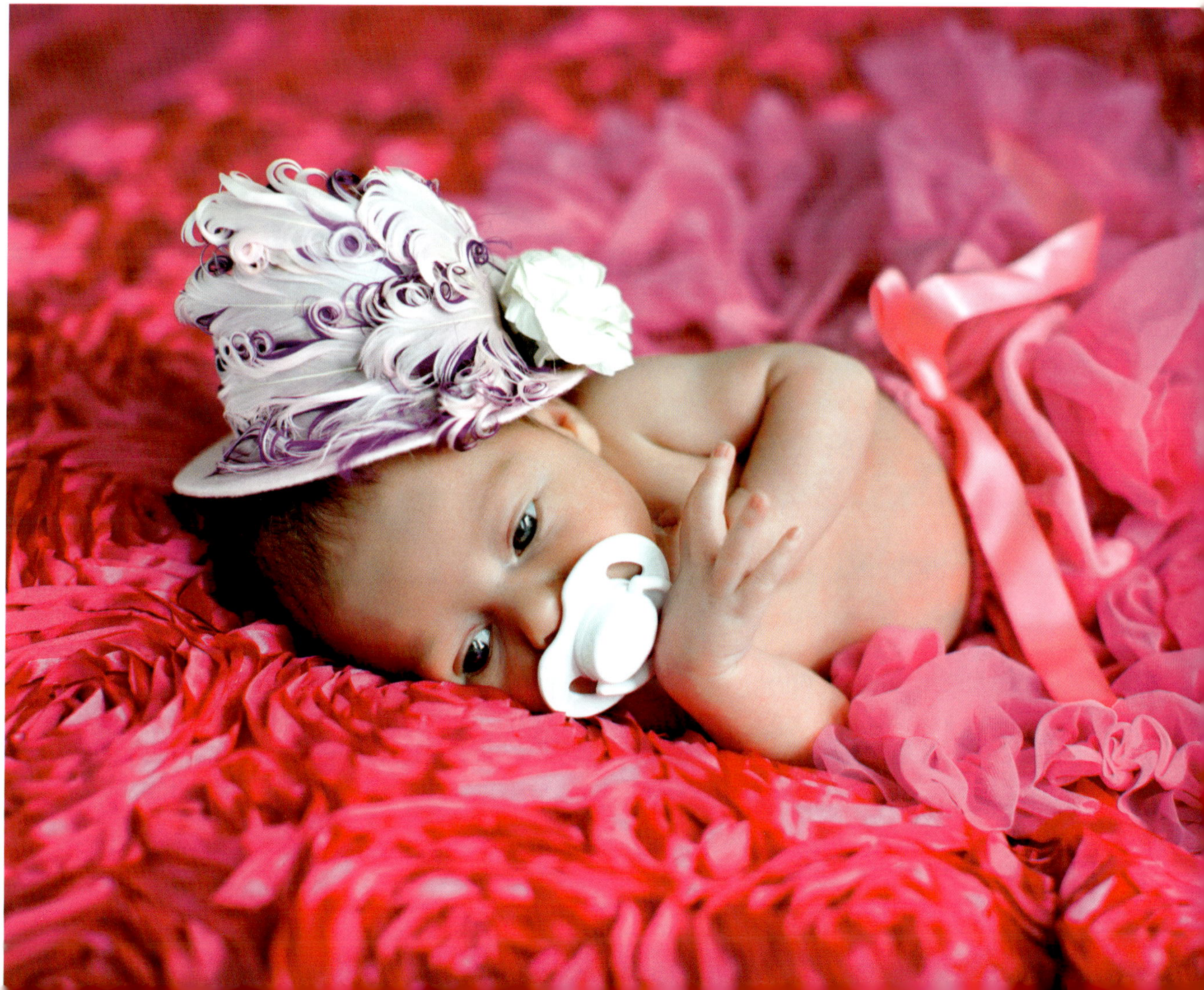

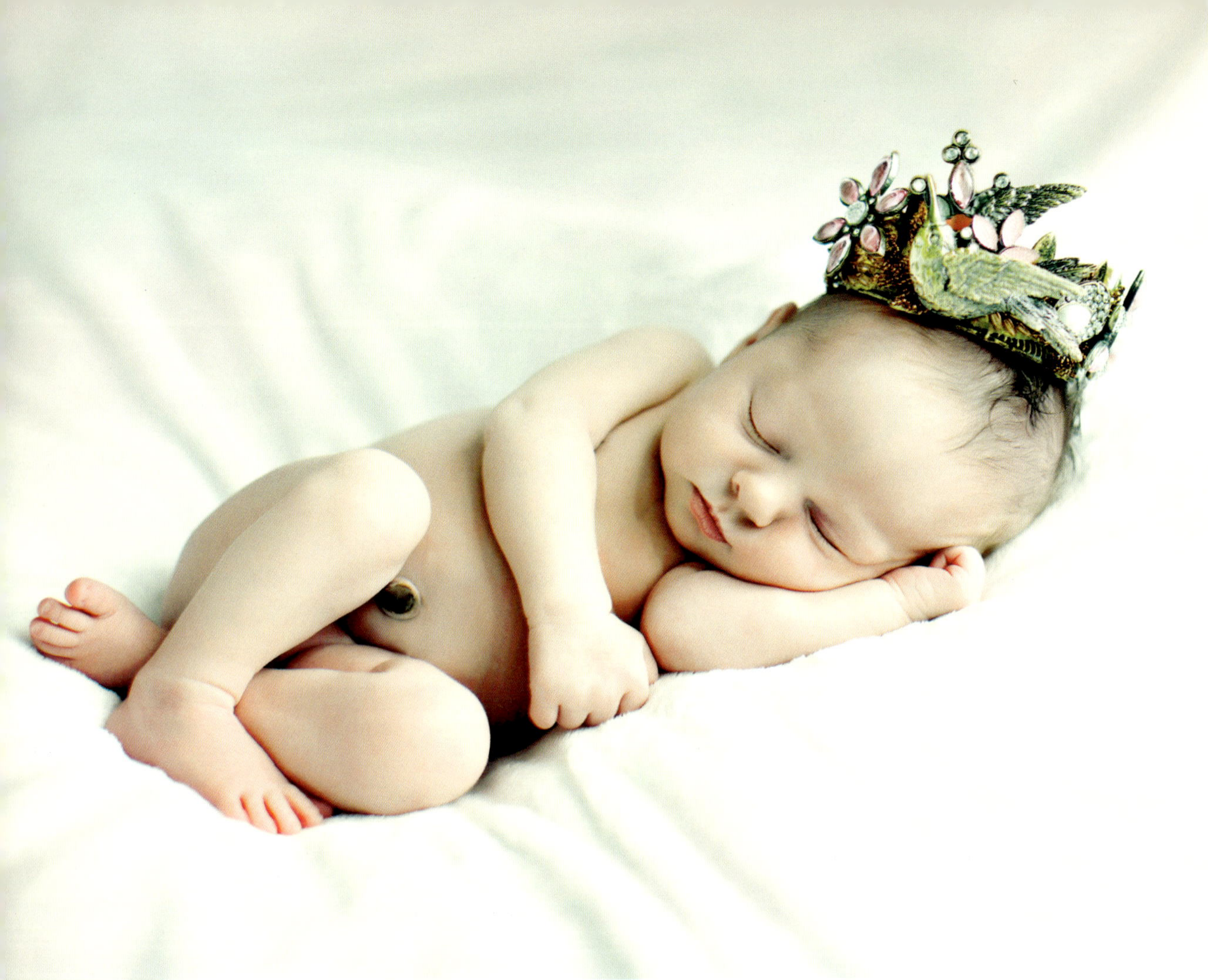

privilege! Keep in mind that as the sun moves across the sky and ducks behind the clouds, the color temperature of the light will change. Since I don't care for the varying color temperature of changing light, I prefer strobe lighting, which produces consistent results.

To find the best window light, shoot at roughly the same time every day. This can be favorable especially when you consider that a newborn baby is best photographed before lunch. Yes, this means an early start for Mom and Dad, but the best, most even light is found between 10:00AM and 2:00PM.

When shooting in a client's home, using their surroundings and decor to tell a story makes great-looking newborn memories.

▲ For the best, most predictible results, try to shoot at the same time every day when using window light.

Understanding Your Camera

It is important to have a proper understanding of how your camera works in order to take control of a lighting situation. Most of the time my light meter lies—it tells me to shoot at f/5, but I prefer f/5.6 to prevent blown-out highlights. This is why shooting in manual mode is a must for complete creative control of one's camera.

With natural light, I tend to shoot wide open at f/2 with a prime lens (50mm f/1.2) to achieve that soft bokeh look. In this scenario, with such a narrow depth of field, Baby can easily become out of focus with slight camera shake. For this reason, I have found that spot metering works best to ensure the point of focus is clear. I usually aim for the baby's eyes or the bridge of the nose. Focusing your lens manually will help to keep your images clean, without allowing the camera and lens to fight each other, continually searching for the point of focus.

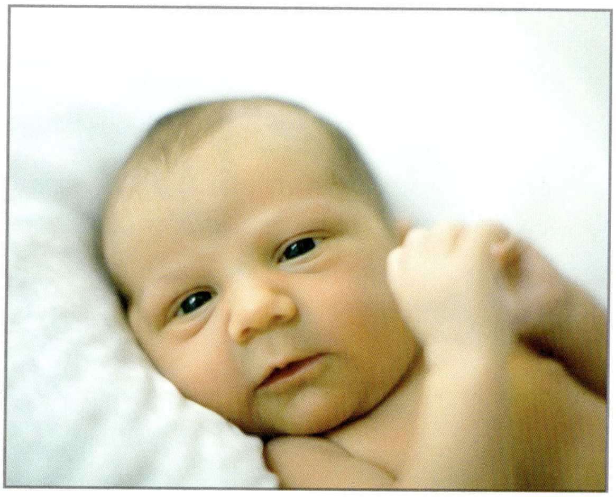

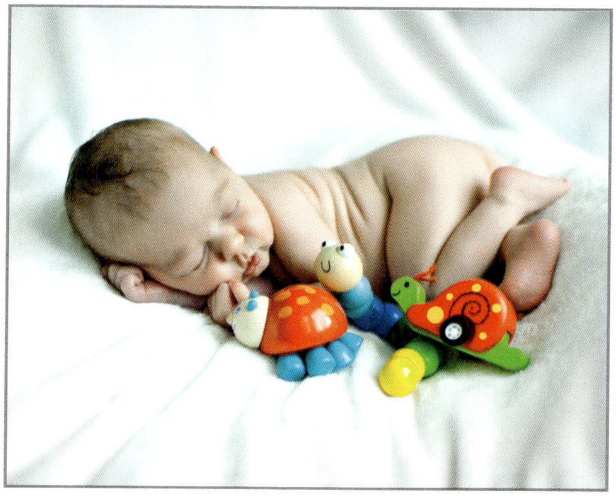

▲ (top) Relying on the camera's autofocus or choosing a too-shallow depth of field results in a blurry image.
▲ (bottom) Manual focus ensures baby's face remains in focus.

▼ (top and bottom) We use the decor of a client's home to tell the subject's story.

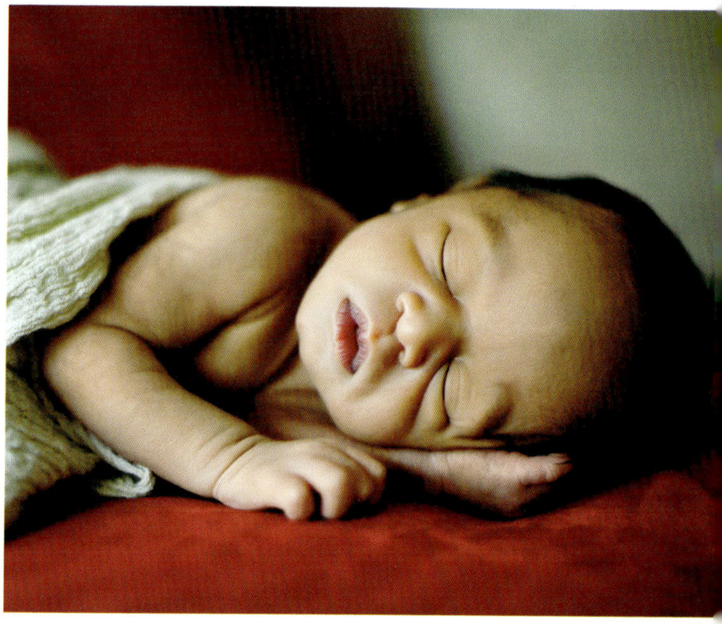

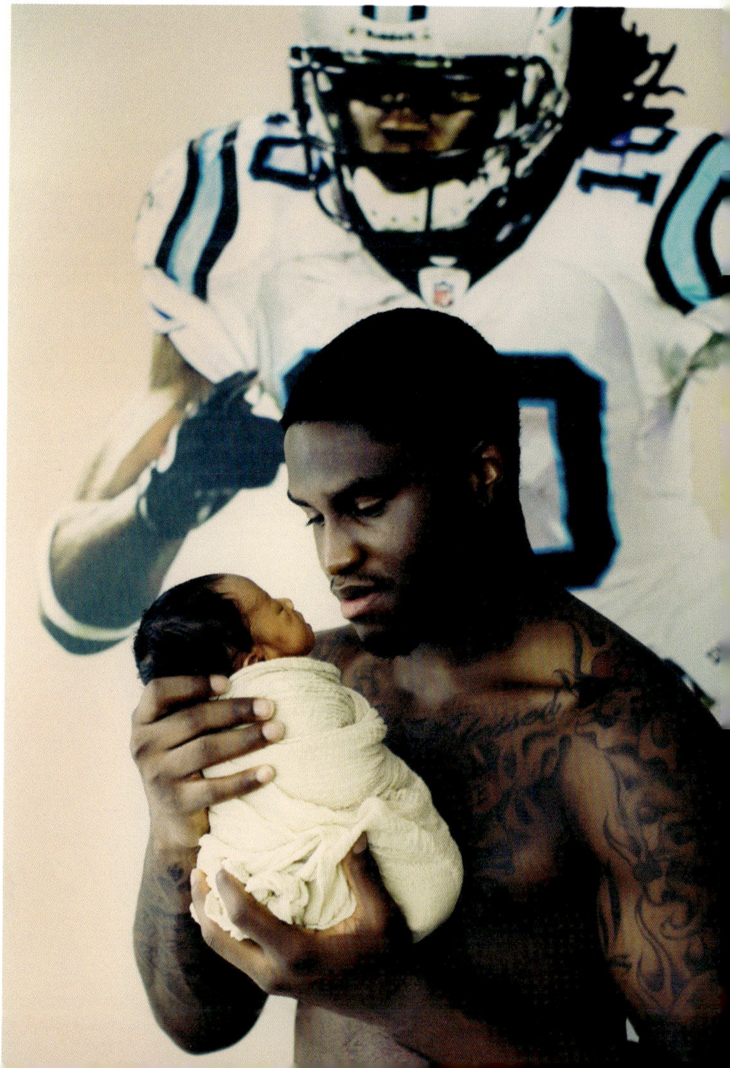

5. Newborn Posing

"A baby is God's opinion that the world should go on."—Carl Sandburg

Preparing for a Newborn Session

Seeing Baby's smile has an immediate positive effect on a mom or dad's mood. There is something about seeing your baby smile for the first time that warms your heart and uplifts your soul!

Baby's first portrait should be taken the moment he or she takes that first breath. Babies grow and change daily, and there are such beautiful moments to capture even in the first few hours, days, and weeks of the little one's life.

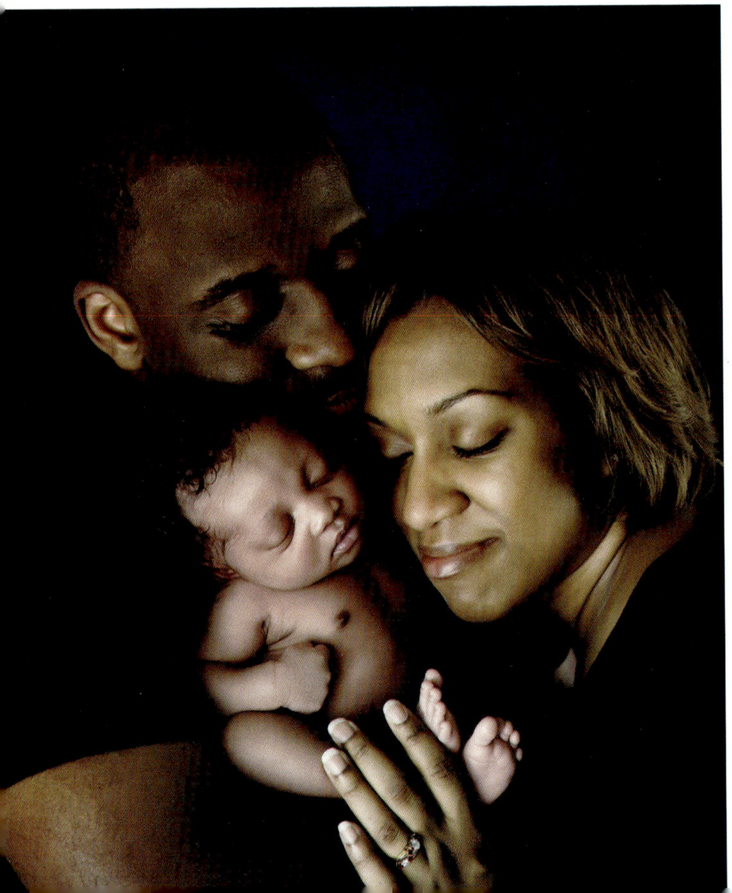

Ideally, a newborn session should be conducted within the first four to seven days after the birth, when baby is a heavy sleeper and is curled up in the fetal position.

By three or four weeks, babies start to stretch their legs and lose that sweet, curled-up look. By three weeks of age, roughly 20 percent of newborns develop baby acne. This is due to the fact the mother's hormones cross the placenta, causing the infant's oil glands to form bumps that look like pimples. This makes retouching and finishing the images time consuming and sometimes difficult.

A visit to your studio may very well be the new parents' first outing with Baby. It's important to create a warm and relaxed environment so that Mom will be at ease. If Mom is stressed out, baby will sense it. Advise Mom to give herself plenty of time to gather a few extra items of clothing, as it is a safe bet that her baby will get sick on her "pretty" clothes just as they walk out the door!

The best time to capture Baby's natural smiles and good mood are in the morning soon

◄ Capturing Mom, Dad, and Baby in a tightly cropped composition shows emotion.
► Newborns under two weeks old are heavy sleepers.

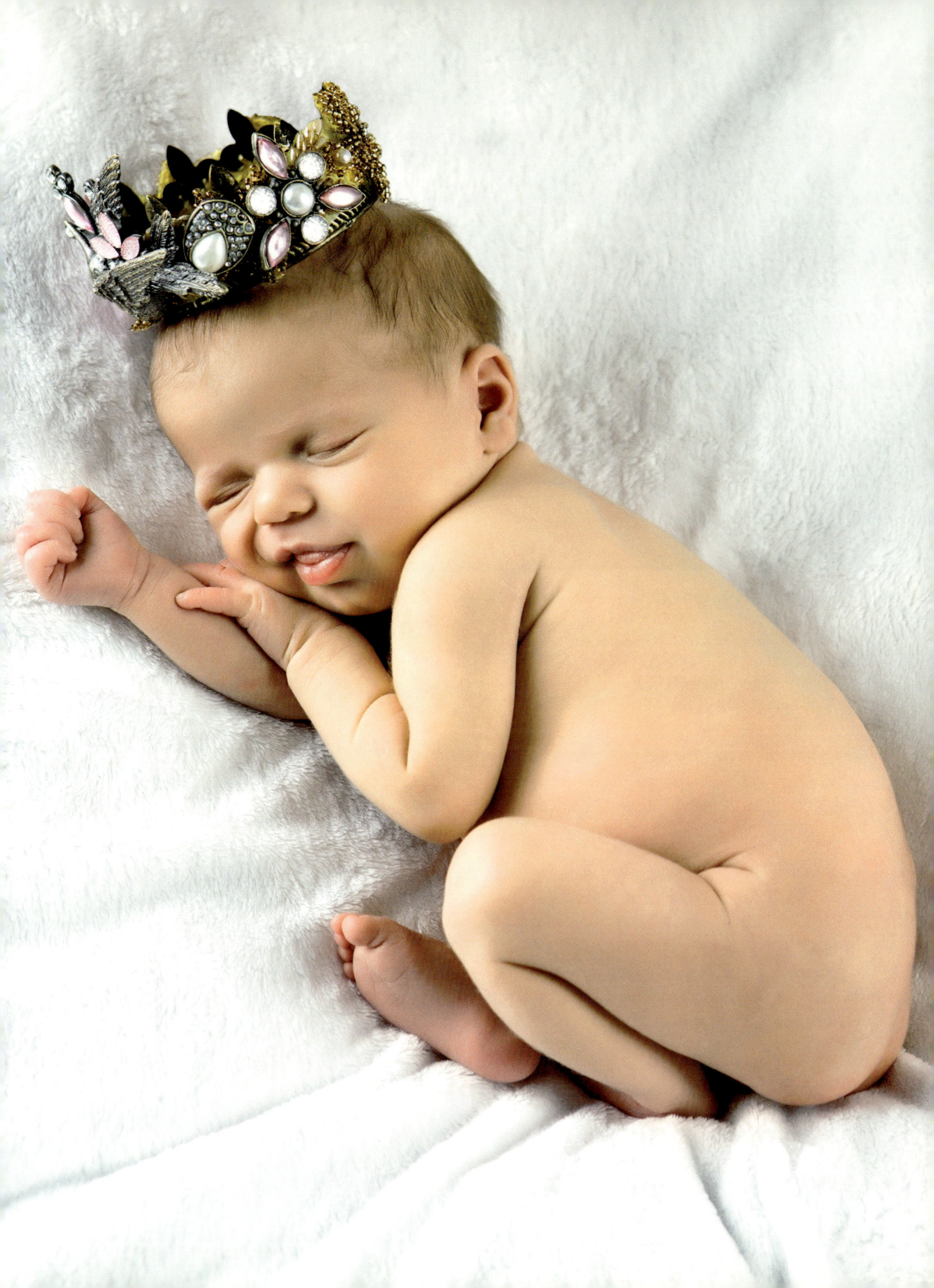

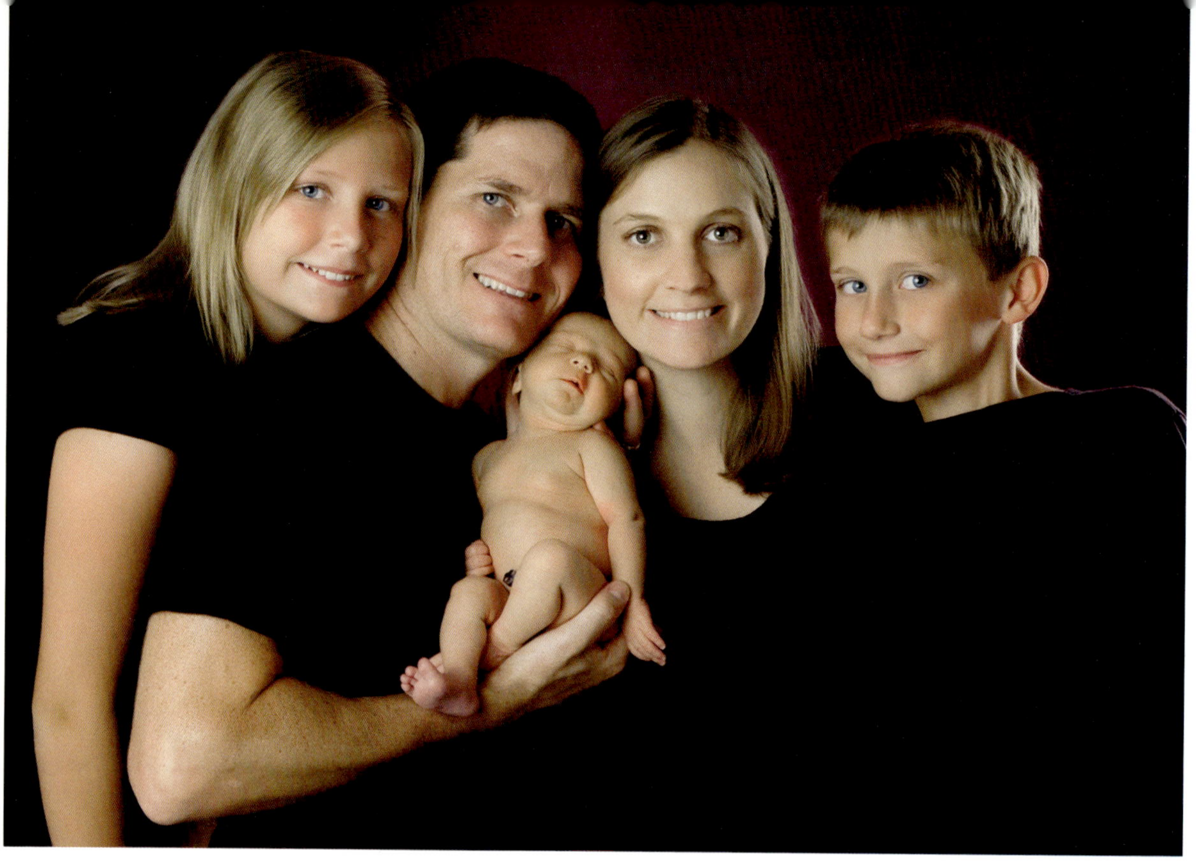

▲ A portrait of the whole family is a huge seller. This is my family when the baby was born. I took the image with the camera on a tripod and used the camera's self-timer.

after they have awakened and have been well fed. Babies have a limited number of smiles, so don't use them up by playing with the baby before the session begins. Babies are unpredictable. If the baby decides halfway through the session that they need a top-off, don't stress. Oblige their needs so that Mom and Baby are content.

Many of the families you photograph will have more than one child. A photograph of a newborn baby is a wonderful keepsake for the parents, but including older siblings can result in additional sales. The majority of families who come to my studio for newborn portraits have other kids under eight years old. Most of these siblings are active toddlers that require a special kind of focus and patience! The best option for photographing siblings is to have them lie down with Baby or sit on a sofa so we can get their faces as close as possible.

Stay in Control

Sleep-deprived parents have little patience for taming a wired toddler. During the session, you want to keep things moving along, so try directing your clients in a calm, friendly, but authoritative tone to maintain control. When older kids are involved in the newborn session, it's important to tell them how things are going to work as soon as they enter your shooting space to avoid any wild behavior or equipment breakage. At my studio, the staff say something like, "Welcome to Mimika's studio. We are going to have fun today! Kids, remember not to grab any of the equipment you see here, as we don't want anyone getting hurt if it falls down. We all need to show that we are good listeners so that we can get a treat from the treasure box when we are done."

Mom and Dad will appreciate your laying down the law. Knowing that you are a professional and fully in control will put them at ease.

When conducting these sessions, the most important rule is to have fun. Enjoy what you are doing, and your enthusiasm will show.

When to Reschedule

When signs of illness are present (runny nose, raised temperature, coughing, and general crankiness), I advise parents to reschedule their appointment when everyone is healthy. Both parents and the baby will enjoy the experience far more if everyone is content and happy. Putting a sick child through the trauma of feeling unwell and having to cope in a foreign studio environment will only result in a crying kid and frustrated parent. We also don't want to infect others. I also advise that immunizations be postponed until after the session.

Wardrobe Planning

As the saying goes, less is more. This is especially true when it comes to planning an appropriate outfit. Solid colors are best. Bright or pastel clothes look best in portraits taken against a white or light background. Blues, white, ivory, khaki, and salmon are lovely outdoors against green foliage. Burgundy, brown, tan, and gray are nice in late autumn. Avoid large or bold patterns, wording, checks, stripes, dots, and spots as they draw attention away from the focus of the photo—the face.

Baby is best photographed in his/her birthday suit. Most clothing swallows up a newborn and distorts their tiny shape. The parents' clothing choice should be simple and neutral. Plain black or beige long-sleeved shirts and jeans work well. These choices help to place the emphasis on the parent–baby bond.

Trying to capture young siblings with a newborn can be challenging, but these are images the parents love to buy.

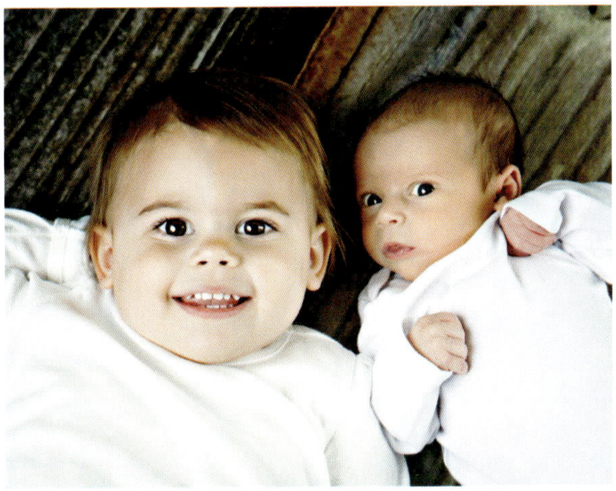

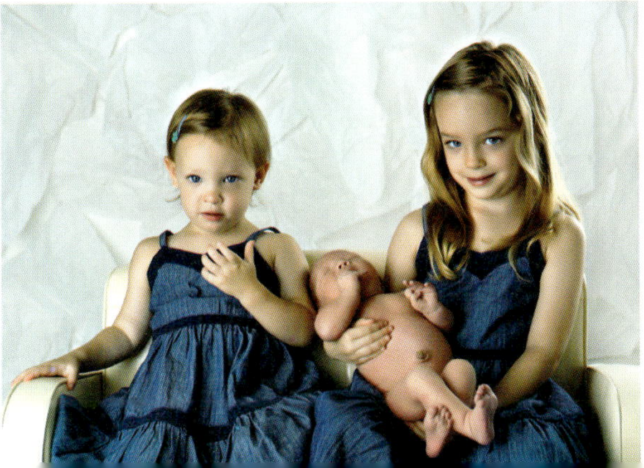

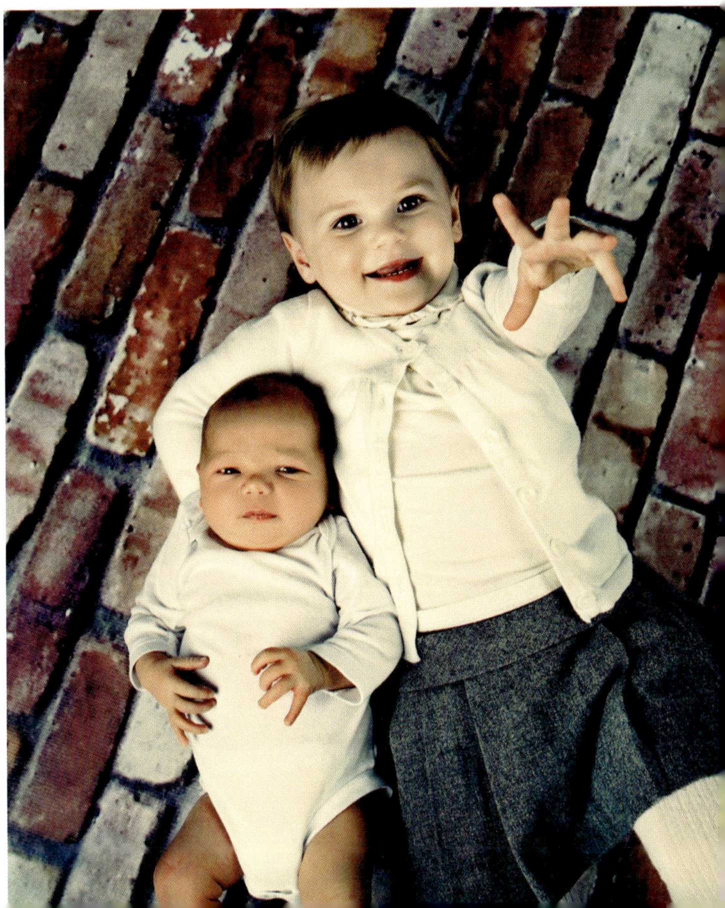

Older kids tend to want to show off their branded or character clothing, but brand names will date the photo and are distracting. Try to steer clothing decisions away from branded items by subtly suggesting a simpler alternative.

When planning for a family portrait, ask your clients to dress in the same style of clothing but not necessarily the same color. It's best not to mix casual and formal attire in the same shot, as formal clothing results in more formal poses. If you are planning a relaxed portrait or will be shooting outdoors, casual and comfortable clothing, like denim, will be an excellent choice. Children look best photographed with bare feet, as shoes tend to make their little feet look much bigger. For Mom and Dad, however, socks are recommended.

You may want to recommend that your clients refrain from getting a haircut immediately prior to the session. Hair has a more natural appearance after it has grown out for a few days. It's always a good idea to bring along a brush or comb to tidy up and tame any flyaway hair as needed.

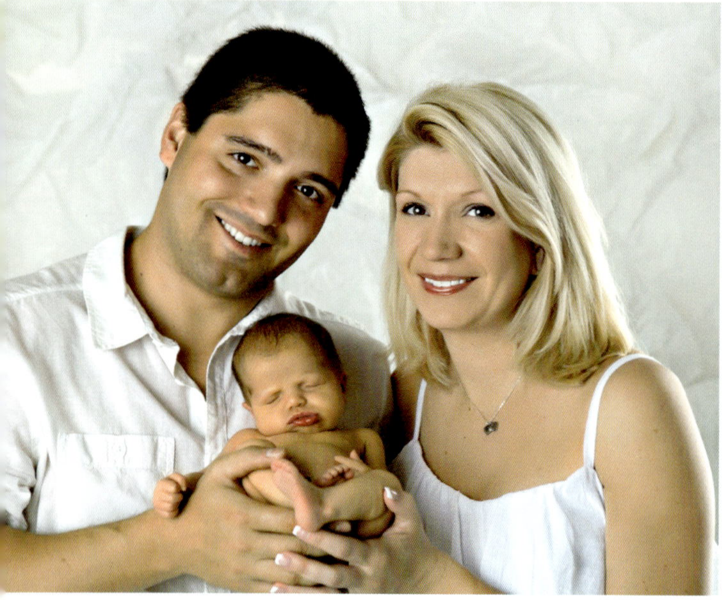

◄ Mom and Dad will treasure photos captured with their baby.

▼ Children look best photographed with bare feet.

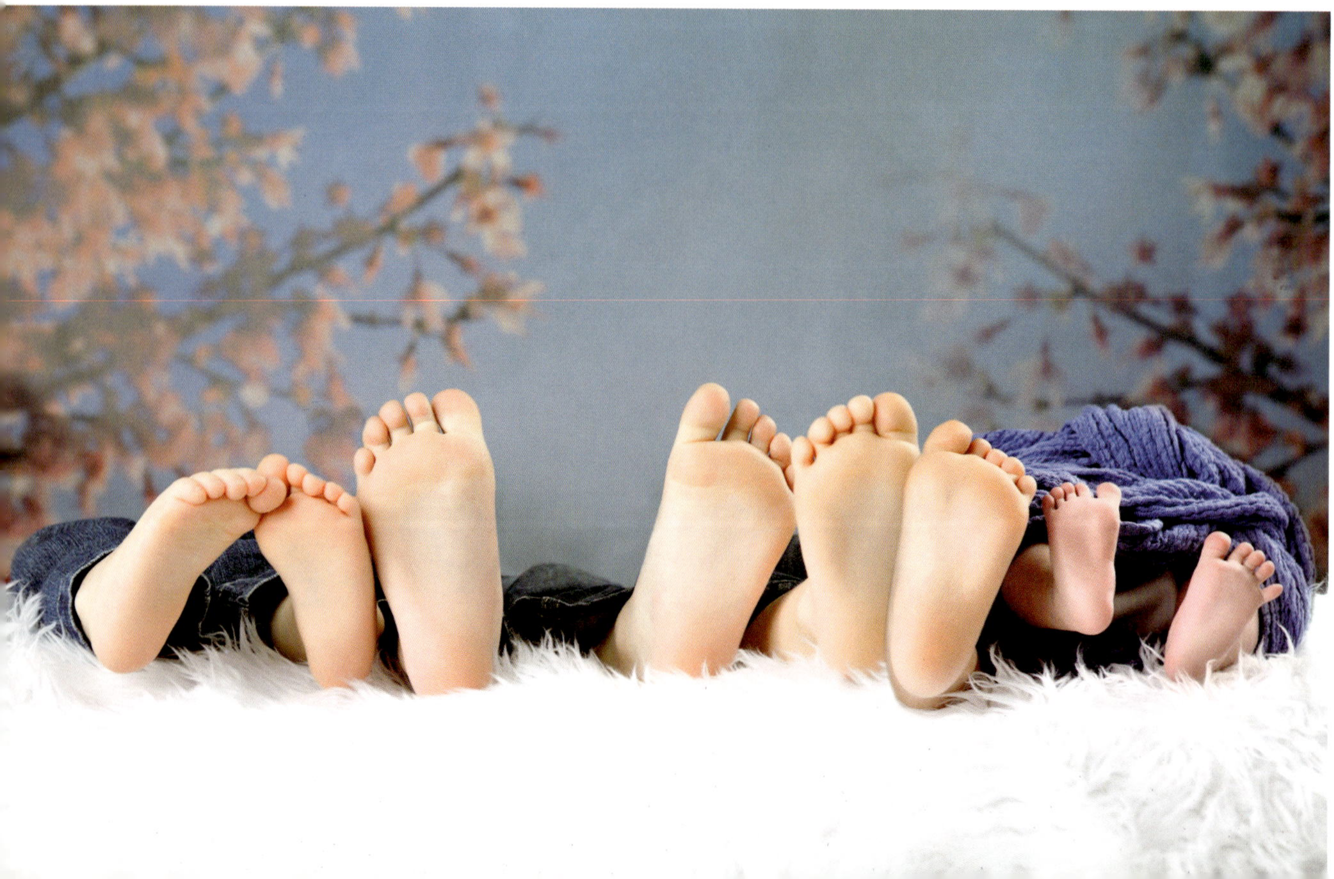

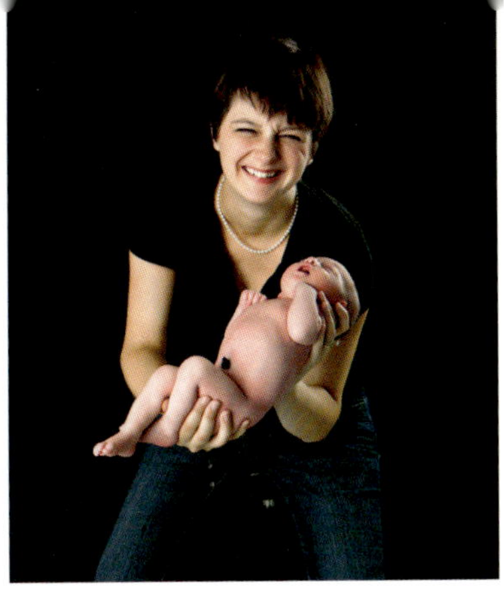

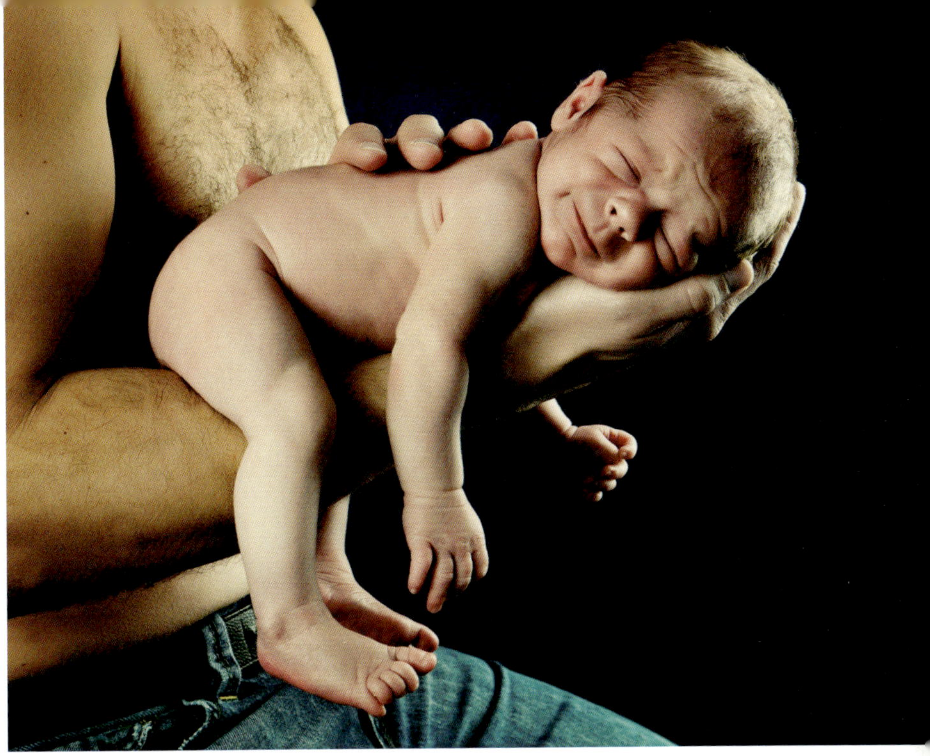

▲ Accidents will happen.
➤ Crying is an expected part of the newborn session—especially right before he or she falls asleep.

Accidents Will Happen

We are only tempting fate when we remove all of baby's clothing and their diaper to get those cute curled-up naked baby portraits. Don't panic, but be prepared for accidents. Have clean-up materials at the ready. In my studio, we have flooring that lends itself to easy cleanup and we keep loads of antibacterial wipes, paper towels, and hand sanitizer available. Often, Baby will warn you that they need to go by crying and wriggling. Place a clean diaper loosely under their buttocks until they settle. I always tell parents it's not *if* but *when* it happens, so expect the unexpected. It's also advisable for the adults to bring an extra set of clothing, as there is a good chance that someone will get sprayed!

"We are only tempting fate when we remove all of baby's clothing and their diaper to get those cute curled-up naked baby portraits."

What to Do When Baby Cries

We all have our good and bad days, and sometimes even adults wake up on the wrong side of the bed. There is a good possibility that the baby may cry during the session. When this happens, it's best to pause the photo taking and give the little one a cuddle to make them feel secure. The bright flashing lights, strange noises, and unfamiliarity can cause uncertainty. Tears may be a sign that the baby has reached his/her limit or is overtired, so wrap up the session quickly. He or she may be unwell or coming down with a cold, and if that's the case, it is best to reschedule the session.

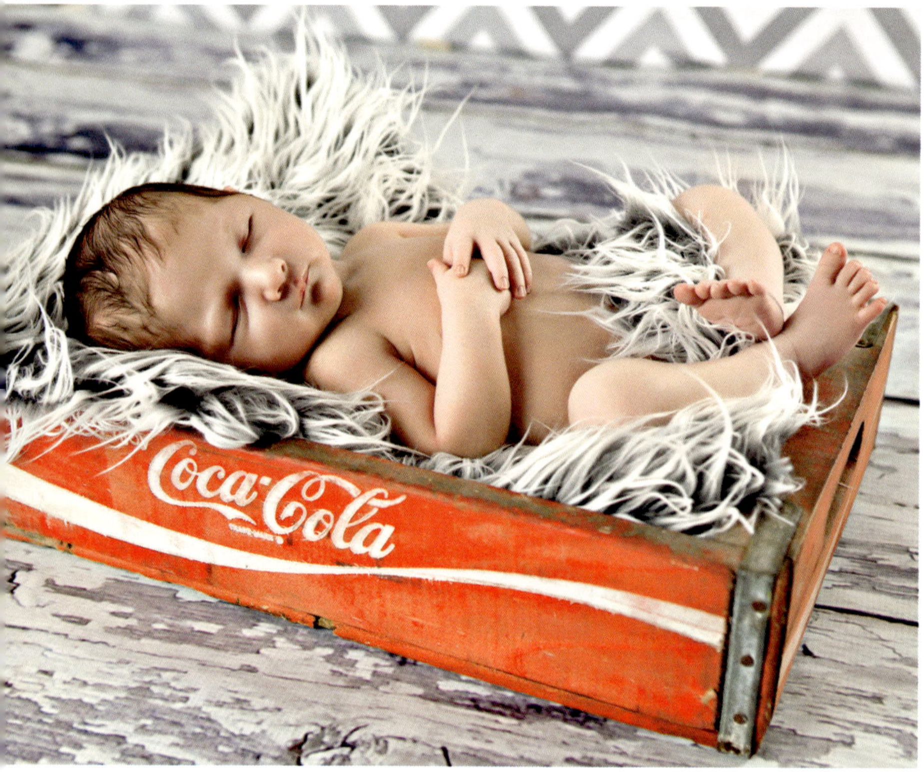

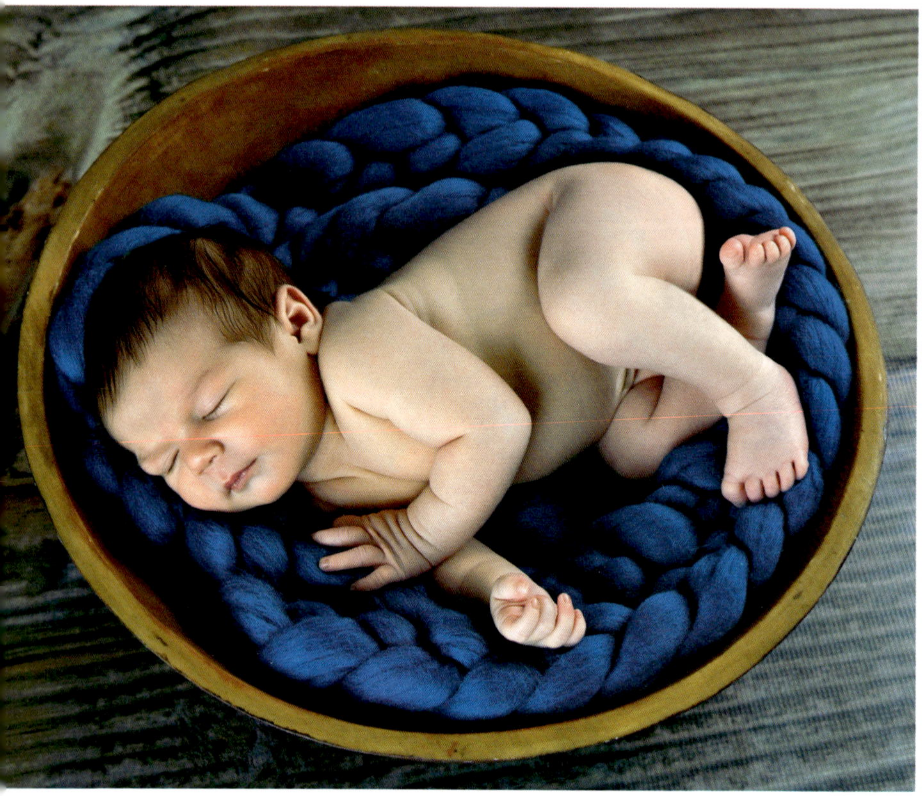

If it is just a case of nerves, it may be possible to offer distractions to Mom and Baby to refocus them.

Props and Posing

Being able to sit or hold their head up is not a requirement for beautiful portraits, as newborns during the first few weeks of life have gorgeous features. I love taking photos of their "kissable" parts such as their hands, feet, ears, eyes, nose, mouth etc., and compiling them in an artistic montage in what is called a Kissable Collection. A newborn baby has much to offer in a portrait, as their little form reminds us how precious and vulnerable new life is. These early days are gone in the blink of an eye, so capturing these subjects when they are itty-bitty is important.

Using props is a great way to showcase the baby's small size and tell a story. Flower boxes, suitcases, hanging baskets, beanbags, glass bowls, wooden boxes, etc., are excellent choices. The possibilities are endless when you make a trip to the craft store and ask yourself, "Will a baby fit in

◀ (top and bottom) Use props to help showcase Baby's size and to tell a story.

▶ The Kissable Collection is a hot seller.

The What-to-Expect Guide

Here is an example of the e-mail I send to clients to help them prepare for a newborn session:

I've put together this What to Expect guide to help you prepare for the session. Make sure to arrive with clean hair, face, and nails, and bring along your selected outfits. I have a bunch of adorable newborn props, blankets, headbands, bow ties, and backdrops, so you need not worry about bringing anything for Baby!

A point to consider: this newborn session is ideally suited for Mom, Dad, and Baby only, as siblings (especially those under the age of five) typically don't cope well with a newborn and the length of the session. Sibling photos are best done when baby is six months old or older. However, if you prefer that siblings be involved, we ask that you bring someone to help who can take older children home or to a park while we conduct the sleeping part of the session to guarantee the best results.

We look forward to capturing your family memories!

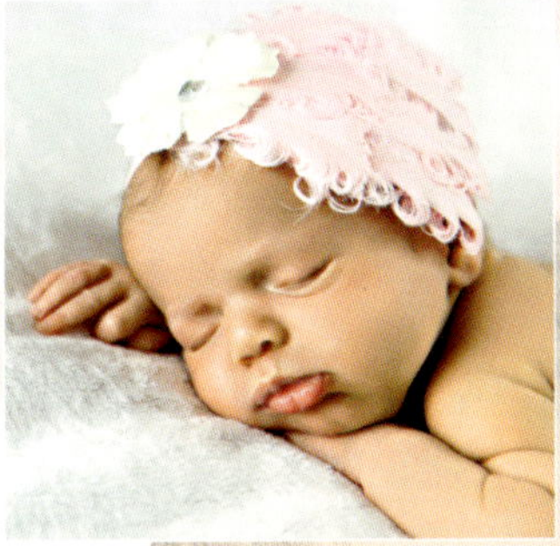
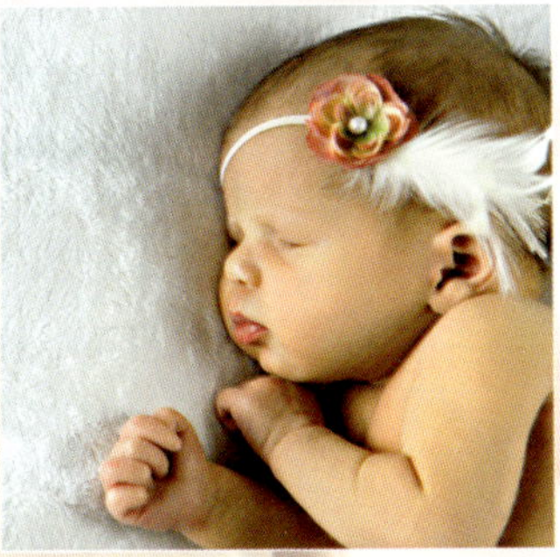
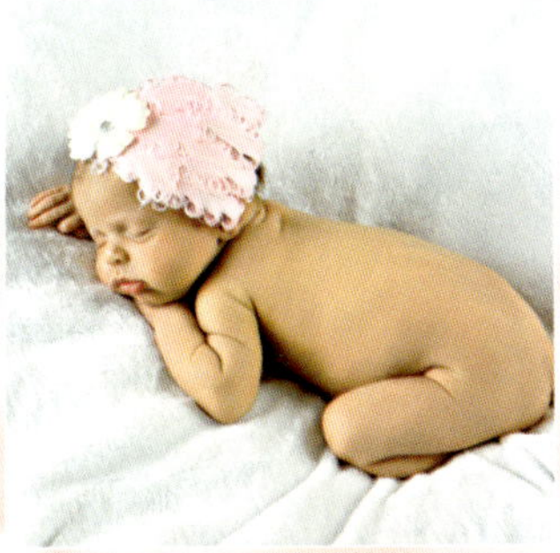
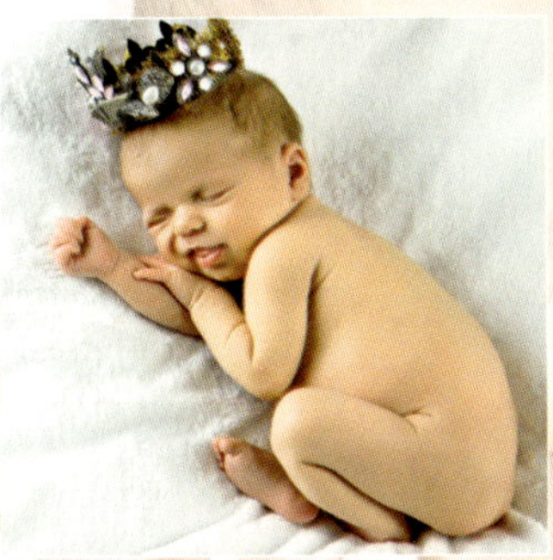
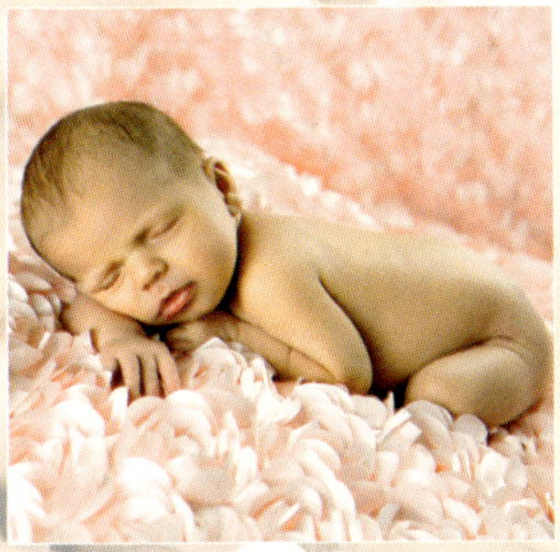
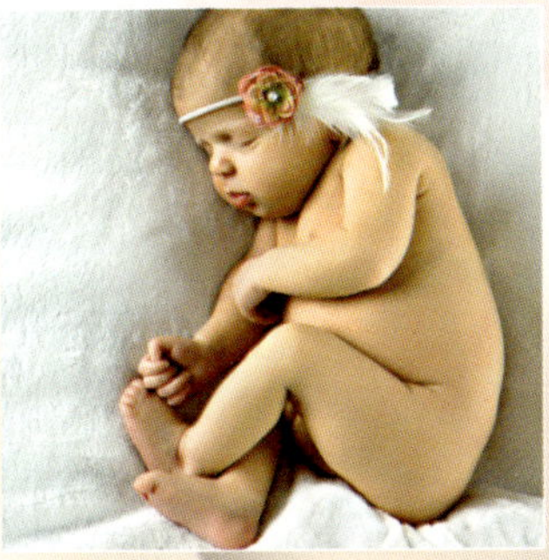
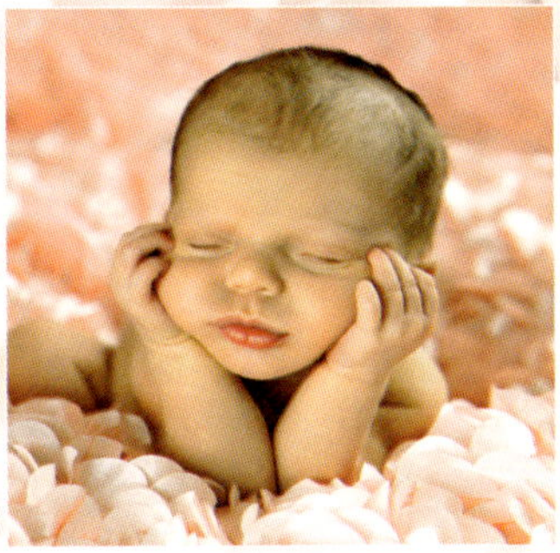
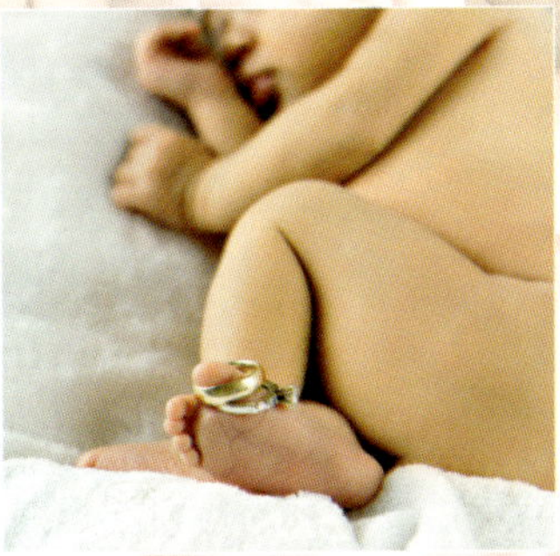
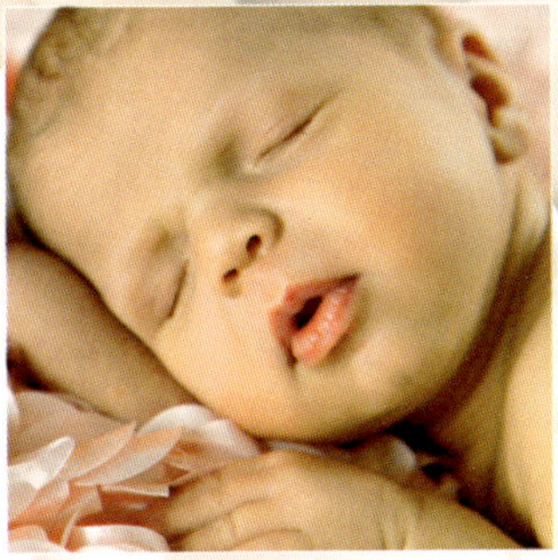

there?" Use blankets, fabric, and rugs for Baby to lie on—they love texture!

Posing for Relationship Imagery. To make a collection more salable, keep a mental note of the poses you photograph. When you get a close-up of Mom holding Baby in the cheek-to-cheek position, remember to do the same when Dad is holding Baby. During the sales appointment, if you have shots to match, you can easily put a lovely collection together.

Moms just love to see Daddy shirtless holding his little baby bundle. It is heartwarming

(below left and right) Relationship imagery is usually sold in a set.

(facing page) Here are some relationship posing ideas.

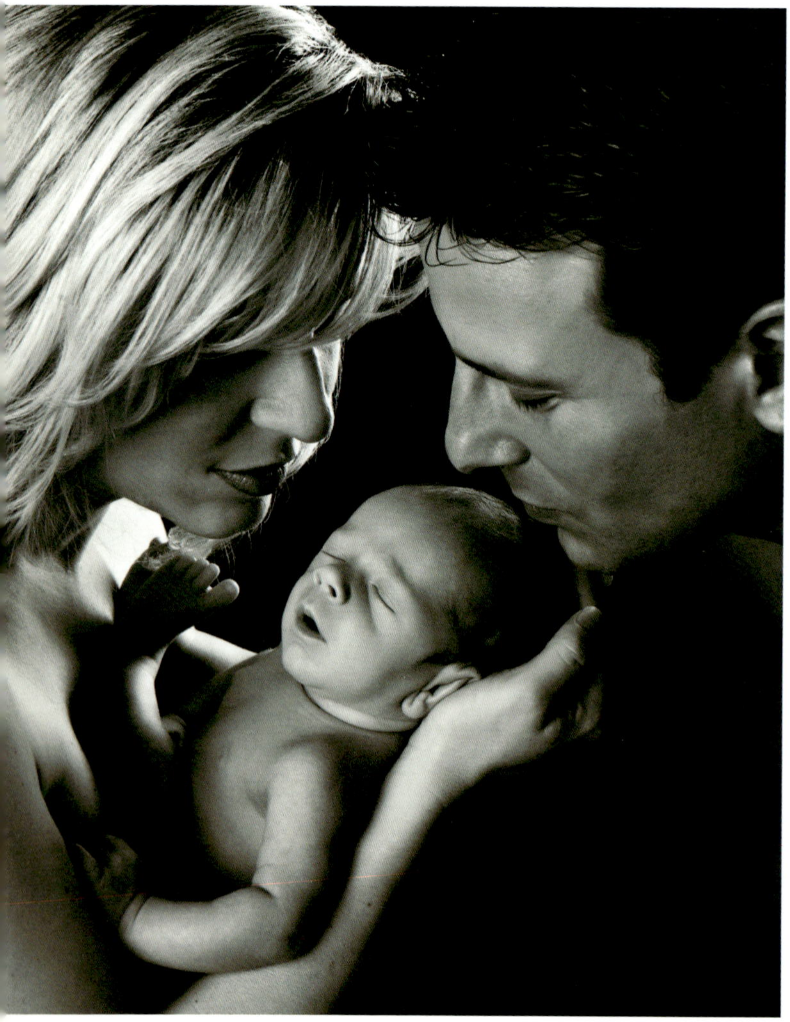

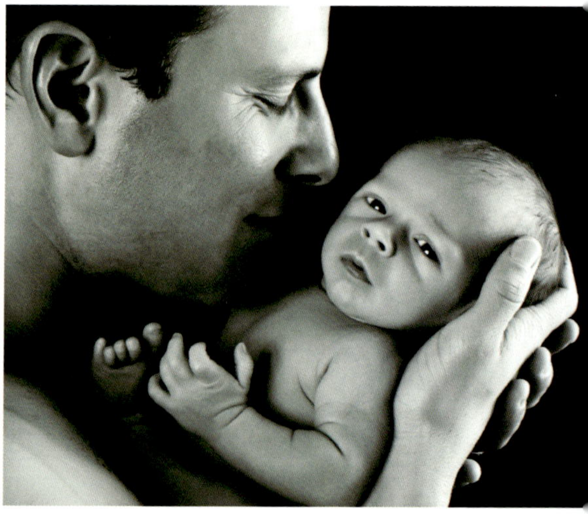

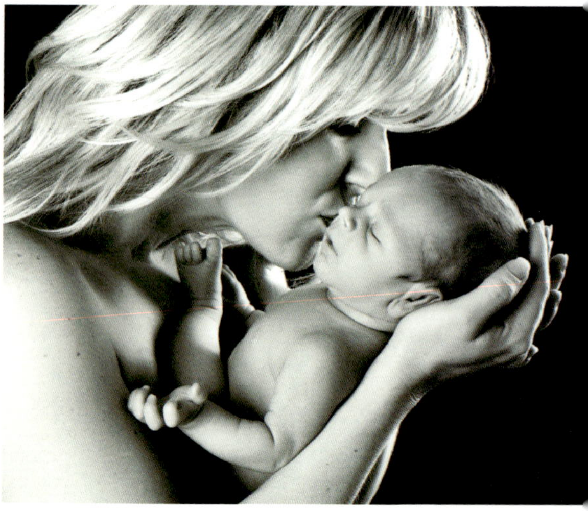

Supply Checklist

Certain staples will make any newborn photographer's job easier. Having the items organized and at arm's reach will help to keep the session moving ahead without interruptions. The list includes but is not limited to space heaters, a firm beanbag, swaddling blankets, a sound machine, rolled prop blankets, wet wipes, antibacterial floor wipes, paper towels, hats/headbands/bow ties, posing blankets, clothespins, tissues, and a pacifier/bottle.

Before you begin, use a big dollop of antibacterial hand soap and thoroughly rub your hands in front of Mom and Dad (without saying anything) to emphasize your attention to cleanliness. This small gesture will put their nervous minds at rest and tell them you care for their baby.

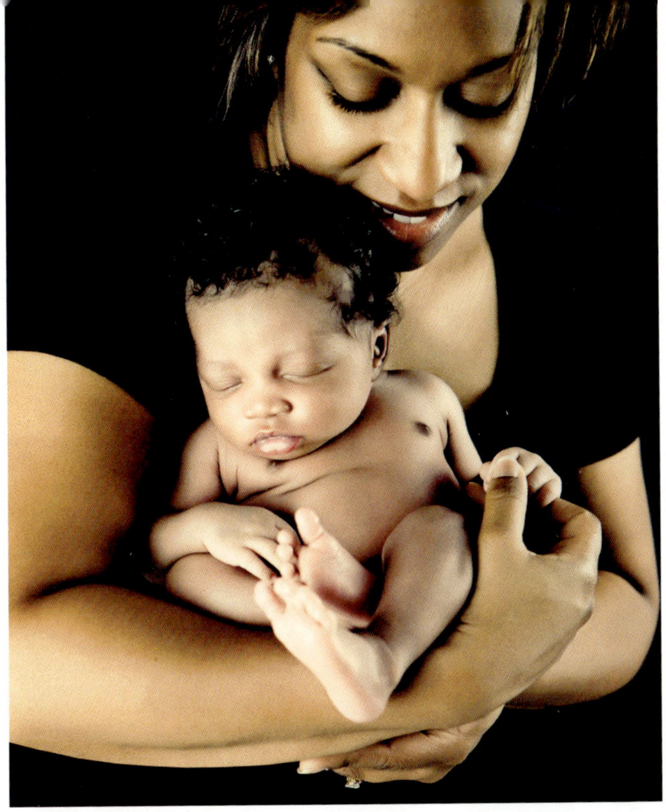
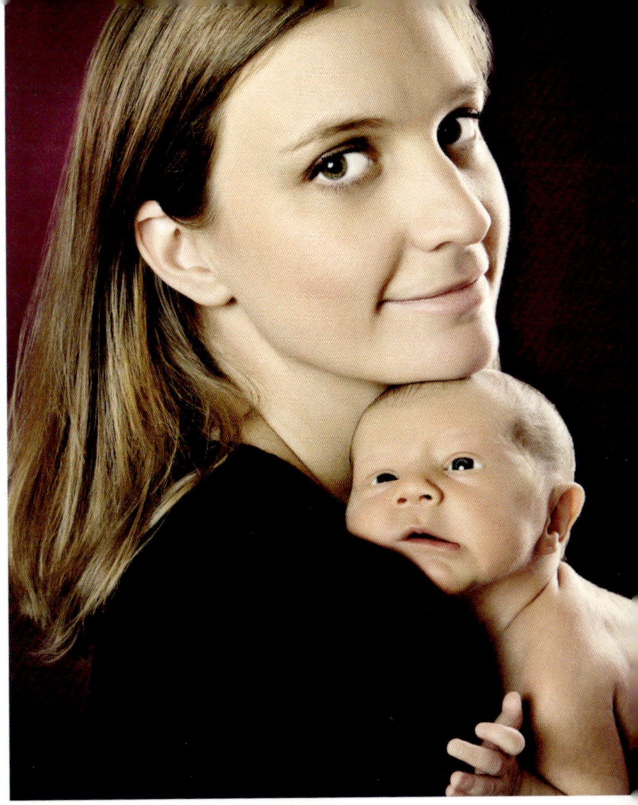
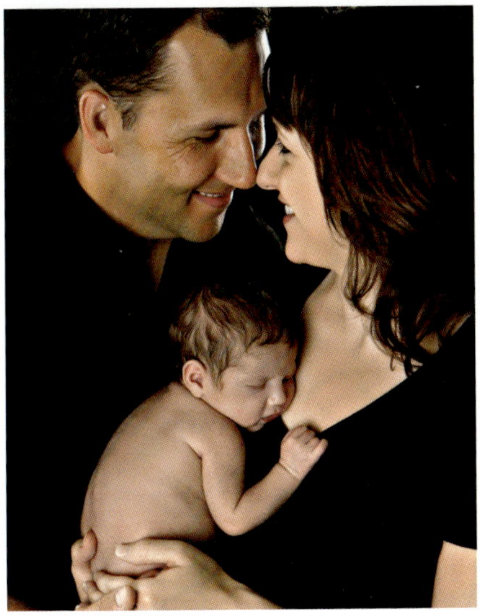
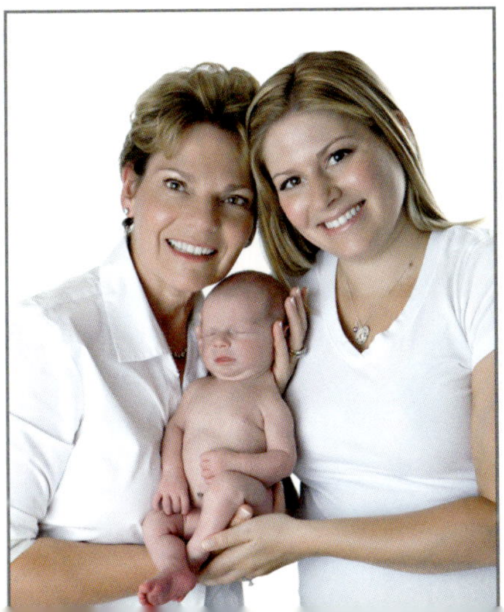
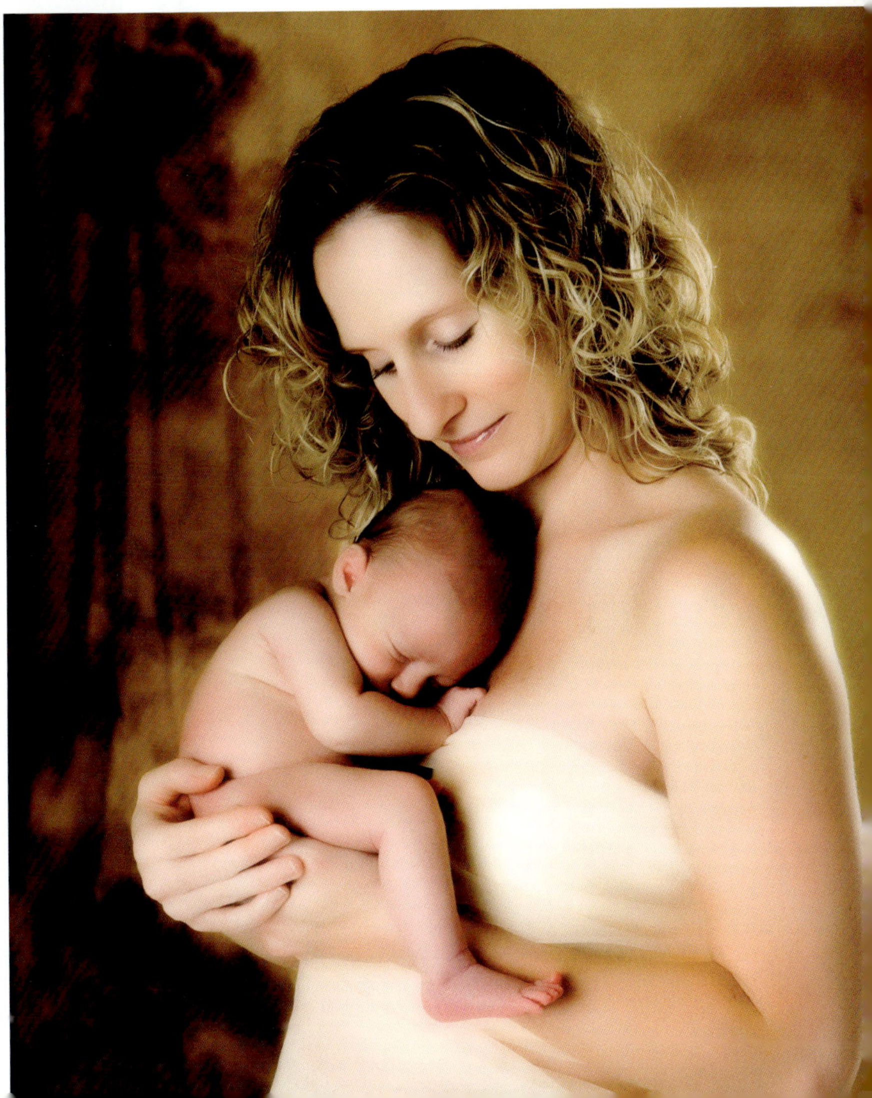

to see Dad's strength juxtaposed with Baby's delicateness. So off with the shirts, Dads! If Dad is not comfortable with his physique, you can use lighting to artfully downplay his arms, and tummy, or other perceived flaws.

Using Parents as Props. During newborn sessions, the parents often serve as props or posing aids. You can cover Mom or Dad with a blanket and pose Baby, then retouch the parent out in postproduction for a seamless look.

Safety First!

Baby's safety is of paramount importance. When possible, work with an assistant, whether it is

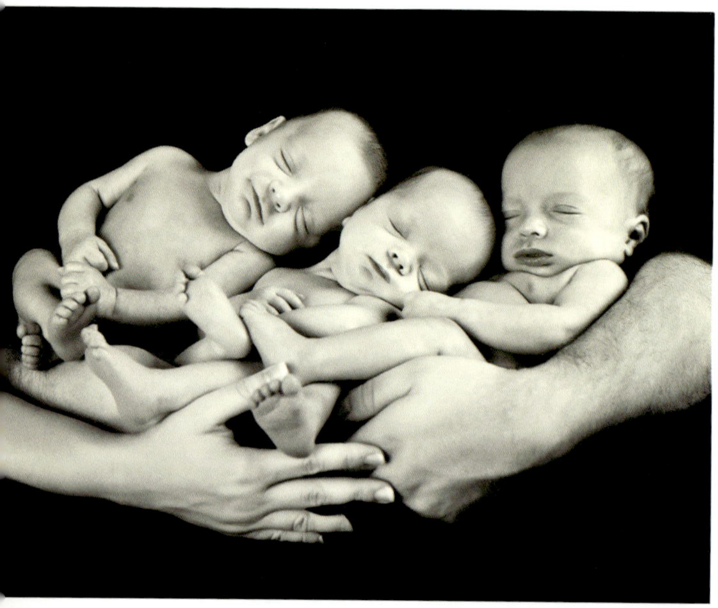

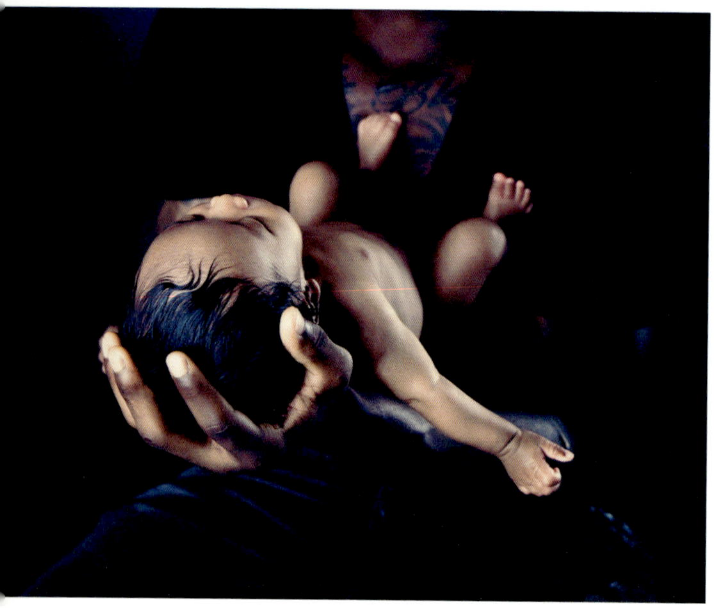

▲ Parents can make great props.

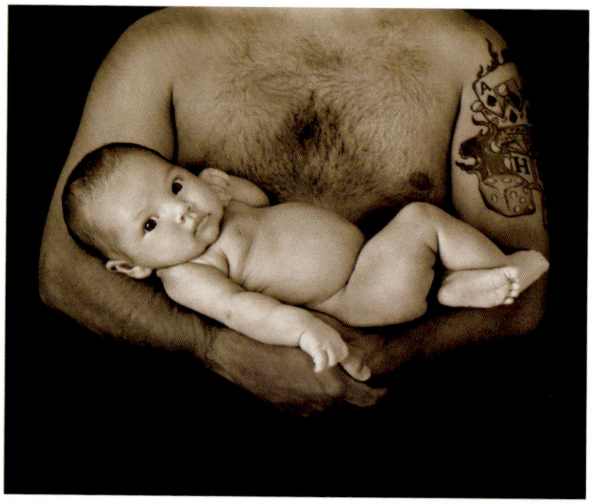

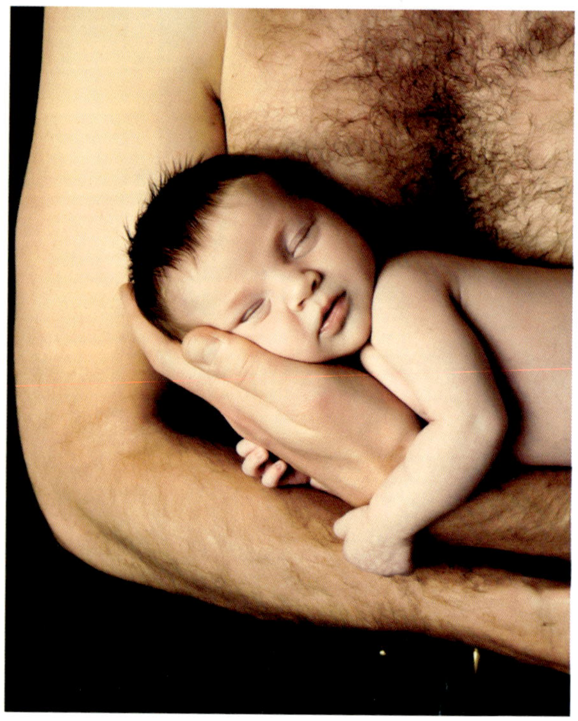

▲ ➤ Shirtless dads are a great addition to the collection.

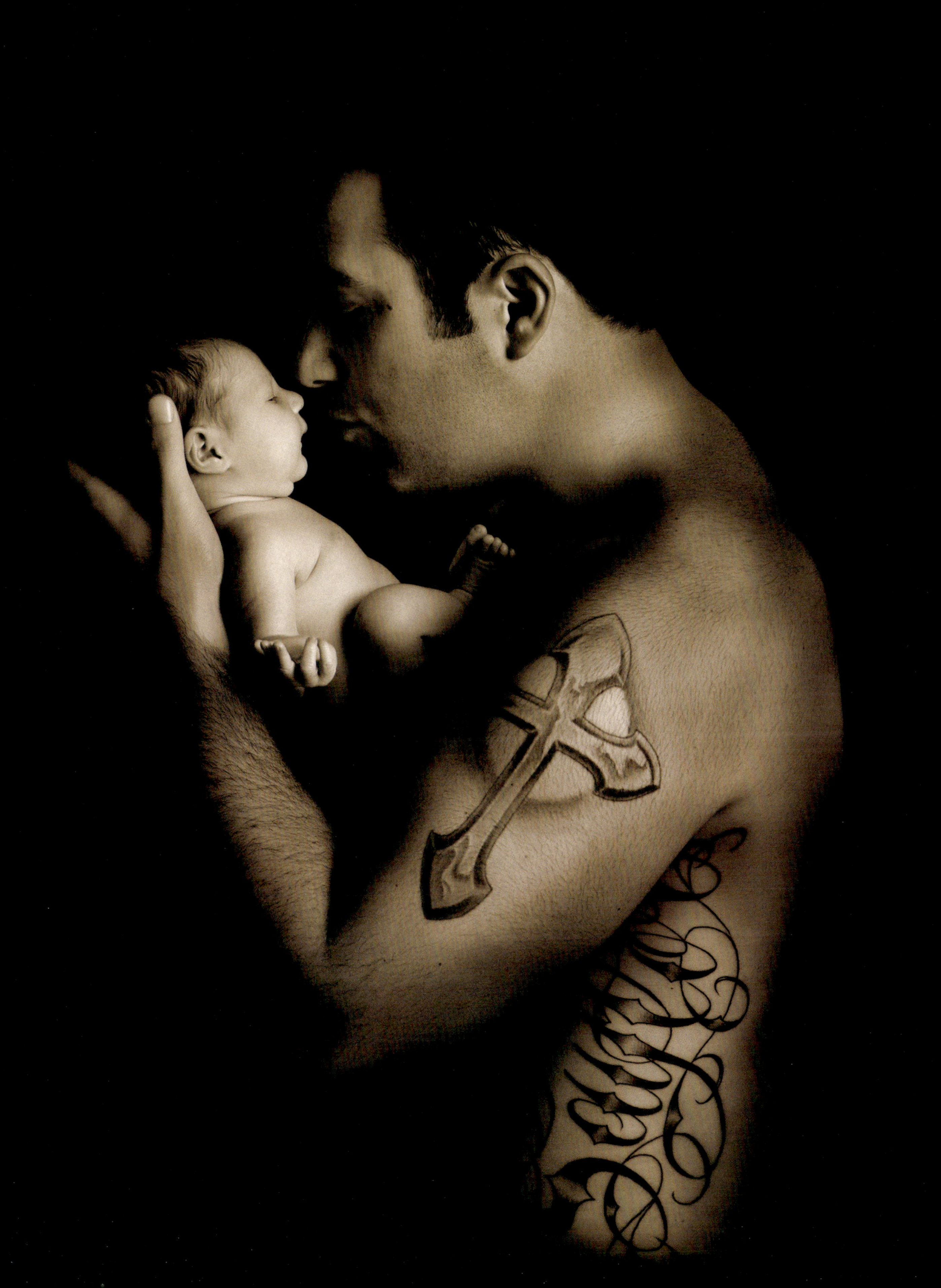

hired help or Mom or Dad. Someone must be within touching distance of Baby at all times to prevent injuries. Whenever I need to get up to move lights or retrieve something, I always ask Mom or Dad to sit with or hold their child. You never want to prevent an opportunity for disaster to strike.

Working with an Assistant

Having an extra pair of hands will make light work when it comes to working quickly with a fussy and tired baby. It takes a lot of patience to soothe a newborn baby to sleep in a new environment, so having an assistant take care of things like changes can allow you to concentrate on the baby and getting the perfect shot.

"Having an extra pair of hands will make light work when it comes to working quickly with a fussy and tired baby."

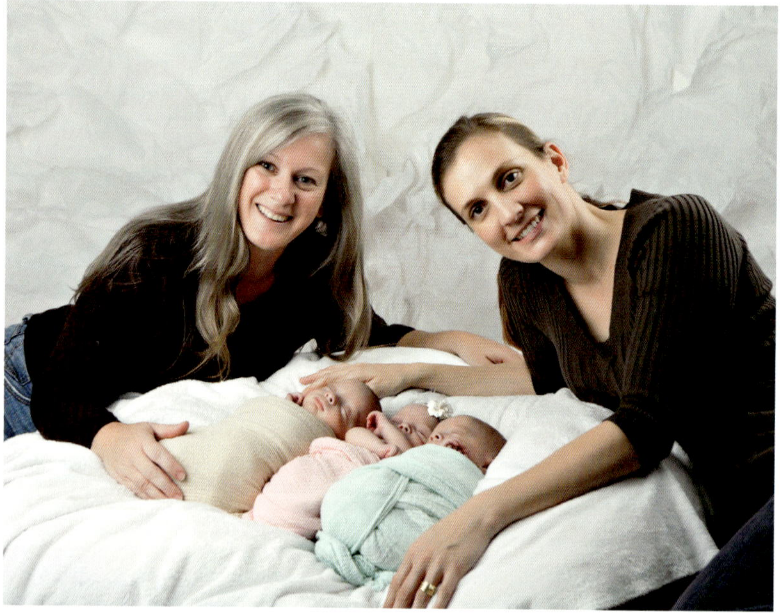

◀ My photographer friend Elizabeth Renee Sanford helped me out with a triplet session.

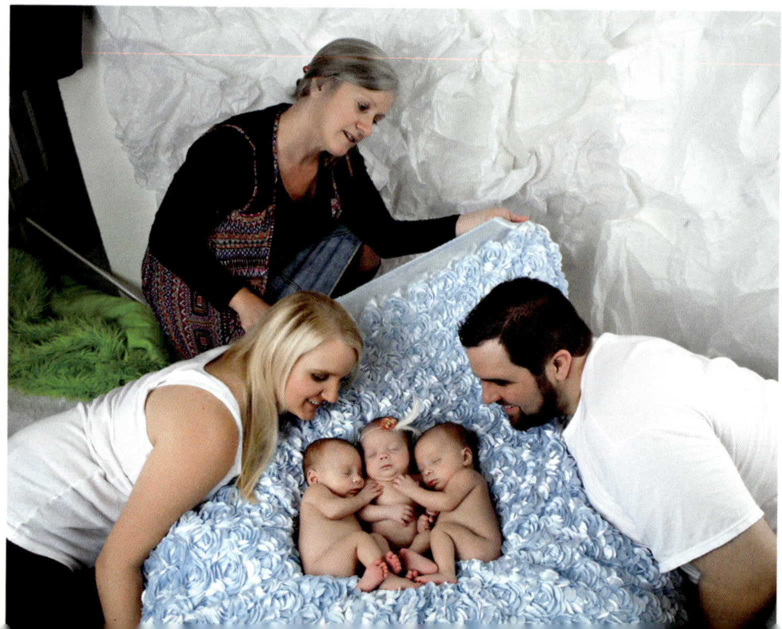

◀▶ Having an extra pair of hands helps keep the session moving without interruptions.

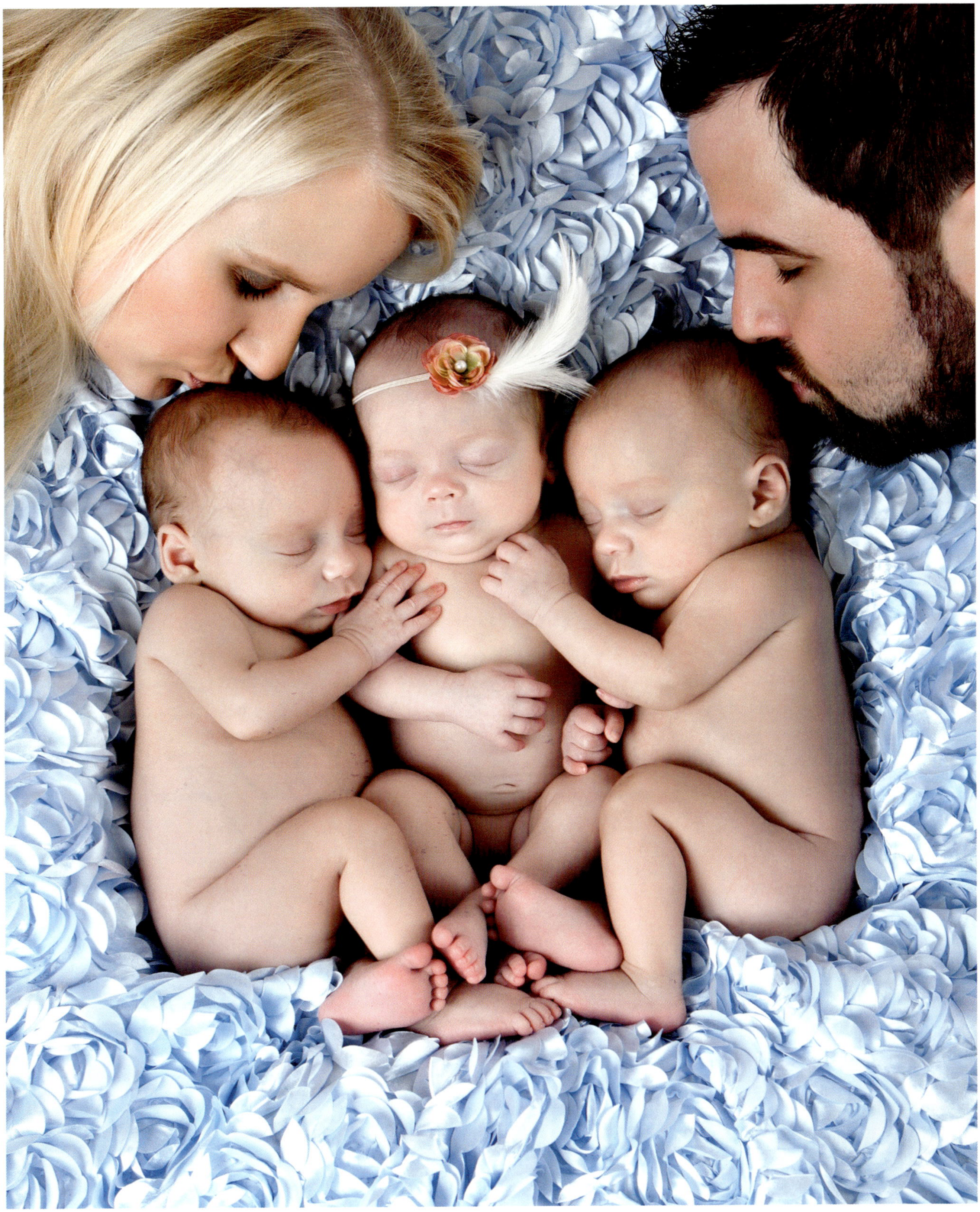

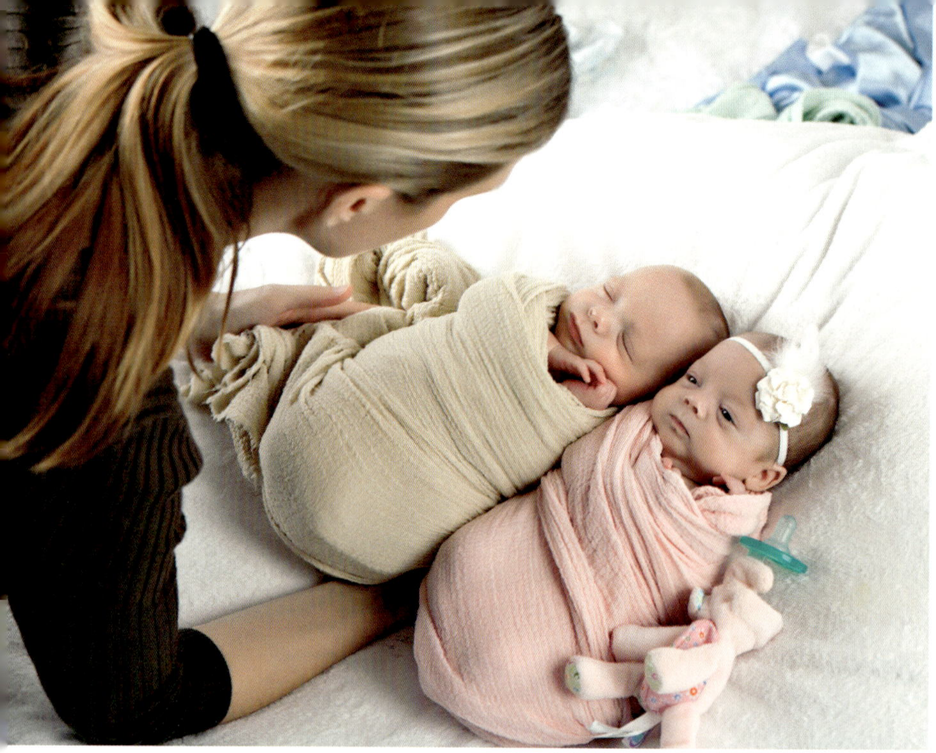

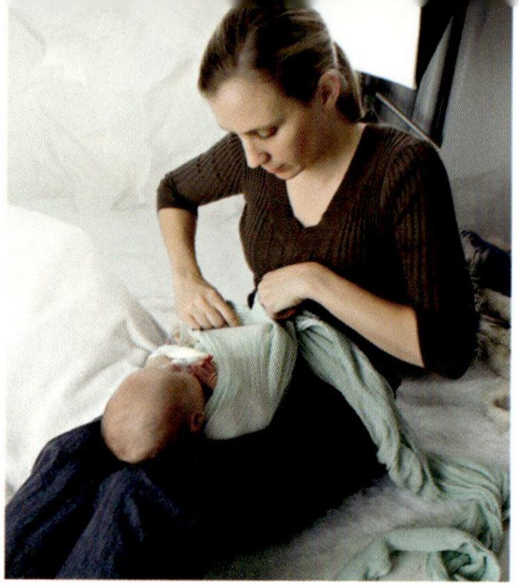

Swaddling helps to soothe a fussy baby.

Soothe baby and keep your camera close at hand so you can capture images quickly.

(facing page) Here are some poses that can be achieved once baby is in a milk coma.

Working Alone

You may need to work alone if Mom and Dad need a breather. When that happens, soothe the baby with your camera close at hand. Once baby is in a deep sleep, you can practically do anything with them and pose them creatively.

Tips for La La Land

The majority of time during a newborn session is spent soothing a newborn to sleep. Once the baby is asleep, he or she can be moved into any pose with little resistance. The trick is getting to this stage.

It takes a ton of patience and some "baby whispering" to soothe a baby quickly. Many new parents have observed me at work and have copied my techniques at home with their baby with thrilling results.

The primary tips for soothing success are:

1. Crank the heat up in the room to 86F/30C. You can turn to space heaters if you wish to warm only your shooting area, or a beanbag, etc.
2. Baby's belly should be completely full. If the baby has been fed recently, a top-off is encouraged. If baby refuses, continue with the session. If baby takes a pacifier, ask Mom or Dad to keep it close by.
3. Use a sound machine with womb sounds at max volume. The repetitive sound of a mother's heartbeat is a familiar and soothing to a newborn. When I started out, I used a machine from my local baby store, but I now use an iPhone app called Womb Sounds.
4. Doing things in threes helps to stop a crying baby because they cannot concentrate on more than one thing at a time. For example, if you are shushing, singing, and rocking or patting, you will find that their crying will stop.
5. If baby cannot be soothed after being fully fed and rocked, swaddling baby tightly will quickly send them to la la land. I use colored

cheese cloth or thin swaddling blankets to get a nice tight fit.

6. Once the baby is fast asleep (i.e., is breathing deeply and is floppy), you are ready to go. Work quickly but gently when changing poses to avoid startling baby awake.
7. Use rolled swaddling blankets to get that tush in the air or prop the head up.

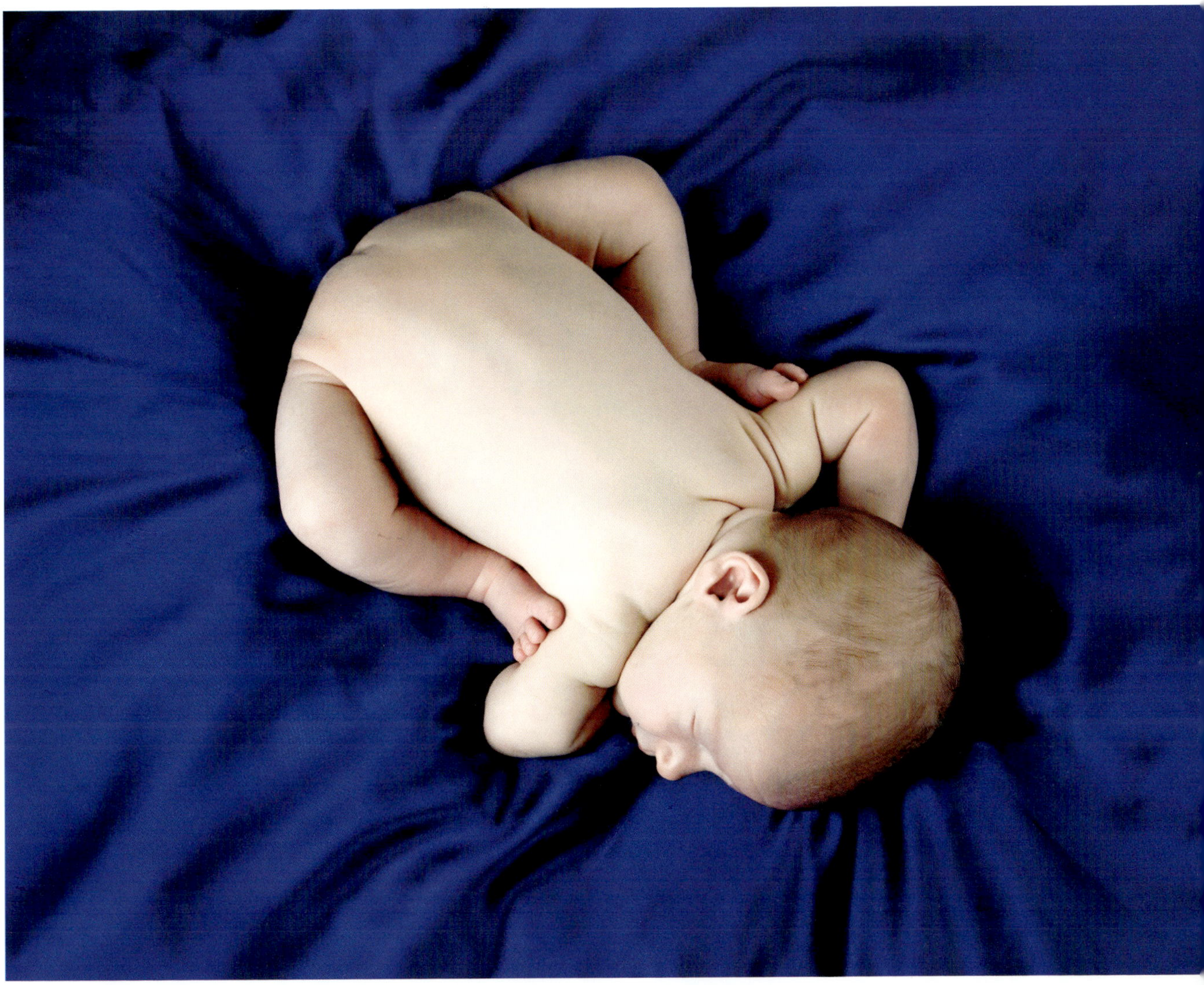

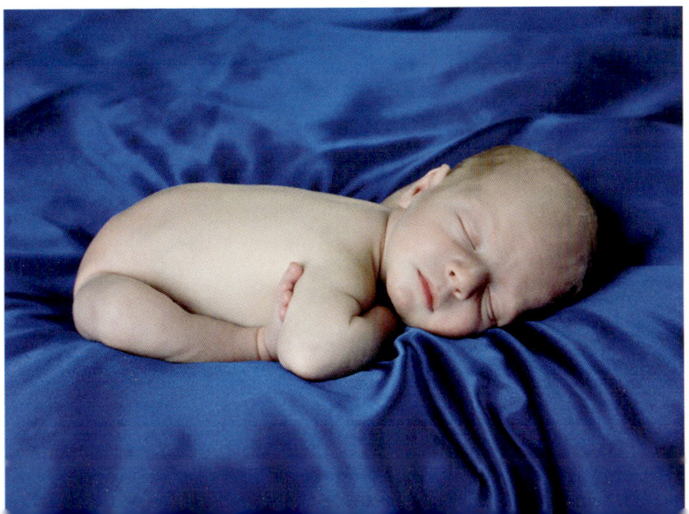

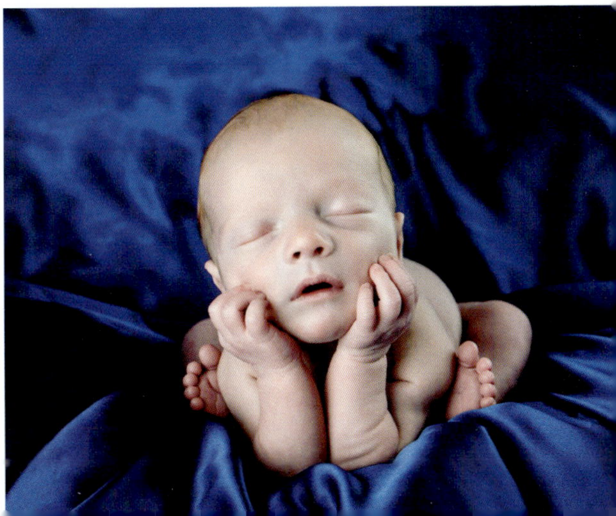

6. Postproduction

"It is not a slight thing when those so fresh from God love us."—Charles Dickens

Programs like Lightroom and Photoshop are designed to enhance your workflow and improve the final product. Relying on them to "fix" a bad photo will result in loss of quality, clarity, and loads of time. It is important to capture the image correctly in camera. If a photo is out of focus or blown out, there is little you can do to salvage it. However, when used correctly, editing software can dramatically improve the artistic quality of your images.

"The best way to speed up your workflow is to batch process your images."

Adobe Lightroom

The best way to speed up your workflow is to batch process your images. I use Lightroom to import my images, adjust settings

▼ This is an example of a processed composite image.

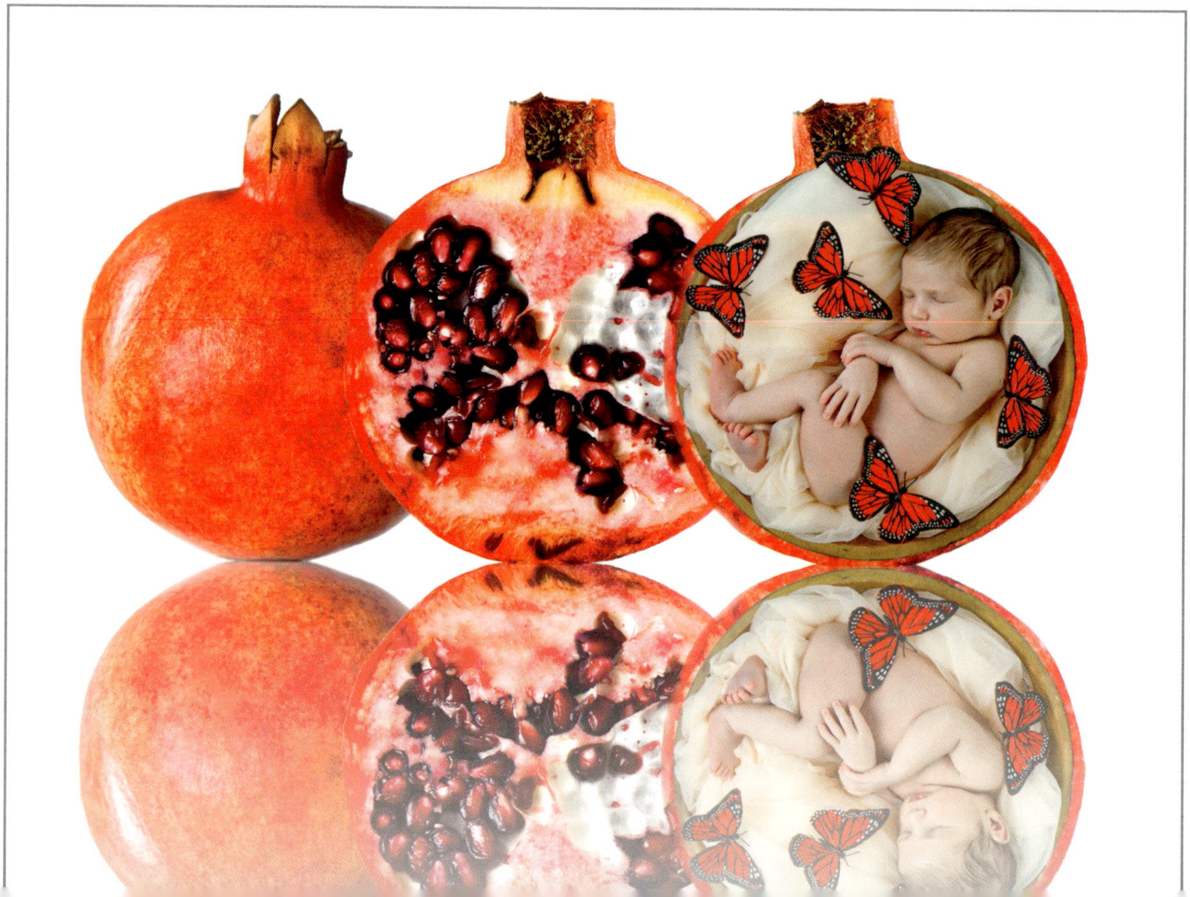

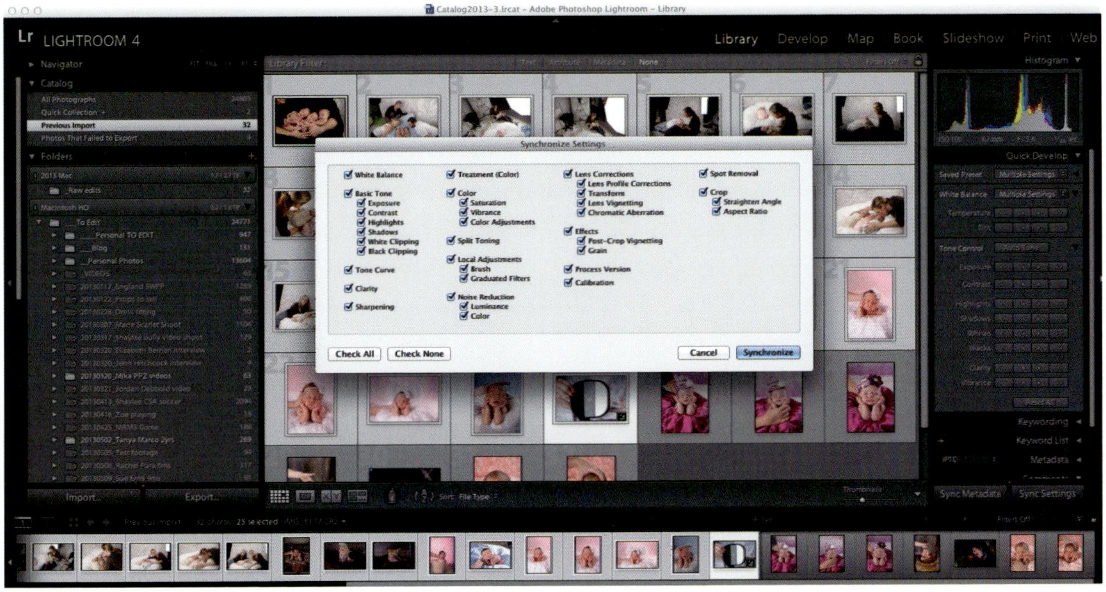

▲ Batching or synching settings saves time.

from white balance to contrast, and then export the final JPEG files.

The best tip anyone ever gave me for achieving accurate skin tones was to photograph a white card under the lighting conditions in which you will be shooting and create a custom white balance. Remember that if your lighting changes after you take your target image (this is often the case when photographing with natural light), you will need to take another test image and create a new custom white balance.

"... photograph a white card under the lighting conditions in which you will be shooting and create a custom white balance."

The white balance adjustment can be done in postproduction as well. Simply import the target image into Lightroom, select the Develop mode, click on the white balance eyedropper tool, and click on the white area of the target. You'll immediately notice a change in the color. If it's too warm or too cool, you can adjust the settings manually.

Once you've got the correct white balance, contrast, exposure, vibrance, saturation etc., simply click on the lead image (the one with the correct settings), hold down the shift key, and select the remaining images. In the Library mode, click Sync Settings, and all the adjustments you made to your lead image will be applied to the balance of your images. With that accomplished, you're done!

Skin-Smoothing Techniques

Many newborns' skin will need retouching. Premature babies tend to suffer from jaundice, giving their skin a yellow tone. Overdue babies tend to have peeling skin. Still other newborns have acne. As photographers, it is our job to make our subjects look as beautiful as possible because no mother wants to remember those early zits!

Thank heavens we have some great tools at our disposal. One of the fastest shortcuts I discovered to creating creamy, gorgeous skin tones is Portraiture, a Photoshop-compatible action from Imagenomic. There are a variety of finishes and smoothing options, but I've found the basic Skin Tones adjustment works perfectly. You can adjust the opacity if you prefer less smoothing—it all comes down to personal preference.

Working with Actions

Using actions can drastically cut down on your editing time, as many options offer one-click adjustments. There are so many actions on the market that you can go crazy buying them all, so spend your money wisely. Note that, like other image editing programs, actions are designed to enhance your work, not fix a bad job.

I love the Florabella Collection. Most of the time I revert to using a handful of the actions to create my signature look. My favorites are the Luxe Collection, and I adore the sharpen/defog set—it helps me to create the "pop" that I love.

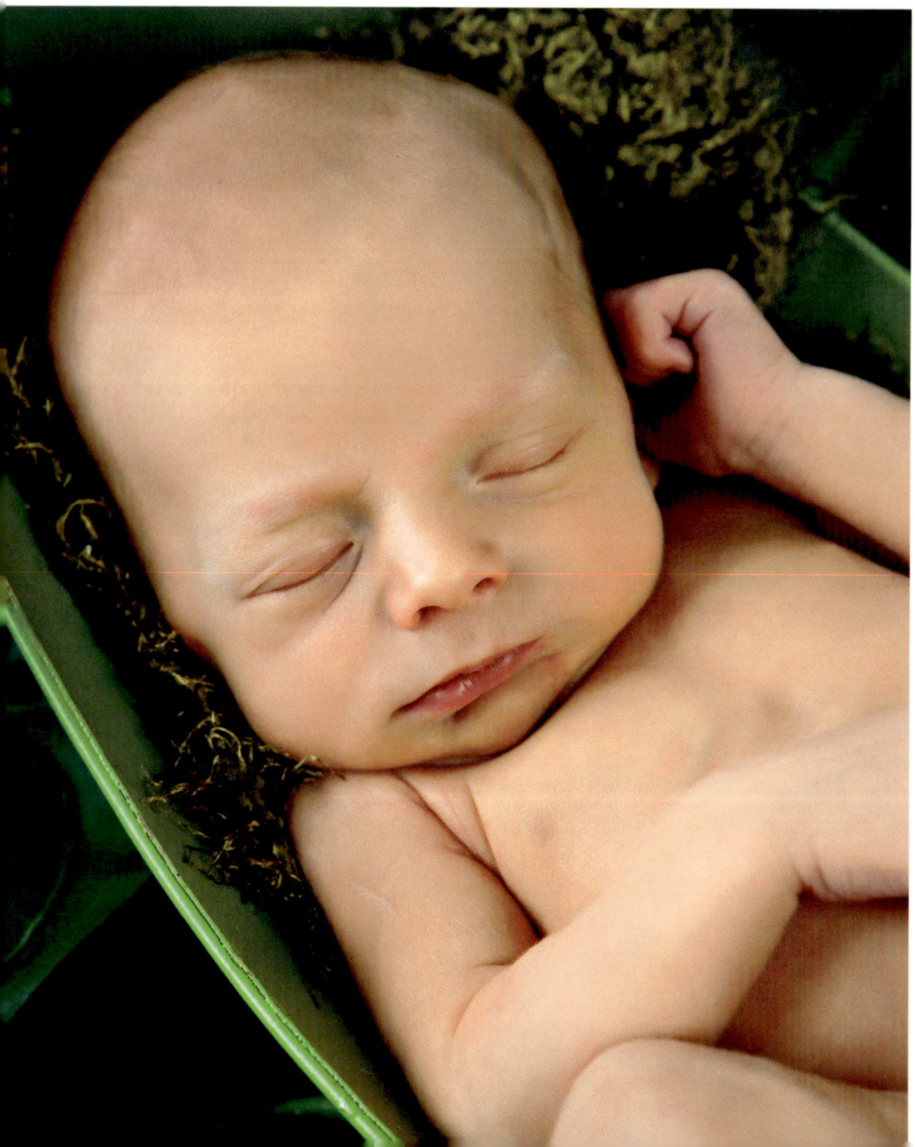

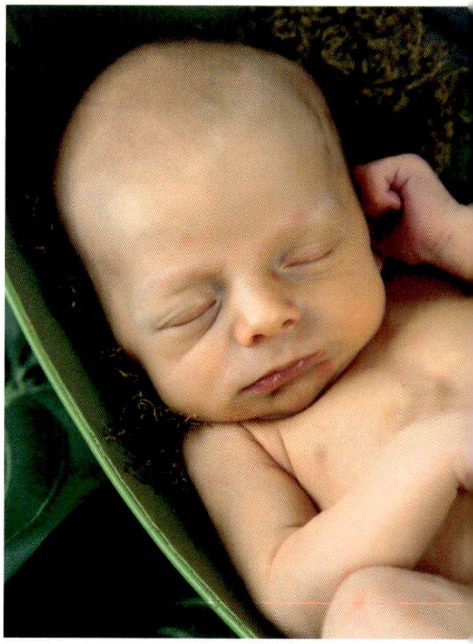

▲ Before blemish removal.
◄ After smoothing and blemish removal.

► (1) Florabella's London action applied. (2) Florabella's Timeless action applied. (3) Florabella's Smitten action applied. (4) Florabella's Black & White Mink action applied.

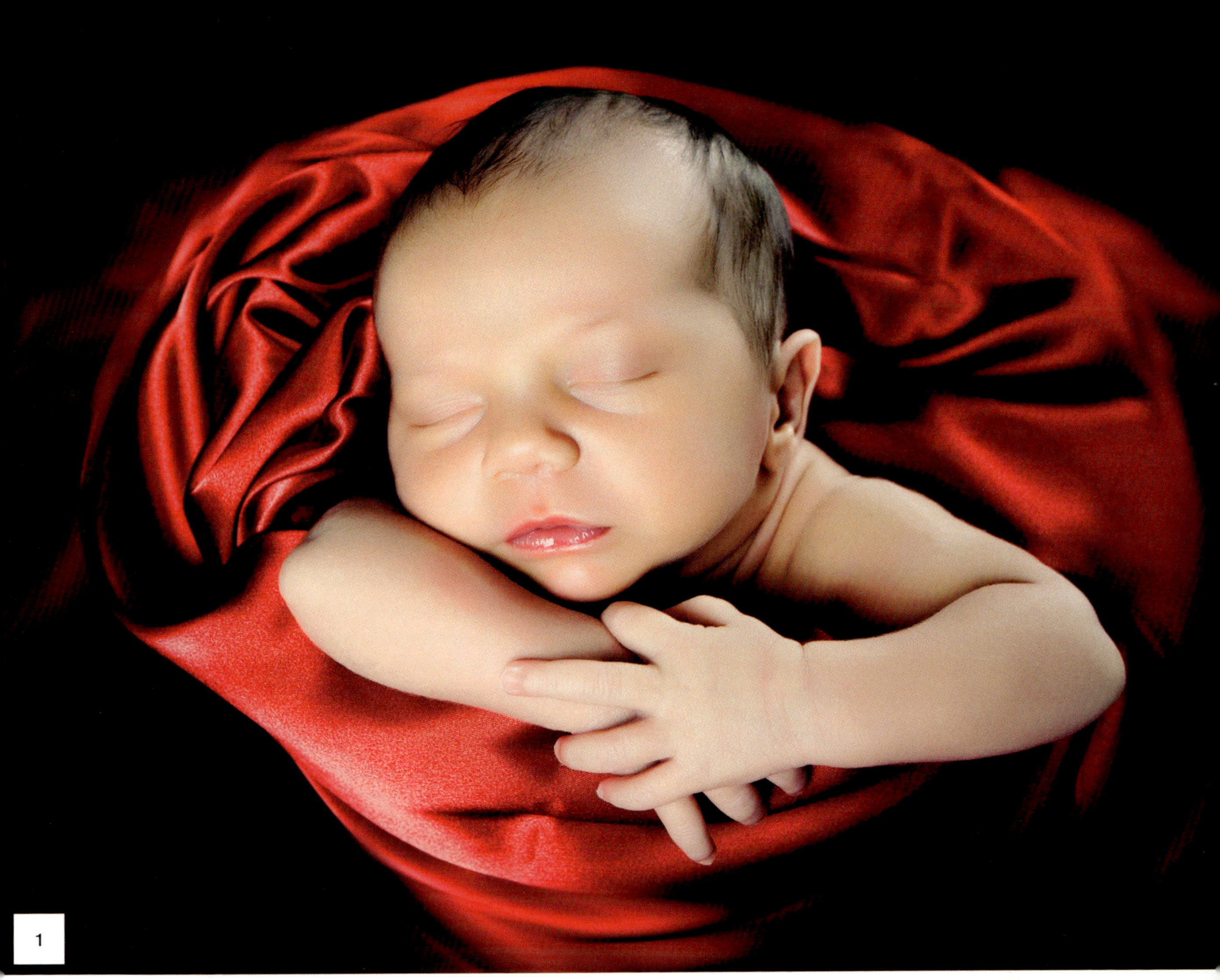
1

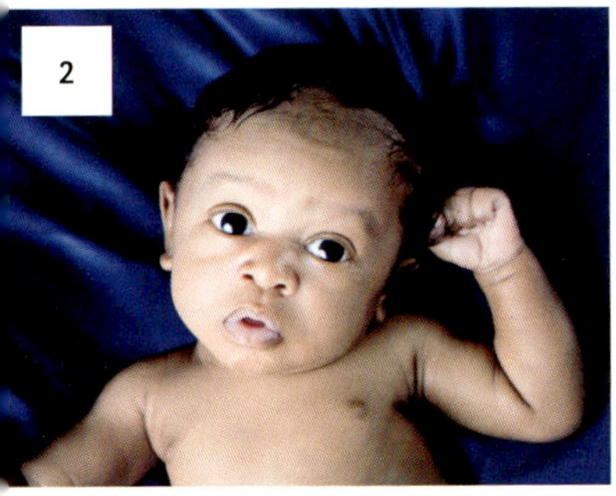
2

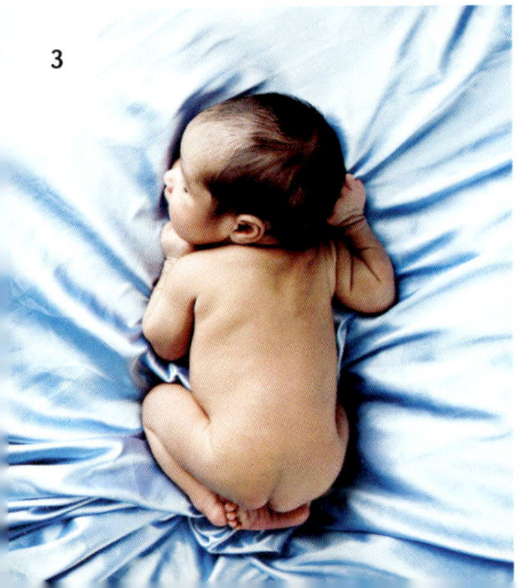
3

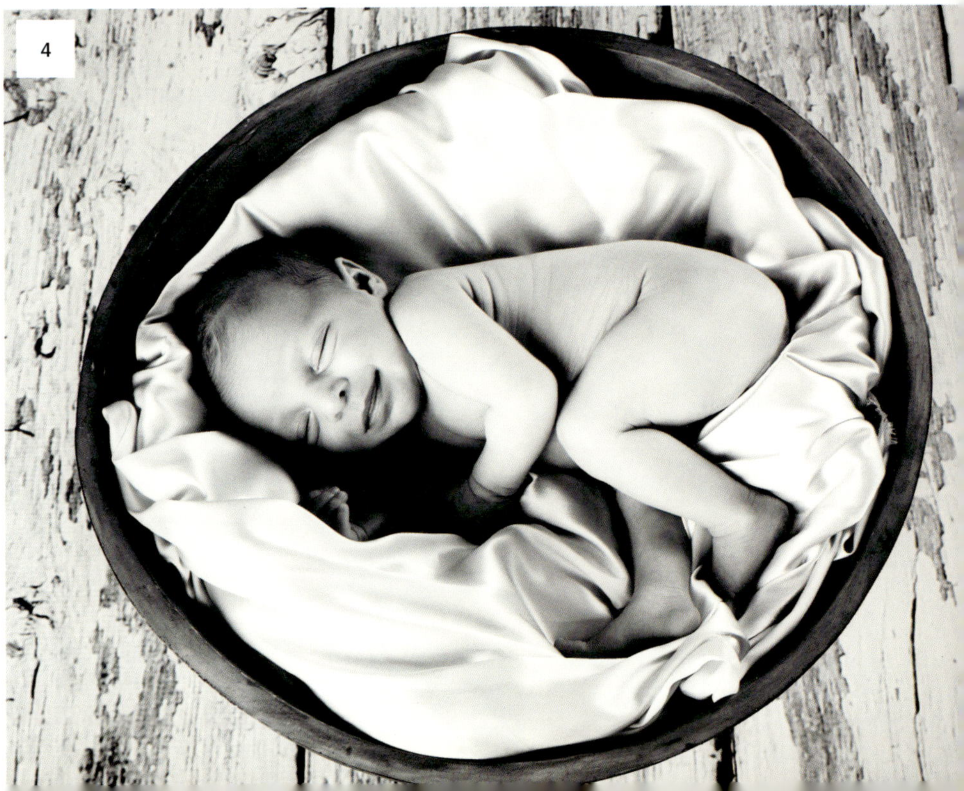
4

Working with Composites

The public doesn't see our postproduction efforts. It's the part of the process that we use to translate the image in our mind's eye into reality. Let me emphasize that safety is the number-one priority when photographing a newborn. You should never place a baby in poses that present a risk to the little one's safety. Too often amateur photographers see images in which Baby appears in midair hanging from a sling or dangling off branches or holding their head straight up. They think that the baby does on his/her own. Wrong! These images are magically created in Photoshop. Assistance is always needed when attempting to photograph such "tricks."

If you have a stylized image in mind, consider the steps you will need to take to create the final look. Shoot the elements that make up the parts and compile the final image using Layers in Photoshop.

"You should never place a baby in poses that present a risk to the little one's safety."

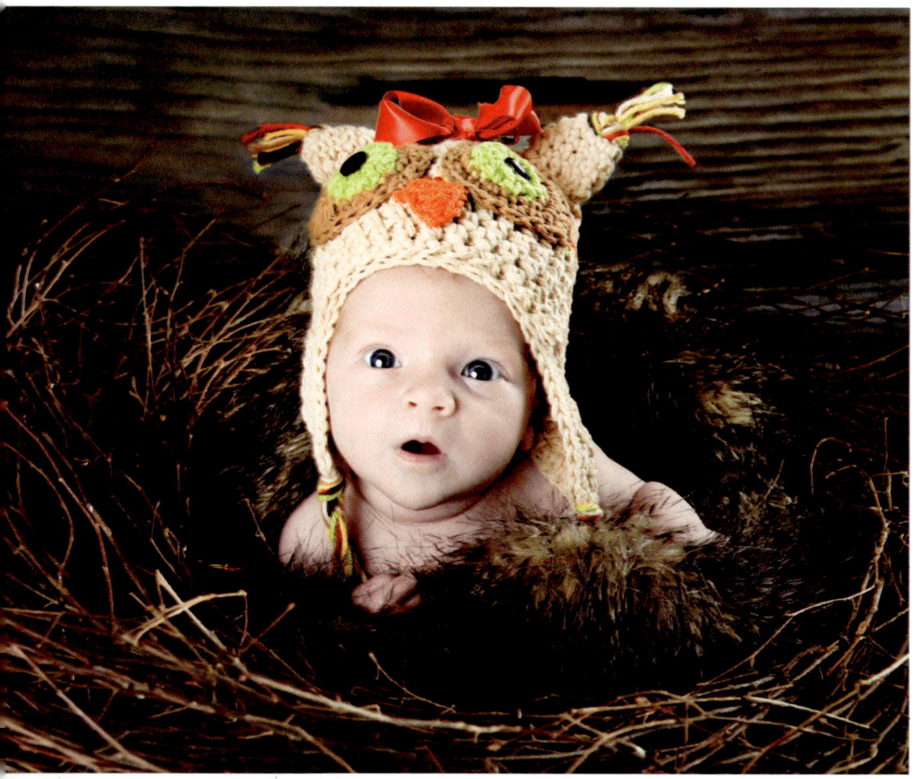

◀ ▼ Postproduction work allows you to produce images that could not be created safely in reality.

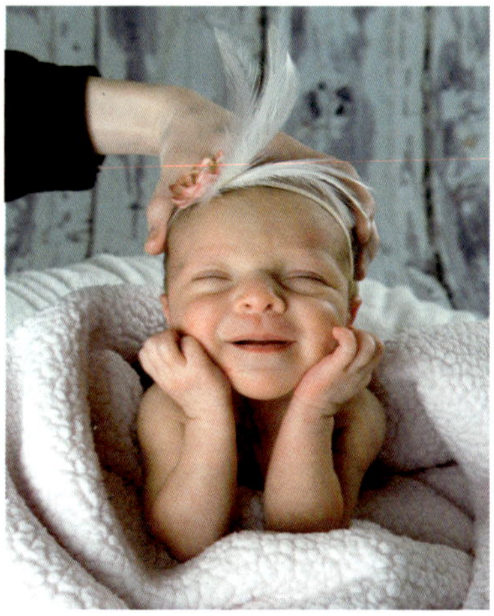

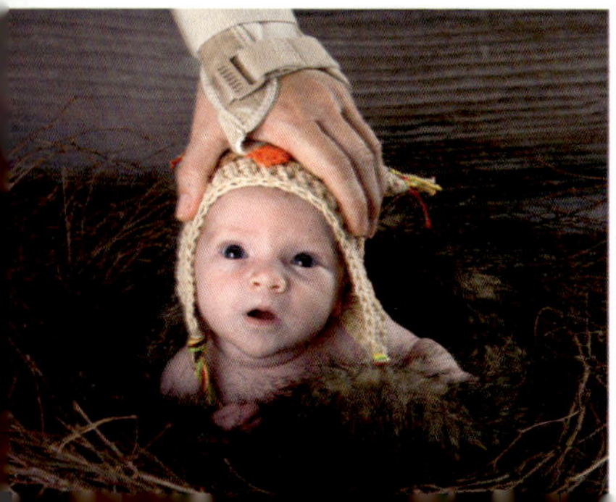

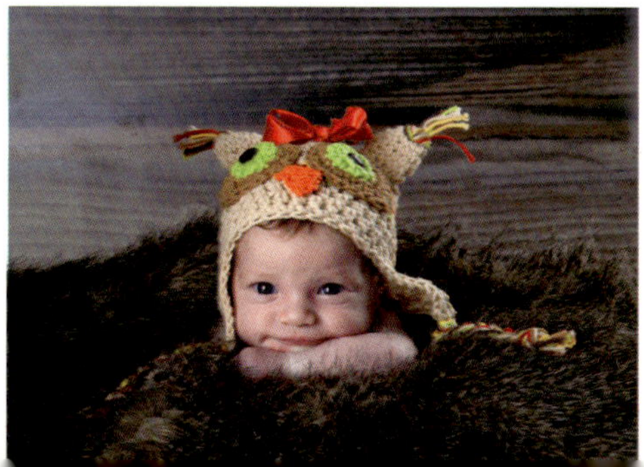

▲ ▶ No artistic or financial reward is worth risking harm to a newborn. Realize that the final image may appear quite different than the physical reality of the setup.

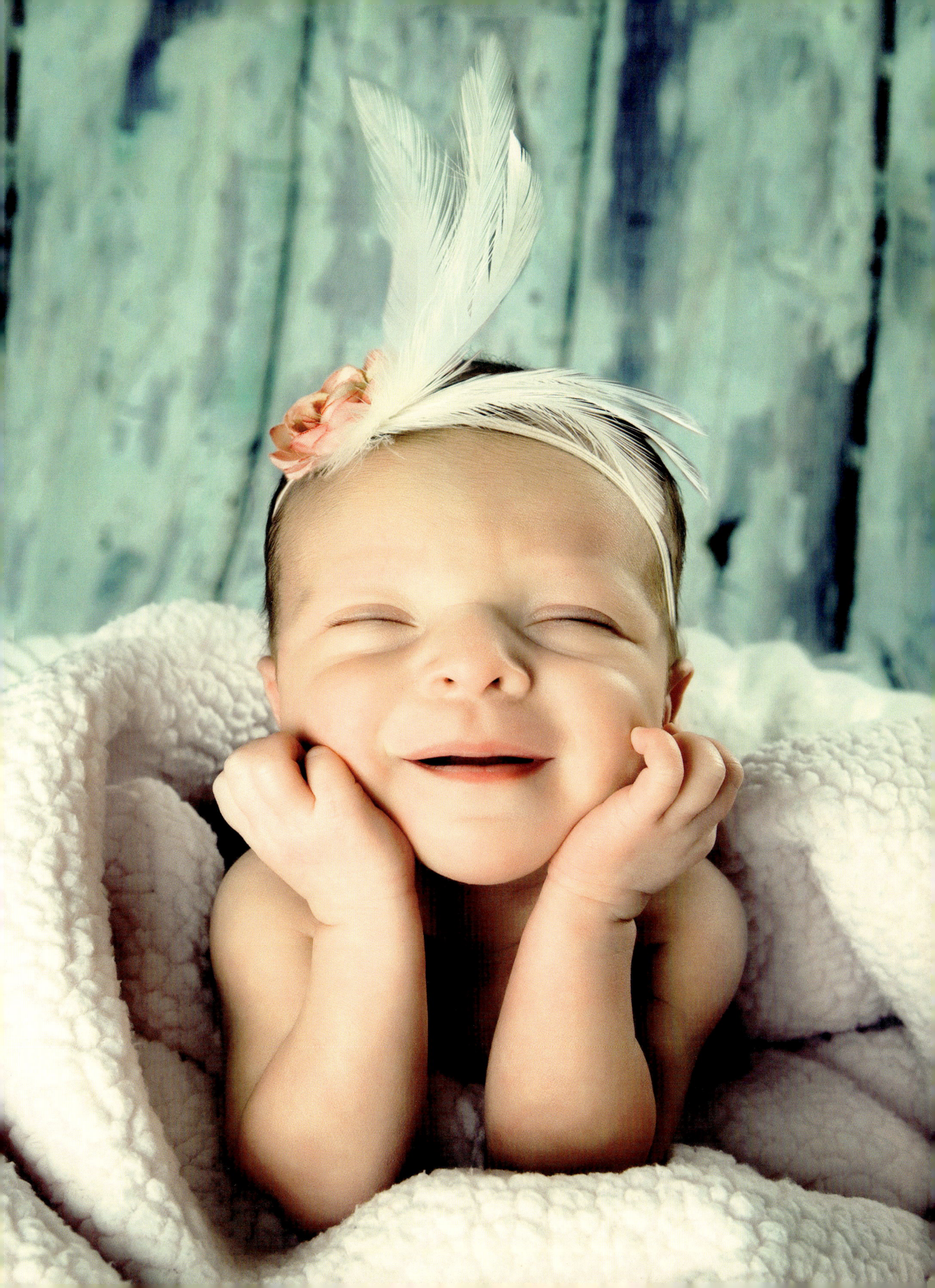

Steps for a Ten-Minute Creative Edit

1. Pick your favorite image with the correct exposure. Retouch the skin and adjust the overall contrast if necessary.
2. Go to Image>Canvas size and stretch the canvas to the desired size.
3. Clone the background using the clone stamp at 15% opacity. Be careful not to affect the subject's hair and face. Work slowly and carefully.
4. Using a layer mask, switch to Difference mode. With a small brush, paint over the subject. Zoom in at 500% to get an accurate view of the subject's head and limbs to make sure you are not losing detail.
5. Add a layer and apply a background texture. Only the background should be affected, as you protected the subject when you selected the layer mask.
6. Add artistic effects to the background (e.g., lens flare, a vignette, etc.).
7. Add a layer of text, flatten, and save. That's it; you're done!

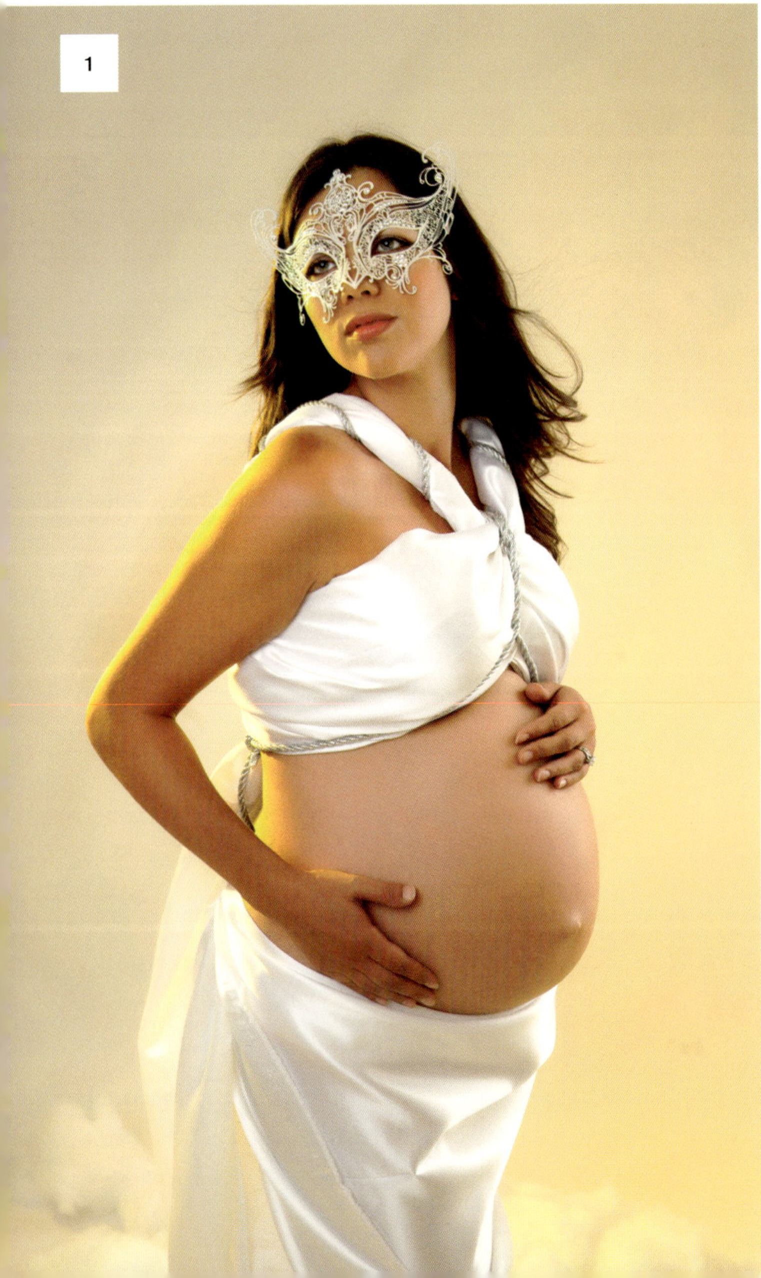

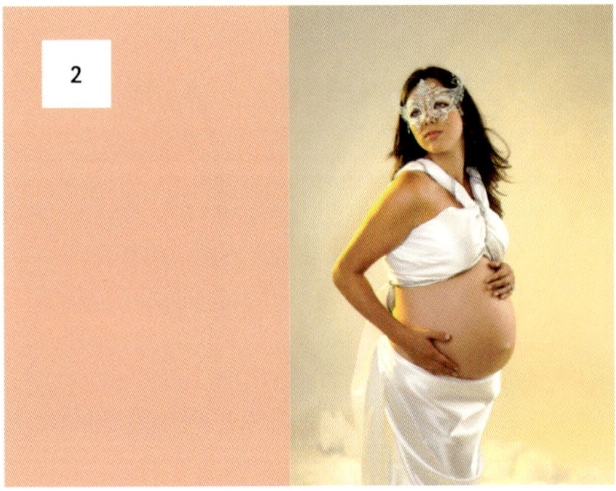

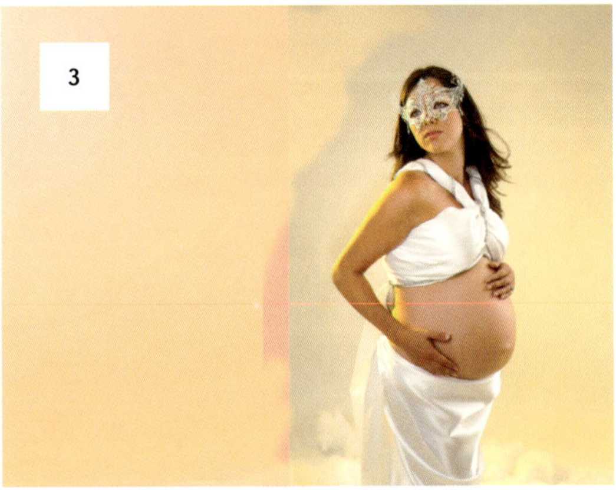

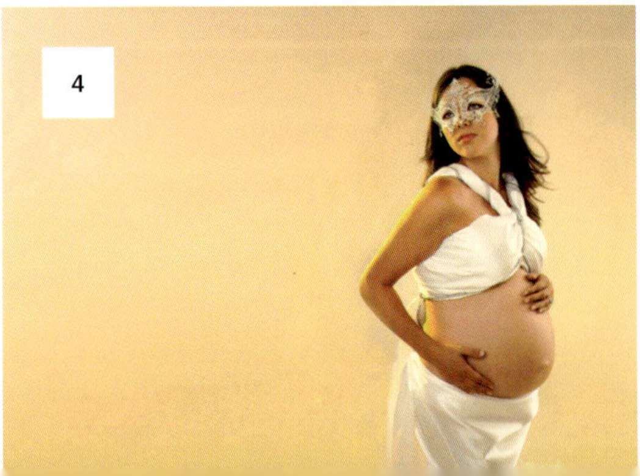

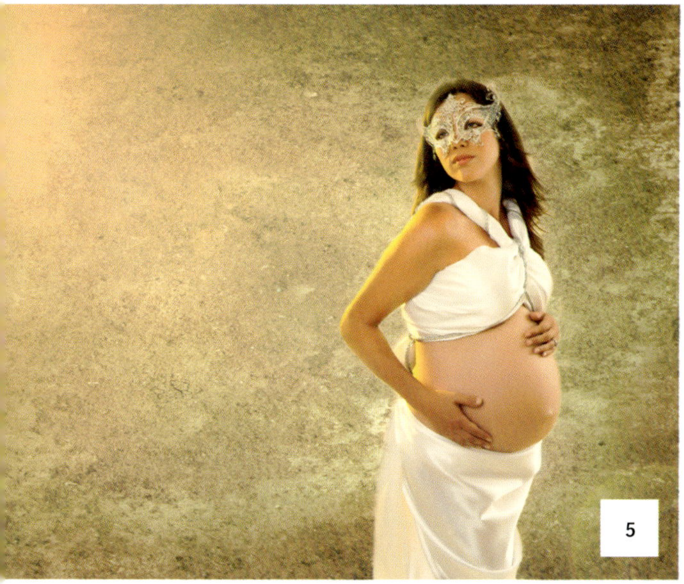
5

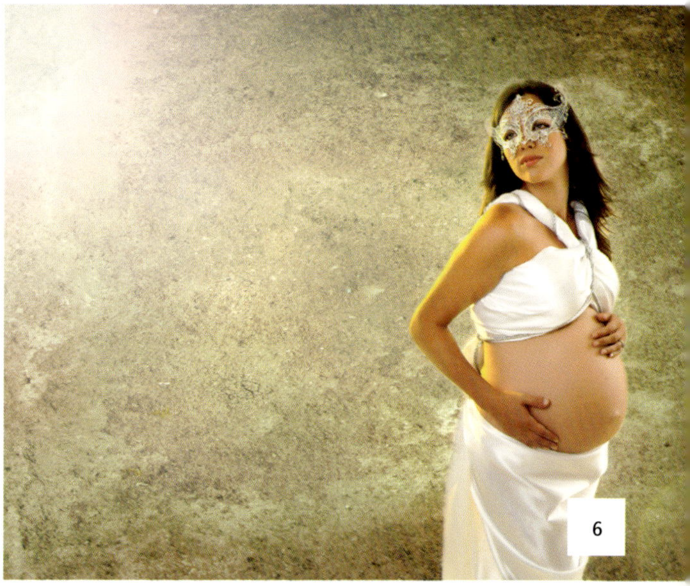
6

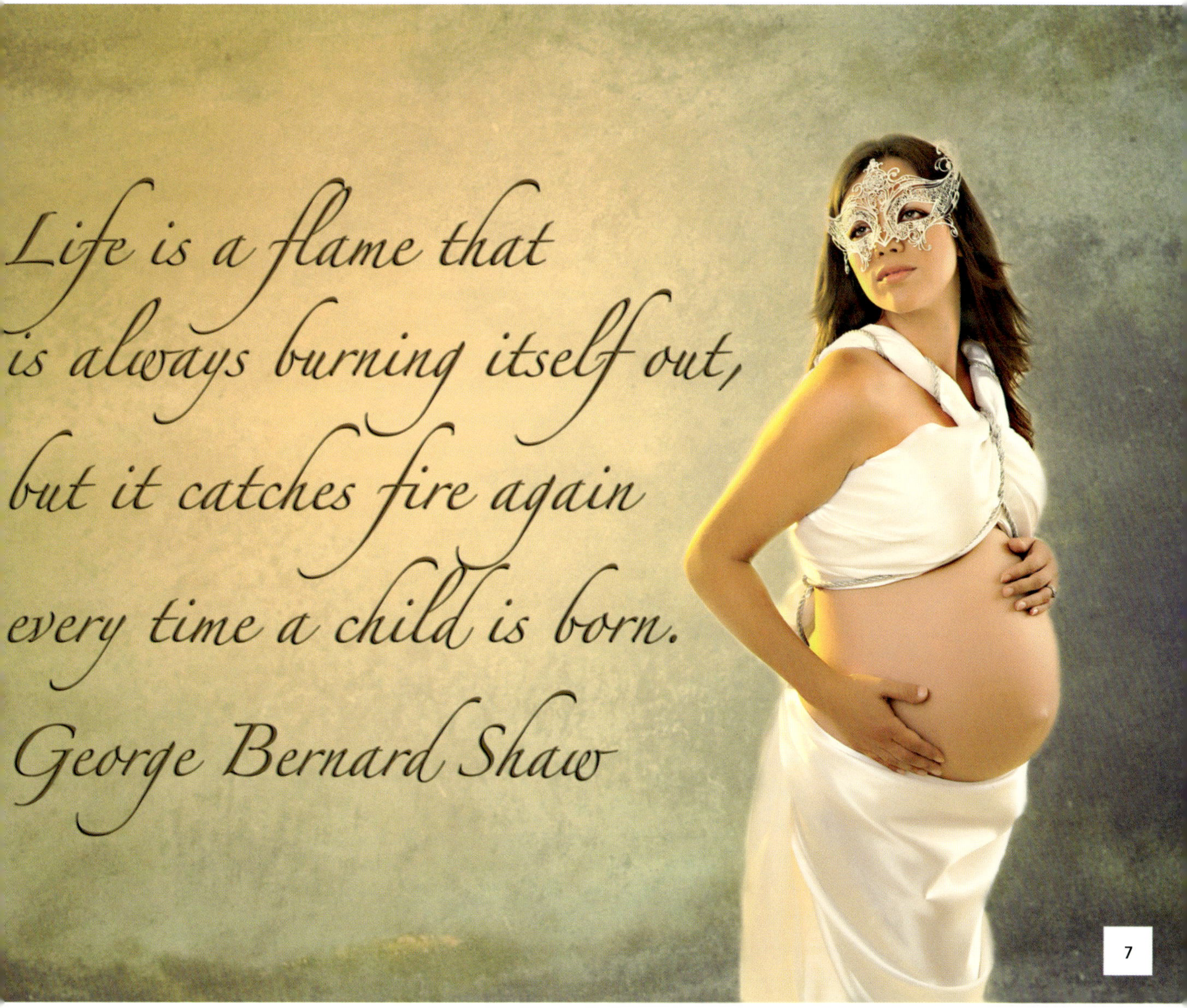
Life is a flame that
is always burning itself out,
but it catches fire again
every time a child is born.
George Bernard Shaw
7

7. Pricing for Profit

"When babies look beyond you and giggle, maybe they're seeing angels."
—Eileen Elias Freeman

Pricing is one of the biggest issues photographers face today. The inherent problem is that potential clients try to assess a service based on several factors, not just price, so pricing is not cut and dry. If all we do is tell our clients to compare apples with apples based on price, competition will be that much more fierce. Instead, we should highlight other aspects of our services for comparison so that price is not the prospective client's sole determining factor. Sure, a buyer needs to ensure that the option

▼ Discerning clients shop for image quality, not price.

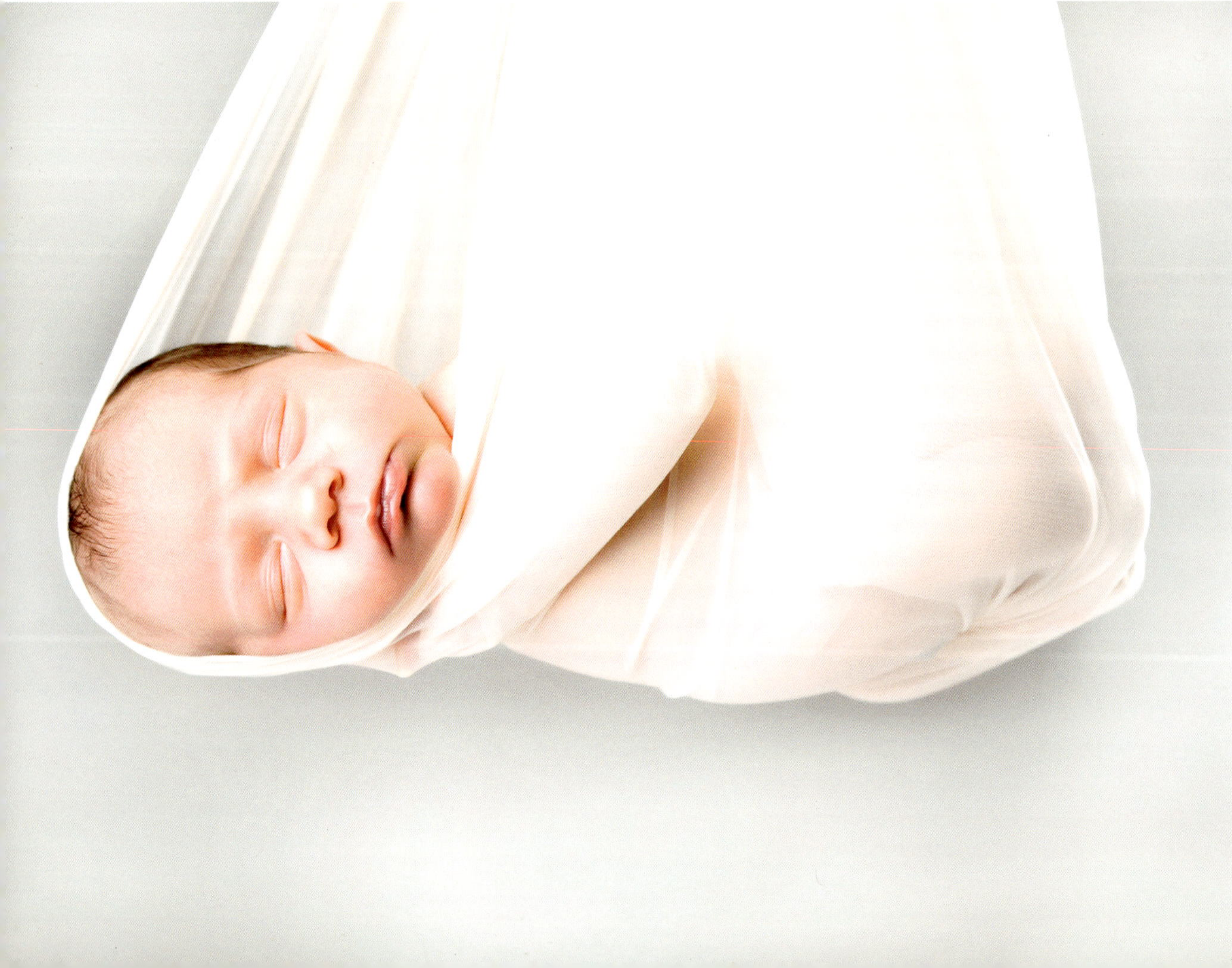

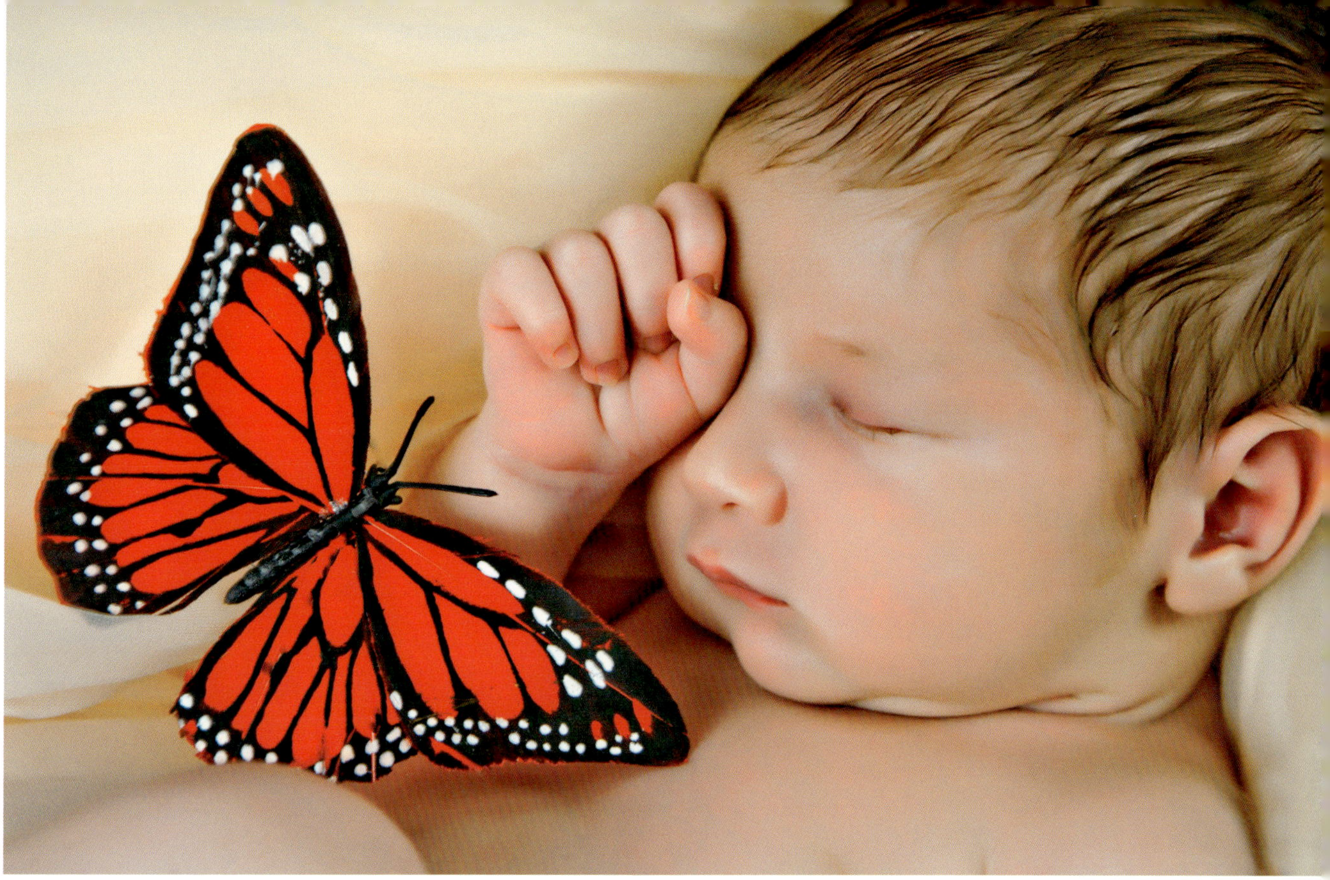

▲ Not everyone with a pulse and a credit card is my ideal client. Be sure the clientele you strive to draw in appreciate your artistic vision.

they select will fit their budget, but when they shop around and see too many options, they may become overwhelmed. A confused mind says no, so it's up to us professionals to make the path clear and the decision easy for the client to select our business.

I have made peace with the fact that not everyone with a pulse and a credit card is my ideal client. Not every person who wants photographs taken is the right client for me. I spent too many years, loads of cash, and many frustrated moments trying to please people who can't be pleased.

Think of the medical profession: just because you need a heart surgeon doesn't mean that any surgeon will do. You will go out of your way to get the right recommendation from those you trust, do your homework, and make a decision based on what is best for you.

Some newborn clients want to have the photos made in their homes. Others prefer the look and styling that can be achieved in a studio. I'm happy to refer away clients who are not a good fit, with the confidence that another photographer can do a better job and be more passionate about servicing the client's needs.

Shoot and Burn and Burn and Burn

Whether to shoot and burn digital files only or sell finished products is a topic of great debate among photographers. I must emphasize that there is no right or wrong way to run your business; it should be based on your personal circumstances. The sales advice I'm about to offer is based on my own experience. I've tested my method time and time again, and every time I have an in-person sales session and offer my

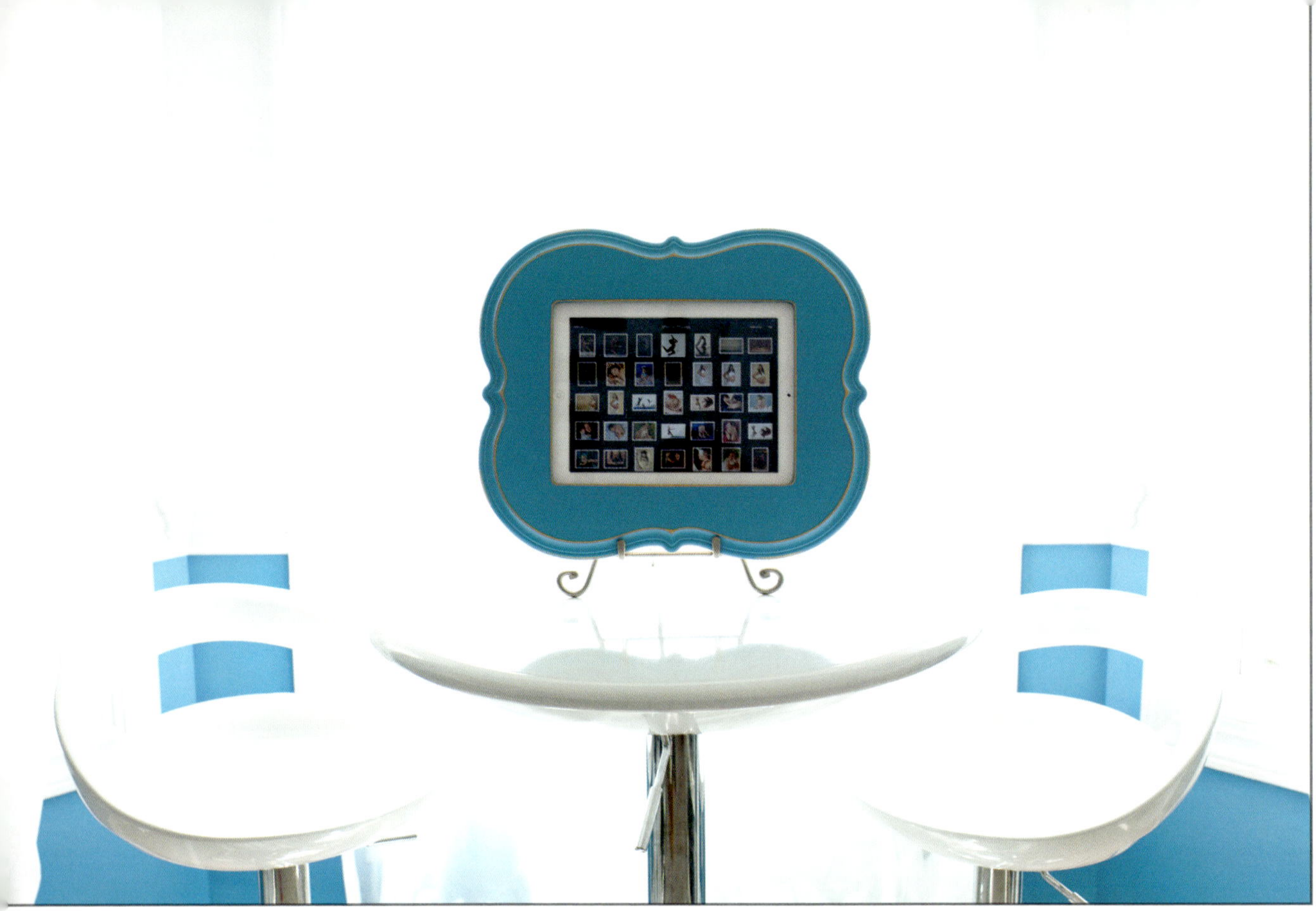

▲ Offering products and selling in person tripled my sales average.

products, I average at least $1200 per sale. When I did online sales and allowed my clients to select and purchase digital files or small prints, my average sale was never more than $400. Face-to-face selling tripled my sales average!

If, like me, you want to work smarter and be more profitable, it makes sense to do what works right? I would rather work with fewer clients and earn more money than wind up frazzled by busying myself with clients who only want digital files.

"If, like me, you want to work smarter and be more profitable, it makes sense to do what works right?"

Let me say this before you get your knickers in a twist: yes, you can be profitable selling digital files only. This is a trade-for-time approach—you trade a certain number of hours for money. However, the drawback is that your time is limited and there are only so many clients you can service in a given week or month.

Priced for Profit

Let's assume you are booked solid and working six hours per day, five days a week. The following charts outline the financial return you might expect when conducting a digital-only proof session versus an in-person sales meeting. The numbers don't lie!

❤ Digital Proofs

Hours available to work per week: 30 hours
Number of sessions per week: 5
Time spent per client: 4 hours
Time spent editing: 2.5 hours
minutes per image: 5 minutes
number of edited images: 30 images
Total hours spent per session: 6.5 hours
Hourly rate as pro. photographer: $50.00/hour
Total cost for session: $325.00
Average sale per session: $500.00
Cost of goods: $45.00
Profit per session: $130.00
Profit per week: $650.00

❤ In-Person Product Sales

Hours available to work per week: 30 hours
Number of sessions per week: 5
Time spent per client: 4 hours
Time spent editing: 0.67 hours
minutes per image: 5 minutes
number of edited images: 8 images
Total hours spent per session: 4.67 hours
Hourly rate as pro. photographer: $50.00/hour
Total cost for session: $233.33
Average sale per session: $1000.00
Cost of goods: $125.00
Profit per session: $641.67
Profit per week: $3208.33

When you sell products, you are more than doubling your income for the same amount of time. Yes, you will spend more time with your clients, but in guiding their purchasing decisions, you can reduce your retouching time. Also, once they've made their purchasing decisions at the in-person sales appointment with your help, there is no need for further delay in getting cold, hard cash into your hands! Who likes to chase a client for money, anyway?

When you are selective about the clients you work with, you can turn business away without the fear that you'll go bust. When there is less pressure to get a high number of sessions booked, you can rest assured that you have a system in place that will allow you to make more money with less effort.

In-Person Selling

The secret to success is that there really is no secret. The face-to-face selling system has been proven to work, and the hundreds of photographers who use the approach enjoy higher sales averages and greater profitability. Granted, not everyone considers themselves a natural salesperson; in fact, the majority of photographers I speak to say they hate selling!

Let's get this clear: in-person "selling" is really not selling—it's meeting your client's needs. As a busy mom, I don't have loads of time to spend on making purchasing decisions. Invariably, something comes up and tasks get pushed aside. I appreciate having help to make my life easier, facilitate my decision-making, and increase my happiness quotient.

When you guide your client through the image-selection process, you are giving them valuable feedback and your artistic direction, and that is something they will appreciate.

Stop assuming every client wants to print their own images on their home inkjet printer. All they know is small prints and scrapbooking. We can thank the tradition of the annual school photo for educating the masses that an 8x10-inch print is "big"!

It's up to us to show our clients just how gorgeous their images can look when hung on the walls as a collection. Think about it: why do we still see models wearing clothing in a catalog? It's because not many people can imagine

"If I had asked people what they wanted, they would have said faster horses."
—Henry Ford

what an outfit will look like when looking at the clothing on a hanger.

Plant the seed by showing your client ideas for putting the best images together. As the artist, you know which poses are the most pleasing. Don't rely on your client to figure it out on their own.

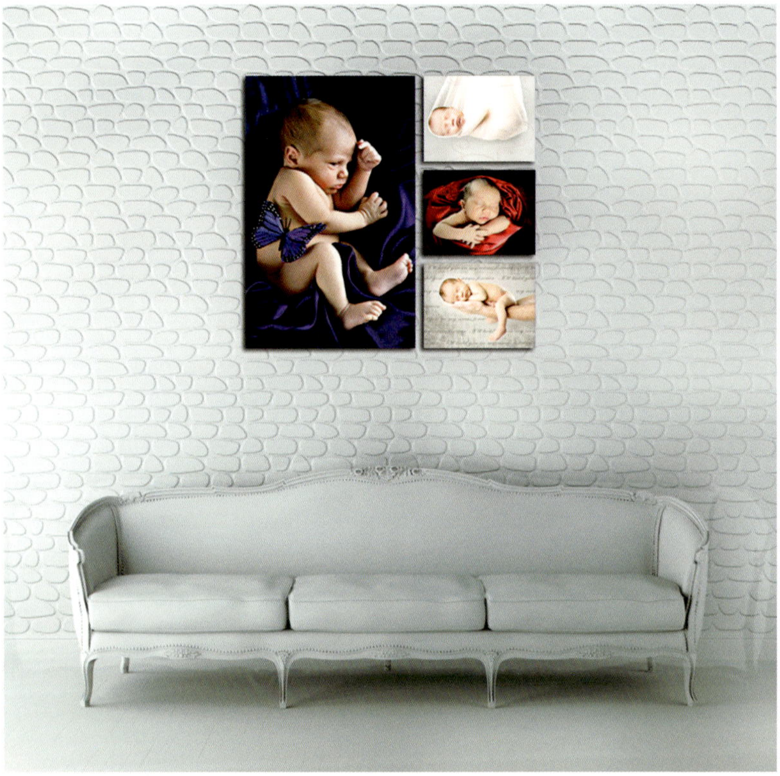

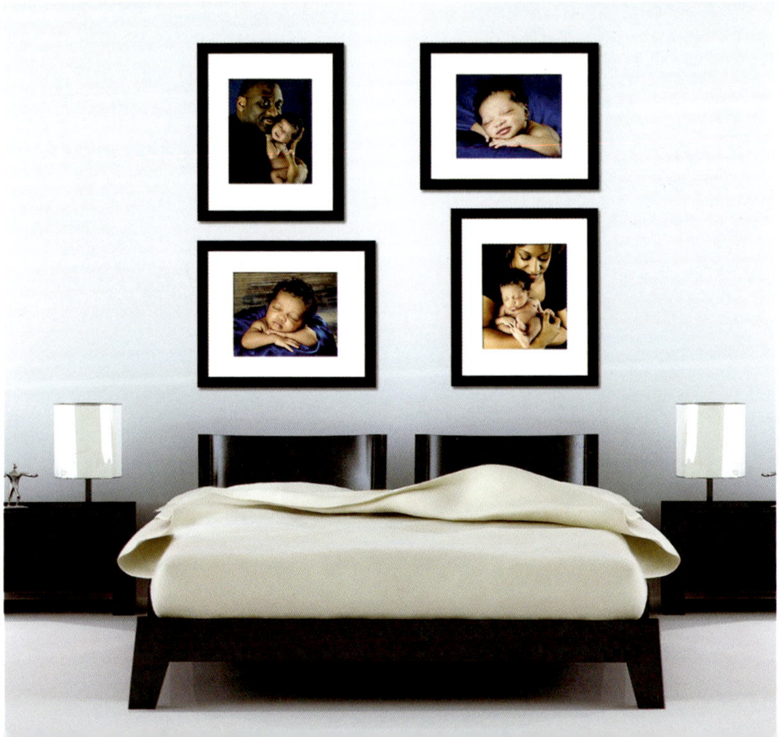

Show, Don't Tell

I have a dedicated studio space in my home for shooting and selling. It took three years to get there, so don't think just because you don't have the same setup that you can't do in-person sales. There are several ways to skin a cat. I used to take my laptop to clients' homes and measure the walls, then sell big!

I've created a space in which I can plant the seed early that my studio creates artistic wall art. There are samples on my walls, so clients can touch and feel the different finishes. Every client who comes to visit for the first time says "Wow! That's gorgeous!"

Most of my clients could never have imagined what they could do with their memories until they saw something they connected with and told me,

◄ Room views provided by Photographer Wall Display Guides.

1
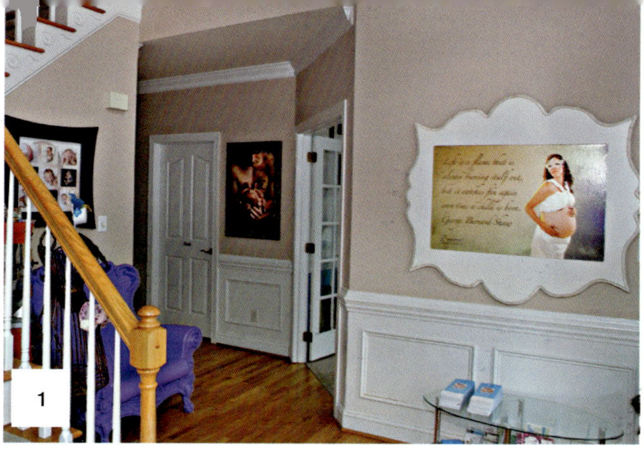

2
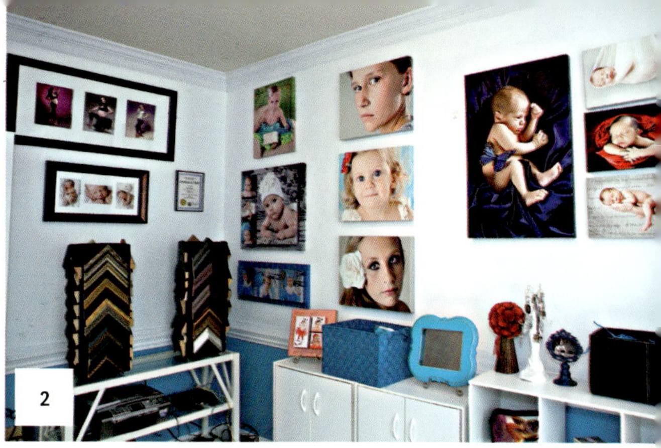

▲ ➤ Here are some images of the various spaces of my studio. (1) My entrance hall. (2) The frame room, showing collections, wall art finishes, frame corners, and layout ideas. (3) The first artwork my clients see when they enter. (4) Frame finishes by The Organic Bloom. (5) View toward the entrance hall. (6) Examples of gallery blocks and canvas by Artsy Couture and Canvas Clusters by Simply Color Lab.

3
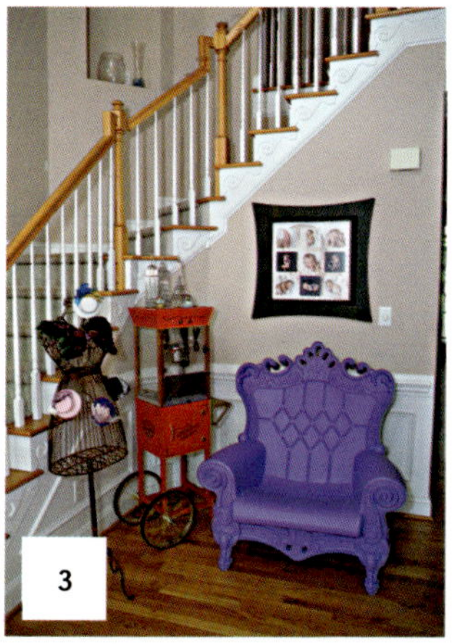

4
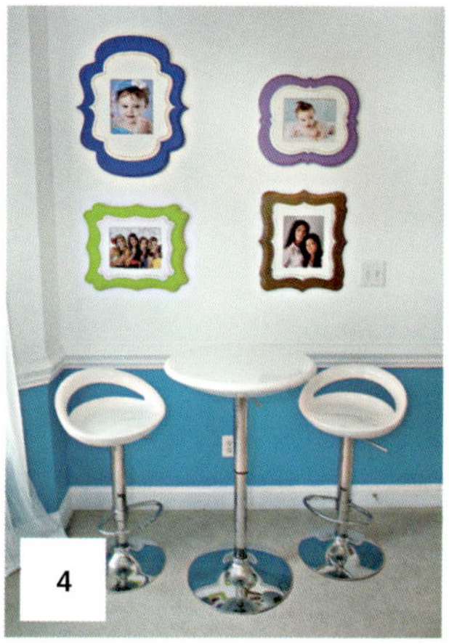

5
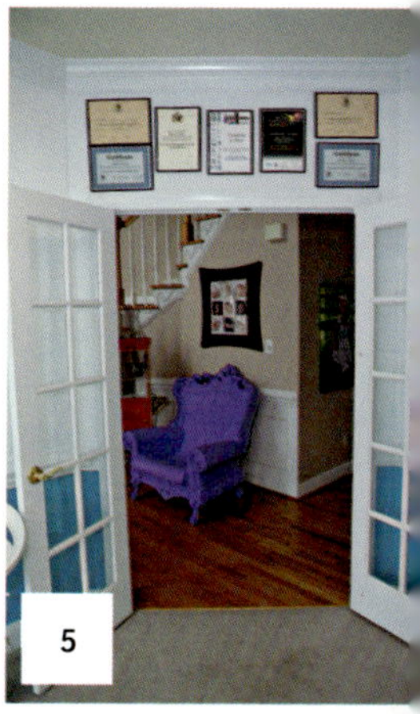

6
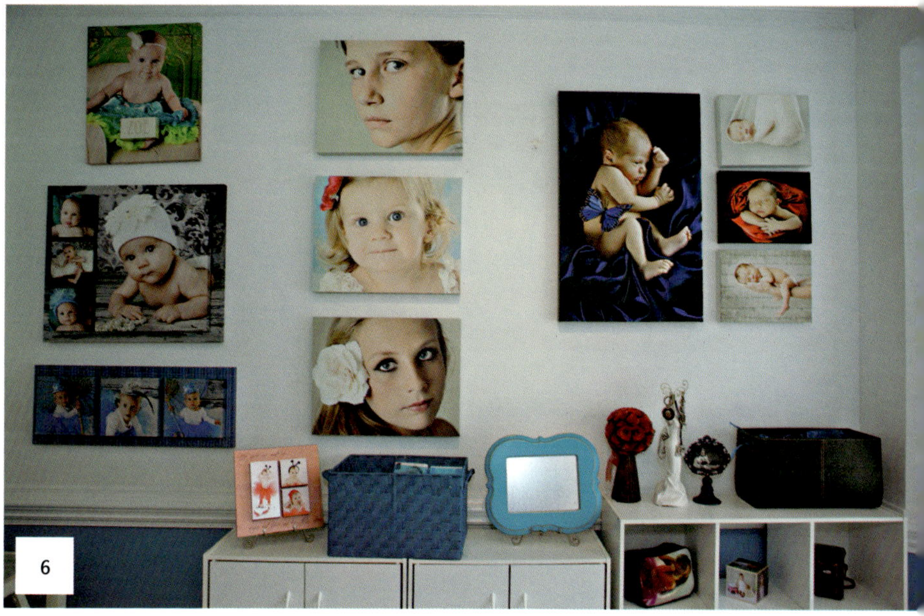

"I want that!" As you can see, that's not selling; the products have sold themselves. I simply provide a little "retail therapy" by showing them options that will make their baby and their home look gorgeous.

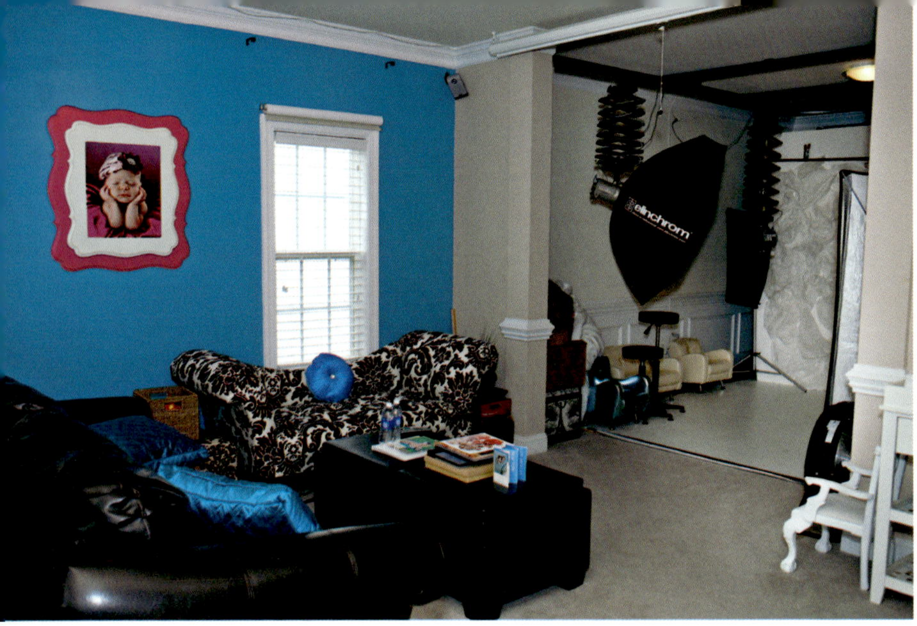

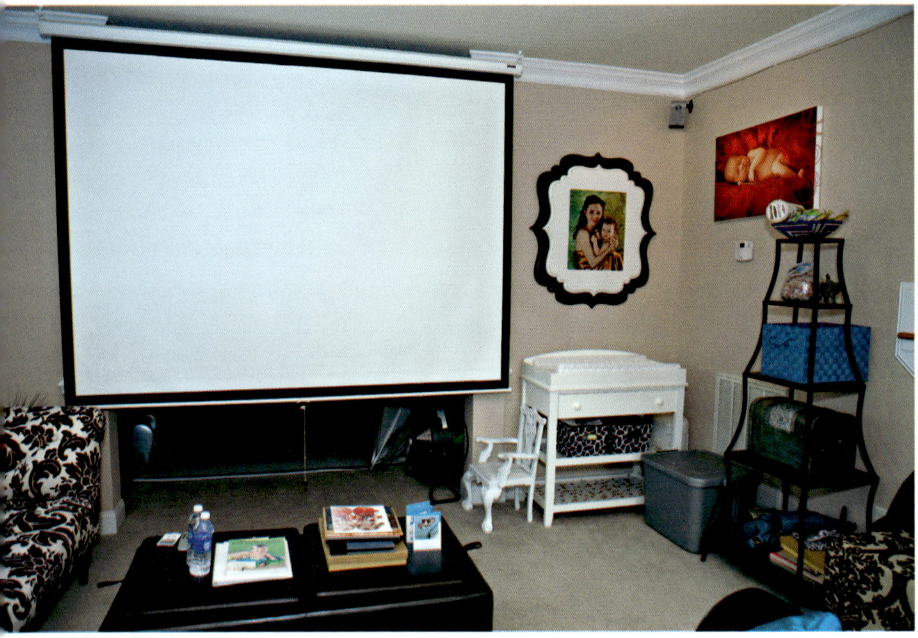

CAPTURE SCHOOL

(top) The viewing area, showing the shooting area.

(bottom) This pull-down projection screen is used for viewing life-size images.

(above) My online photography school's logo.

Selling the Experience

Building anticipation by creating an exciting sales experience makes the job of getting an order much easier. When you pay a premium to see a movie at the theater rather than waiting to see it on DVD weeks or months later, it's the experience you're paying for.

Using music to build emotion is key to getting people to buy from their heart and not their head. When they are emotionally invested, they are more open to suggestions and feel better about the money they spend. This is not to say you are "tricking" them

"Building anticipation by creating an exciting sales experience makes the job of getting an order much easier."

into buying—they will buy images of their baby no matter what—but you are creating the optimum environment for them to invest more. More tears means more money!

I use surround sound synced to music with lyrics when displaying slide shows. I've found that using a song with lyrics helps to keep my clients focused on the show and discourages idle chatter. You want your clients to be fully engaged so they take in the whole experience. In the past, before I had surround sound and a projector to present the slide show, I'd simply use Photoshop or Bridge to play the show with the music on my stereo turned up.

Selling Using ProSelect

Using software like ProSelect, Preveal, or Shoot and Sell will help you sort the images and speed up the viewing process. I tell clients "Think of it like being at the eye doctor, where you play spot the difference with yes, no, and maybe." I love ProSelect for my studio viewings, as I can show the images life-sized, stack them next to each other for comparison, and create layouts for collections. Selling collections with more than one image has dramatically increased my average sales.

I've found that it's advantageous to offer incentives to clients placing big orders. When my clients spend a certain amount, they earn a bonus or free gift. This approach allows me to build the perceived value of the products—it's a critical strategy for making your clients feel like the money they invest with you is well spent. I prefer not to offer discounts, but I do offer my VIP recurring clients a 10 percent discount on wall portraits.

Selling is both a science and an art form that can be learned. When you take a consultative approach to servicing your clients, selling isn't "salesy." At the end of the day, we want clients that are so happy to do business with us that they will brag about us to their friends.

Want to learn more? In my online school, I teach sales techniques geared toward photographers who want to build a more profitable business. I've developed a system that works to guide clients down a path to where they invest top dollar in photography. For more information, visit www.captureschool.com.

"Selling collections with more than one image has dramatically increased my average sales."

If you want more free resources and advice from some of the most successful photographers in the industry, watch my free "Mimika TV" interview show at www.mimikacooney.com.

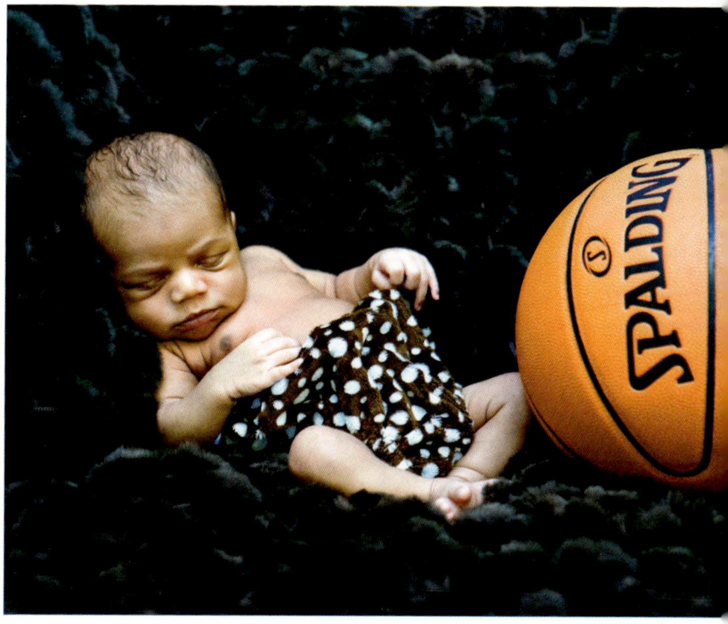

8. Interview with the Pros

"Everyone is born a genius, but the process of living degeniuses them."
—Buckminster Fuller

Interviews with professional newborn photographers revealed several similarities and several differences in working habits. The way we approach our craft influences the final outcome; it makes us all unique.

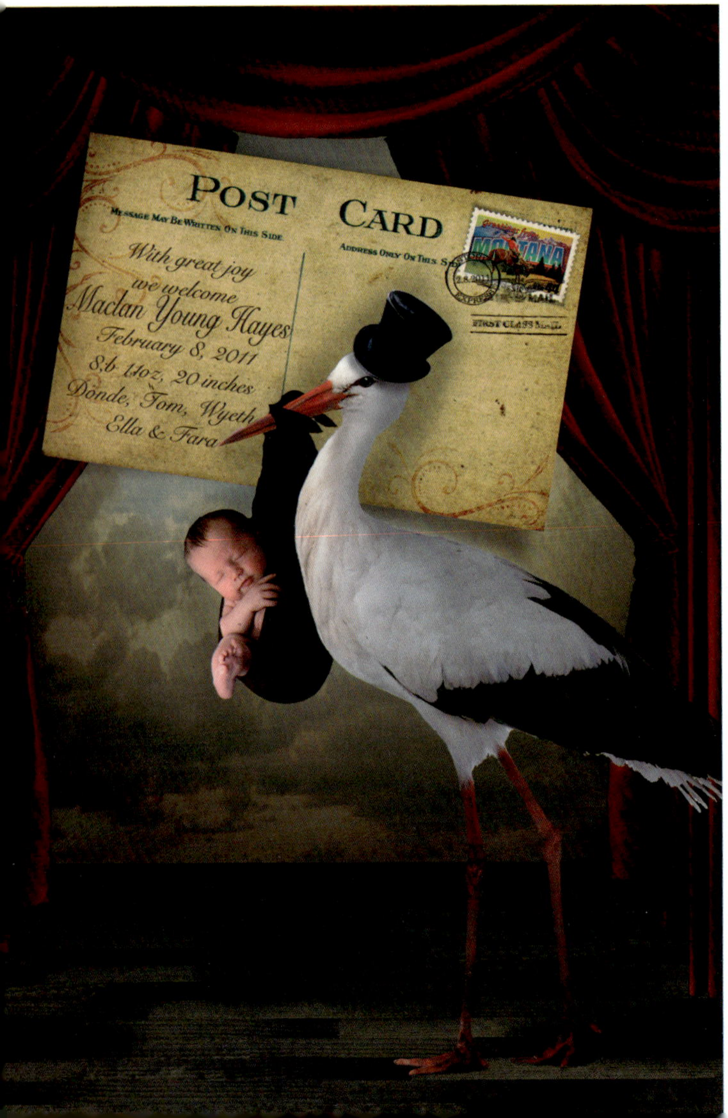

Contributors

I'd like to thank the following photographers for sharing their knowledge and their work:

Amy Coe
www.inspireportrait.com

Kelli Annison
www.photobella.com

Emily Lapish
www.emilylapish.com

Sandi Ford
www.bumpsbabesandbeyond.co.uk

Louise Fullbrook
www.louisefullbrook.com

Melissa Morrissey
www.melissamorrisseyphotography.com

Angela Randall
www.angirandallphotography.com

Brenda Horan
www.brendahoran.com

Heather Dougherty
www.doughertyphotodesigns.com

◀ Photograph by Amy Coe.
▶ Photograph by Brenda Horan.

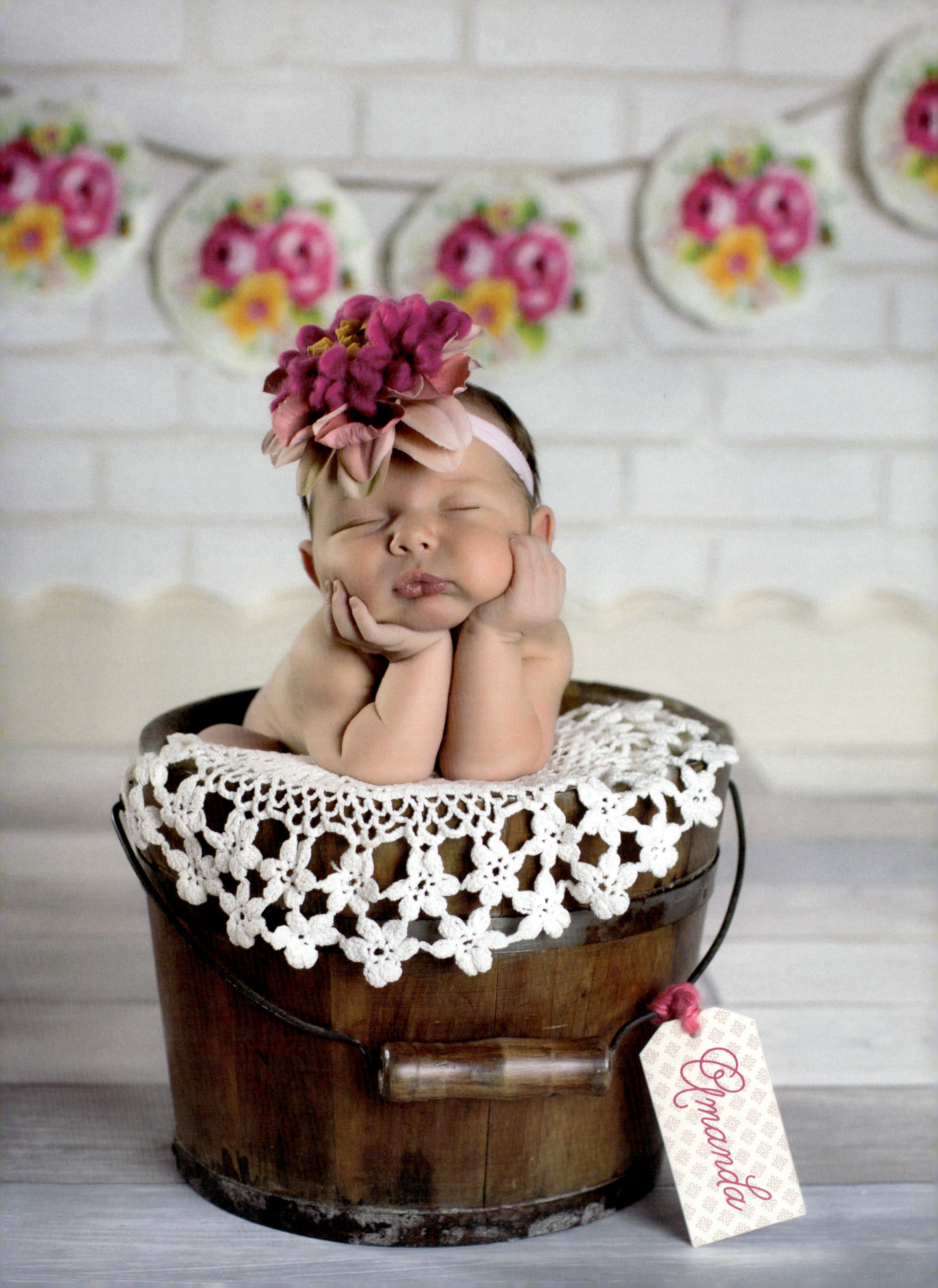
Amanda

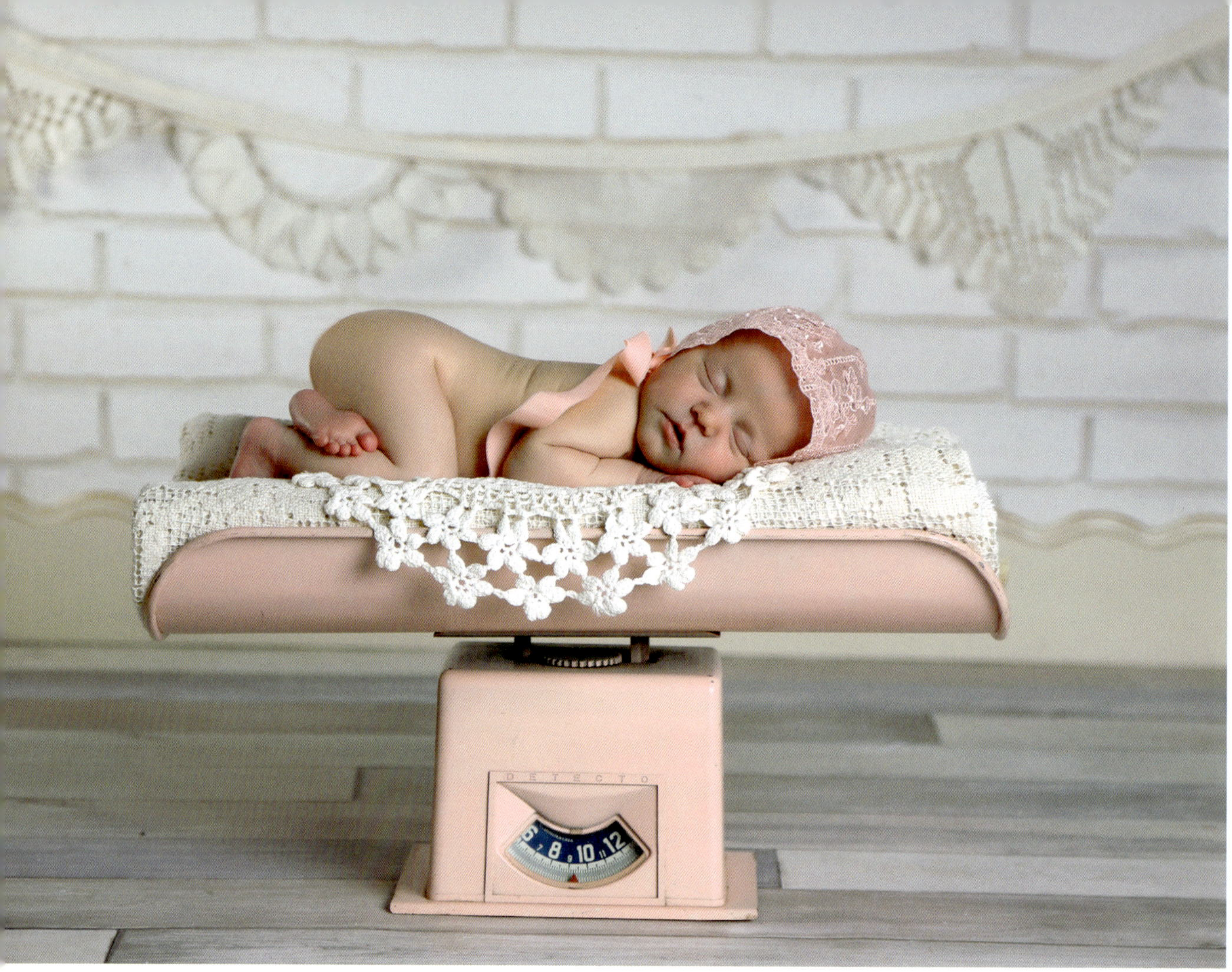

▲ Photograph by Brenda Horan.

How long have you been a newborn photographer?

Amy: Ten years in business, five years photographing primarily babies.

Kelli: Three years.

Emily: Four-and-a-half years.

Sandi: Sixteen months.

Louise: Two years.

Melissa: Two years.

Angela: Four years.

Brenda: Fourteen years.

Heather: Six years in business, two years specializing in newborns.

How did you learn about newborn photography?

Amy: Trial and error, talking to friends in the industry.

Kelli: I attended in-person workshops, purchased a book, watched online videos.

Emily: Workshops, reading, and practice, practice, practice!

Sandi: Attended in-person workshops, watched online videos.

Louise: Purchased a book, watched online videos.

Melissa: Trial and error, putting my work out there for critique.

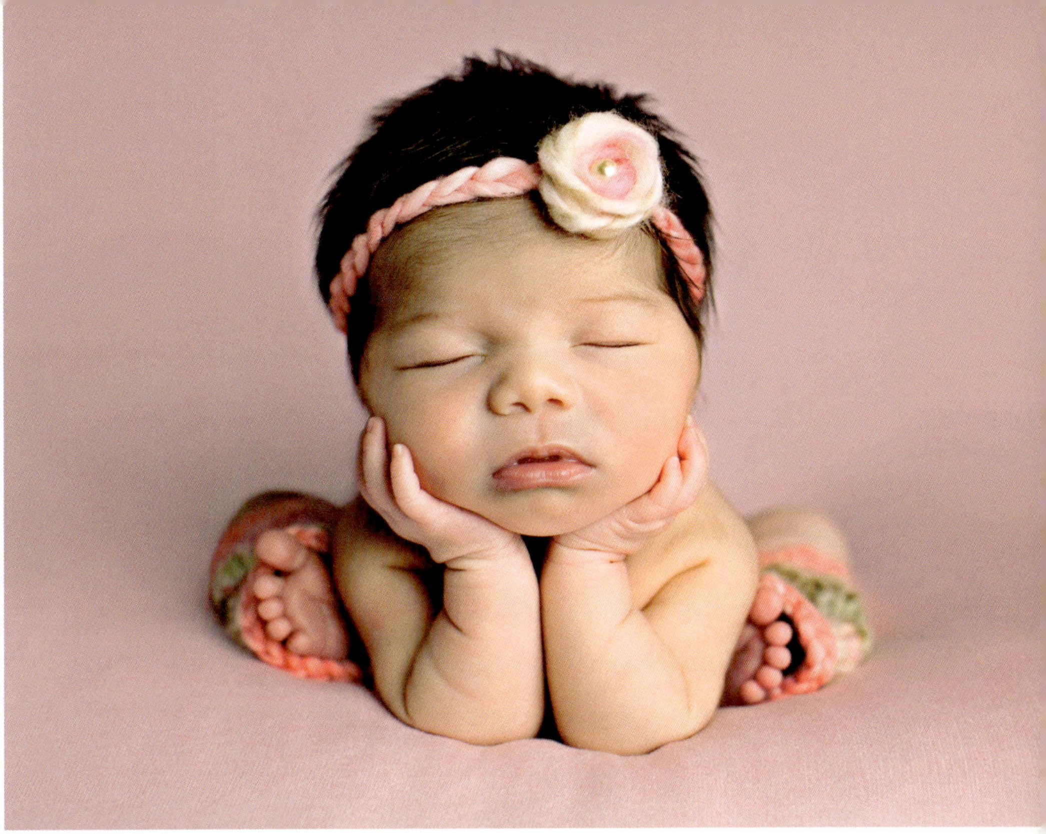

➤ Photograph by Heather Dougherty.

➤ Photograph by Melissa Morrissey.

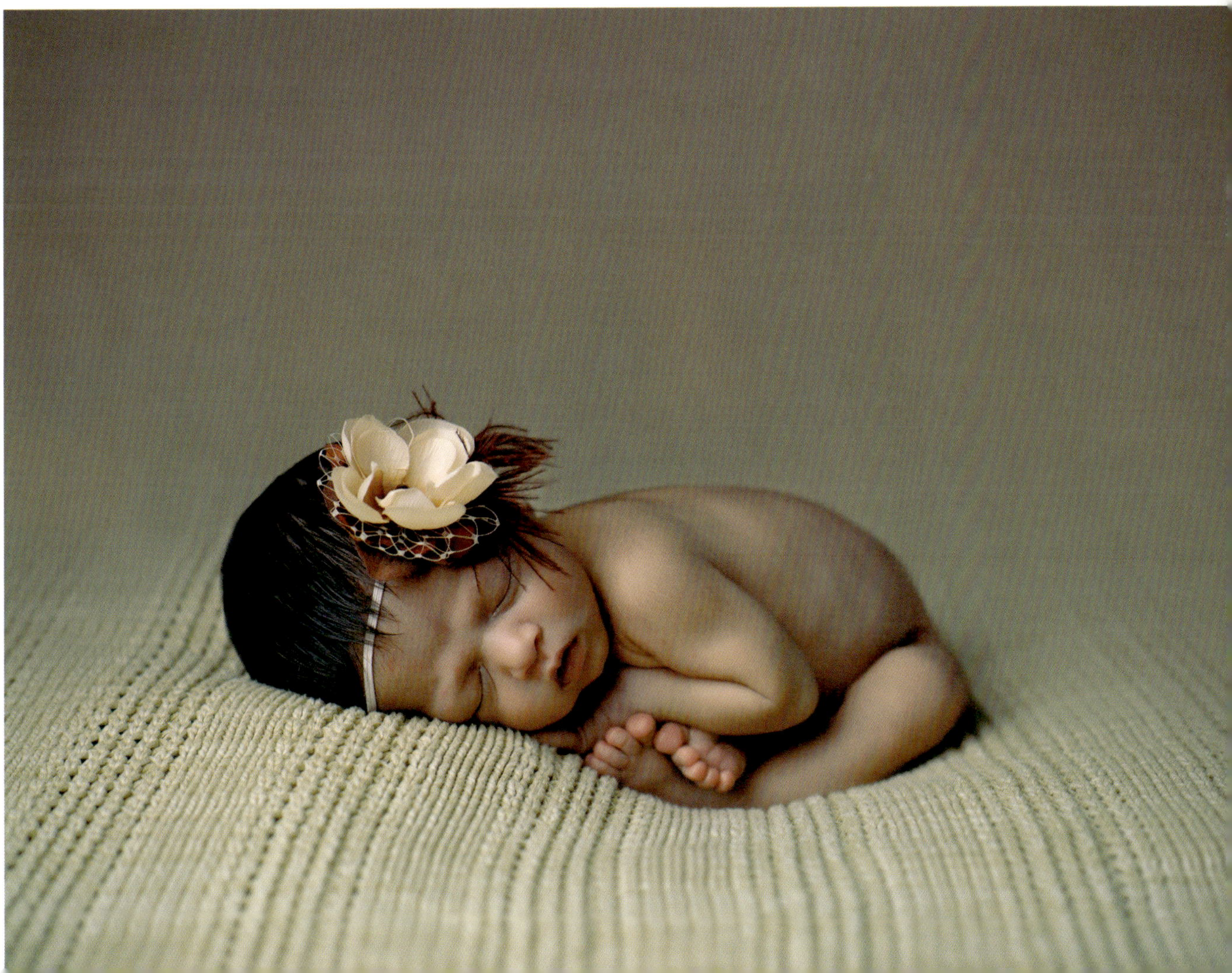

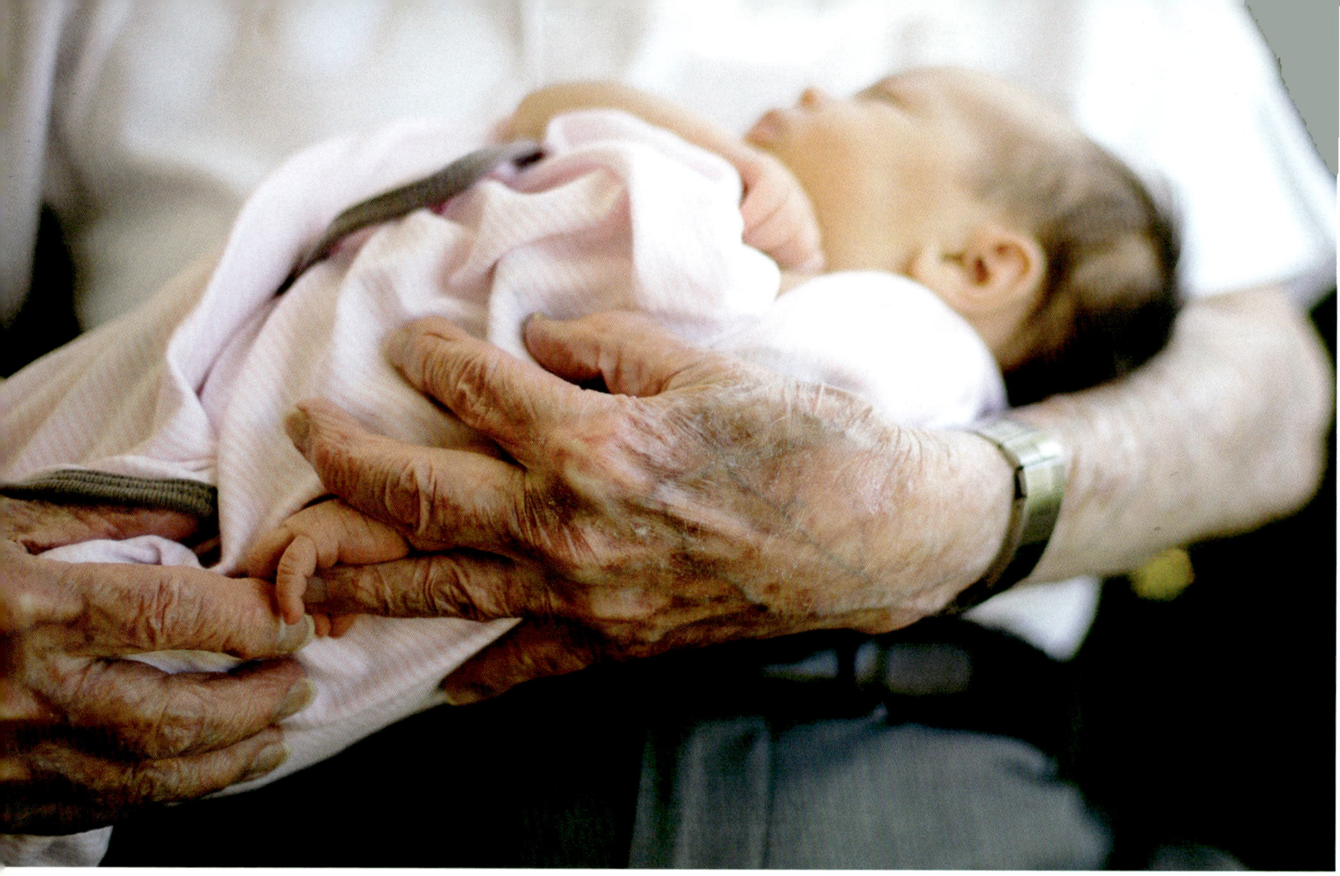

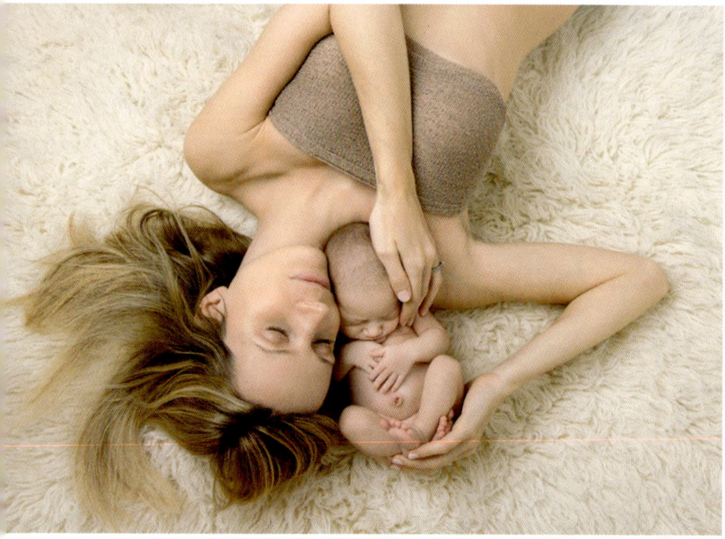

▲ Photograph by Emily Lapish.
◄ Photograph by Sandi Ford.
► Photograph by Emily Lapish.

Angela: I attended an in-person workshop, but I became more interested in newborn photography when I had my own children.

Brenda: Workshops, books.

Heather: I attended an in-person workshop and learned on my own.

How long do your newborn sessions typically take to complete?

Amy: Two to four hours.

Kelli: One to two hours.

Emily: One to two hours.

Sandi: Four or more hours.

Louise: Two to four hours.

Melissa: Two to four hours.

Angela: Two to four hours.

Brenda: One to two hours.

Heather: Two to four hours.

How many newborn sessions do you photograph per month?

Amy: Two to six.

Kelli: Four to six.

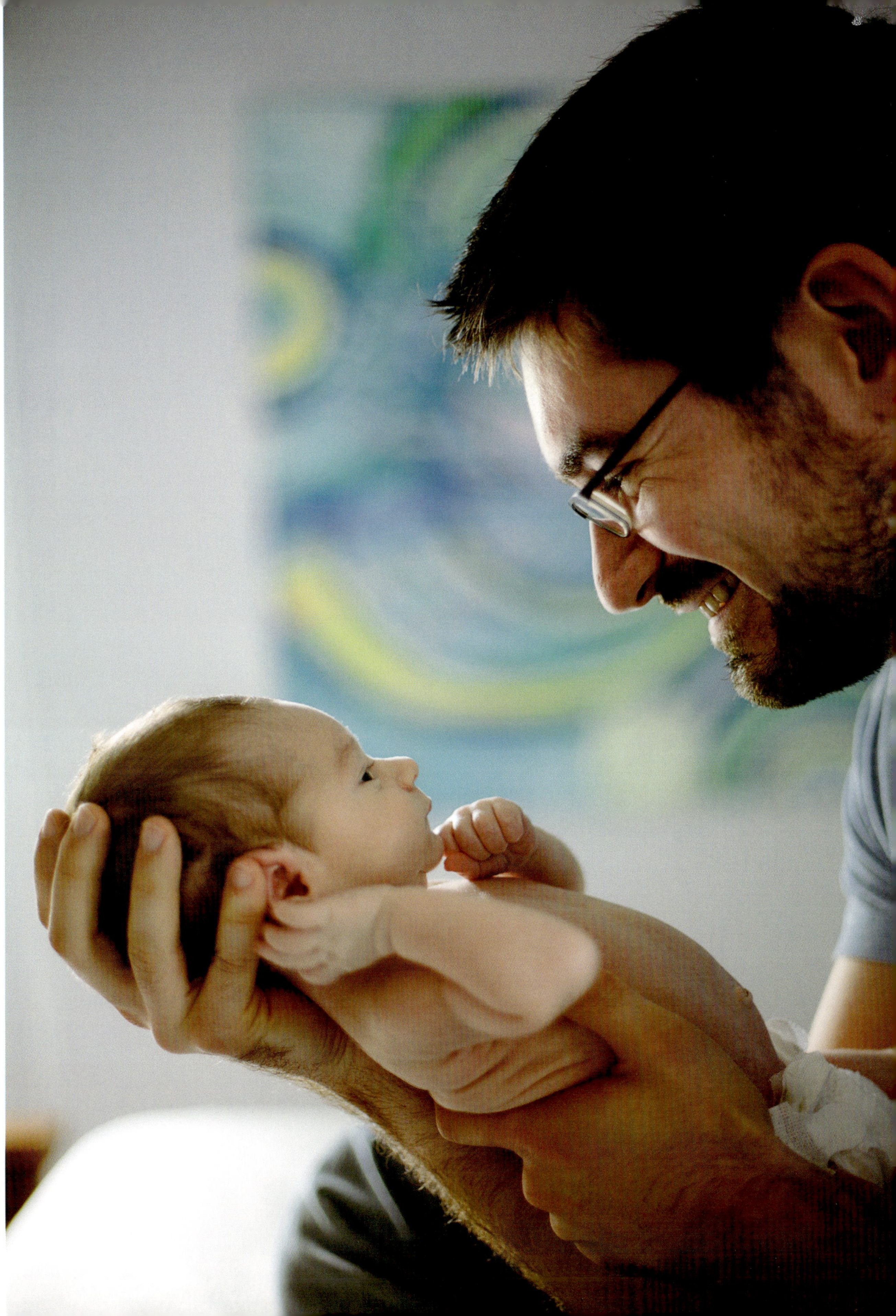

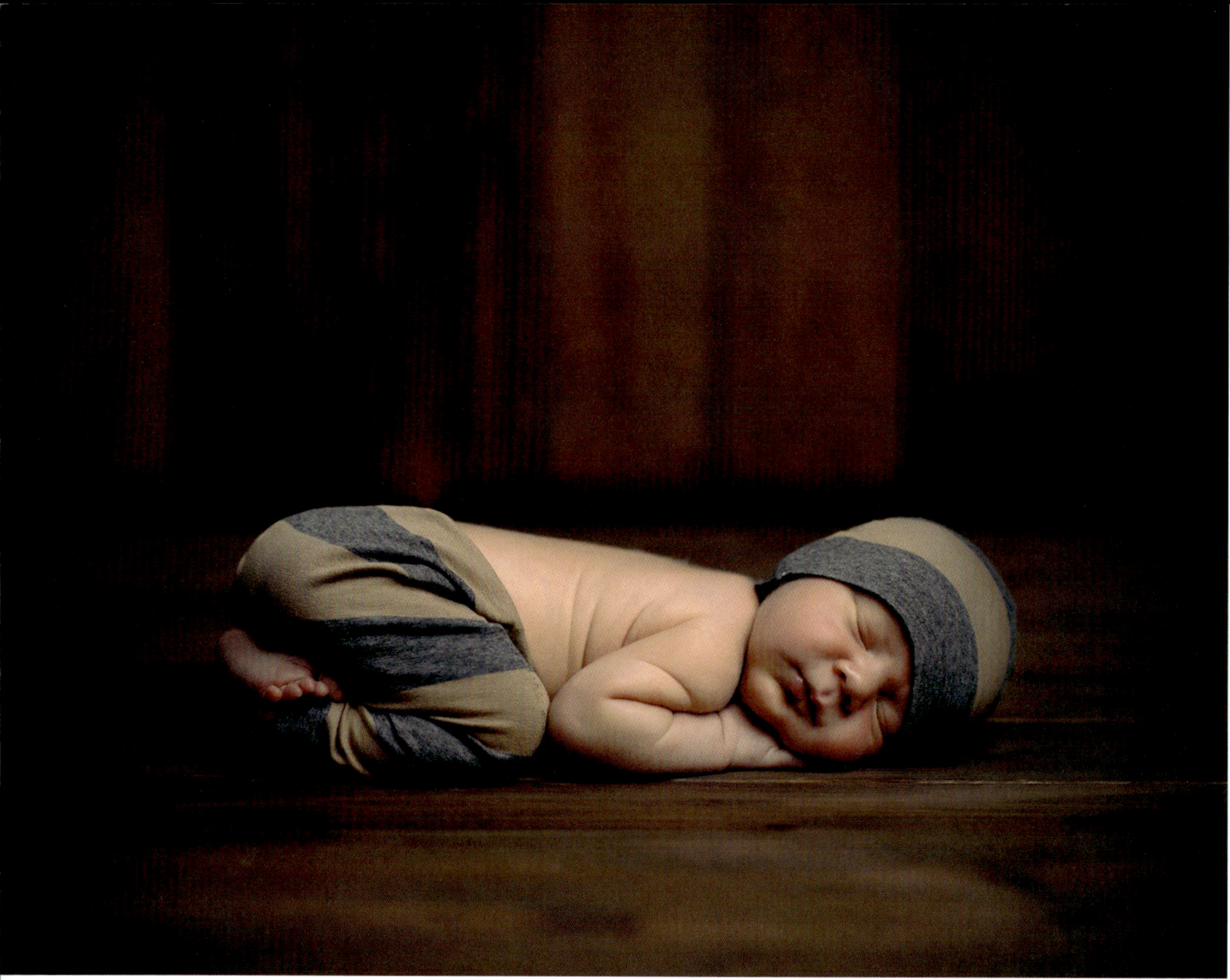

▲ Photograph by Melissa Morrissey.

Emily: Two.

Sandi: Six to ten.

Louise: Twenty or more.

Melissa: Six.

Angela: Four to eight.

Brenda: Four to eight.

Heather: Three to eight.

Do you use natural light, studio light, or a combination of lighting methods?

Amy: I use studio lighting only. I use a medium softbox and an AlienBees 400 for newborns. I also use a big white bounce card to fill in shadows.

Kelli: I use an Interfit Cool-Lite. I find that it works perfectly for newborns. The light is continuous, so I don't have to worry about a flash waking Baby, and it never gets too hot. My light is usually placed at a 45 degree angle, to camera right, with the baby's head pointing toward the light. On camera left, I have a large reflector or large white board sitting up against the wall.

Emily: All my newborn photography is lifestyle, done in my clients' homes, using only natural light. Window light is an amazing thing in newborn photography.

Sandi: I use studio light. When I am shooting on wood floors, I prefer the richer tones and colors that I get with natural light, and there is no glare!

Louise: I am about to embark on a new learning course for studio flash, but right now I'm very happy with the results I get from continuous lighting, which I have used from the start. I also try a little bit of natural light when possible, but my studio is not well lit with natural light, so I only get to do this when visiting new parents at their homes.

Melissa: When photographing newborns on a beanbag, I use one AlienBees studio strobe. For prop shots, I often add a reflector.

Angela: In my studio, my lighting setup is pretty simple. I use a 4x6-foot softbox and 3x4-foot softbox for some of my setups. I also like to use just the 4x6-foot softbox with a reflector.

Brenda: I use a combination of natural light and studio light. I prefer natural light when working on my posing table, and I use studio lighting for my prop photos.

Heather: I use an AlienBees 400 strobe with a 50x50-inch Westcott softbox.

What's in your photo bag?

Amy: Canon EOS 5D Mark I.

Kelli: Canon EOS 5D Mark II, 50mm f/1.4 lens, and 100mm f/2.8 on macro. I believe in simplicity in all things, including equipment.

Emily: I shoot predominantly with a Canon EOS 5D Mark II and usually gravitate toward my 24–70mm f/2.8L and 50mm f/1.4

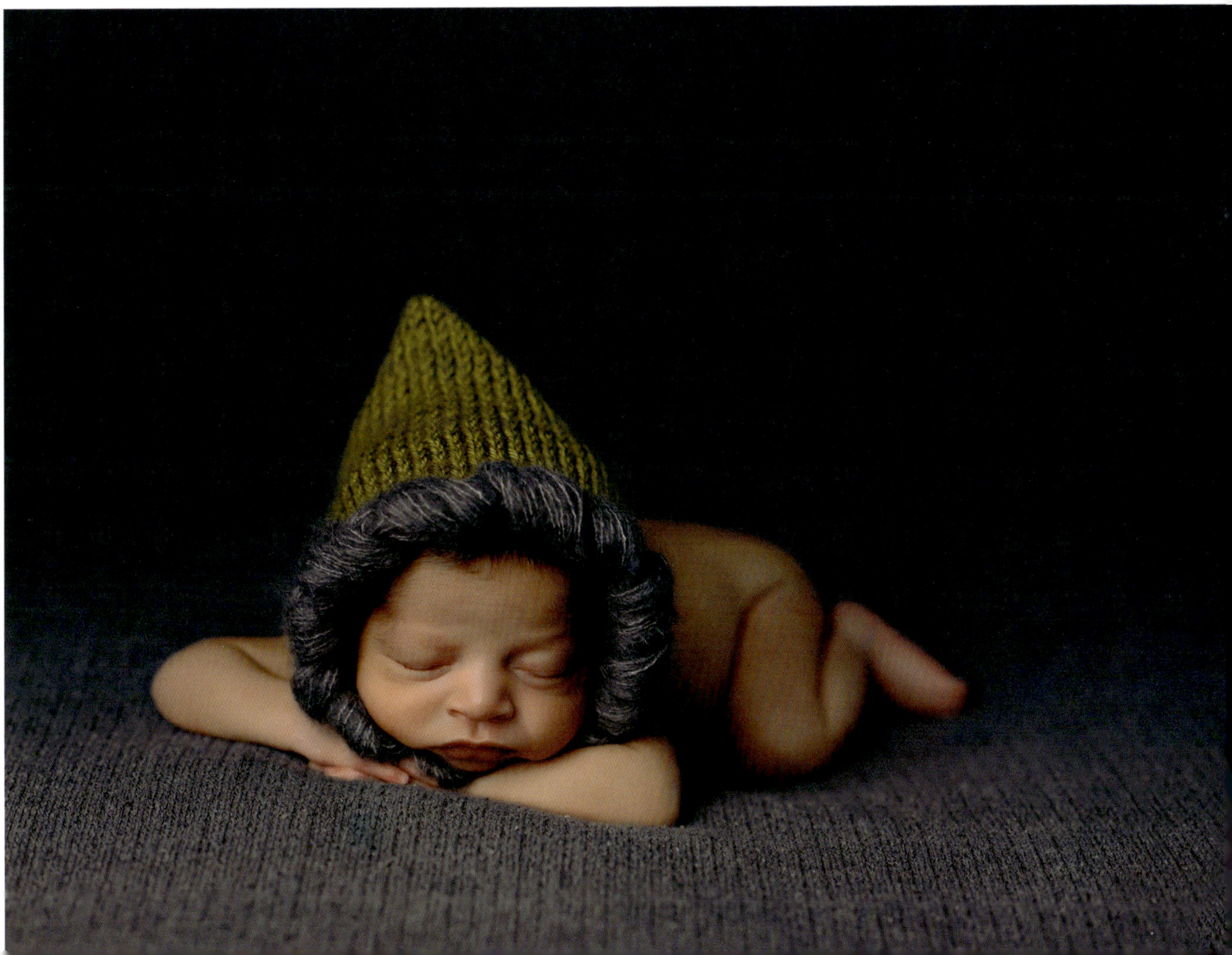

▼ Photograph by Melissa Morrissey.

lenses for photographing newborns. I travel light for newborn sessions. I used to do more of a studio setup in my clients' homes, carrying in tons of heavy equipment, props, etc., but I found that to be very overwhelming for new parents. My calling is to take real, honest lifestyle portraits, and I don't feel that props, elaborate posing, and costumes fit into my business model.

Sandi: I carry a Canon EOS 5D Mark III, 50mm f/1.4 and 24–70mm f/2.8L lenses, and a gray card.

Louise: Two Canon EOS 5D Mark IIs (one for backup), 580EX II Speedlites, 50mm lens (my favorite), 100mm macro for close-ups of baby features, a 12–24mm lens for family sessions, and an 80–200mm lens just because I wanted it! I also carry a Trek-Tech Optera 460 Pro tripod with a Manfrotto 390rc2 head, tons of batteries, and two grips.

Melissa: I carry a Nikon D700, a Nikon 85mm f/1.4G lens, which I use for almost everything, including newborns—it's the best lens hands down! I use a Nikon 50mm 1.4D when I need more space.

Angela: What is in my photo bag? I have a Canon EOS 50D and two lenses: a 70–200mm f/2.8L and a 50mm f/1.4. My go-to is the 70–200mm lens.

Brenda: I use a Canon EOS 5D Mark III. I use a 50mm f/1.2L lens for newborns.

Heather: I carry a Canon EOS Mark III, a Canon 50mm f/1.2L lens, and PocketWizards.

▼ Photograph by Kelli Annison.

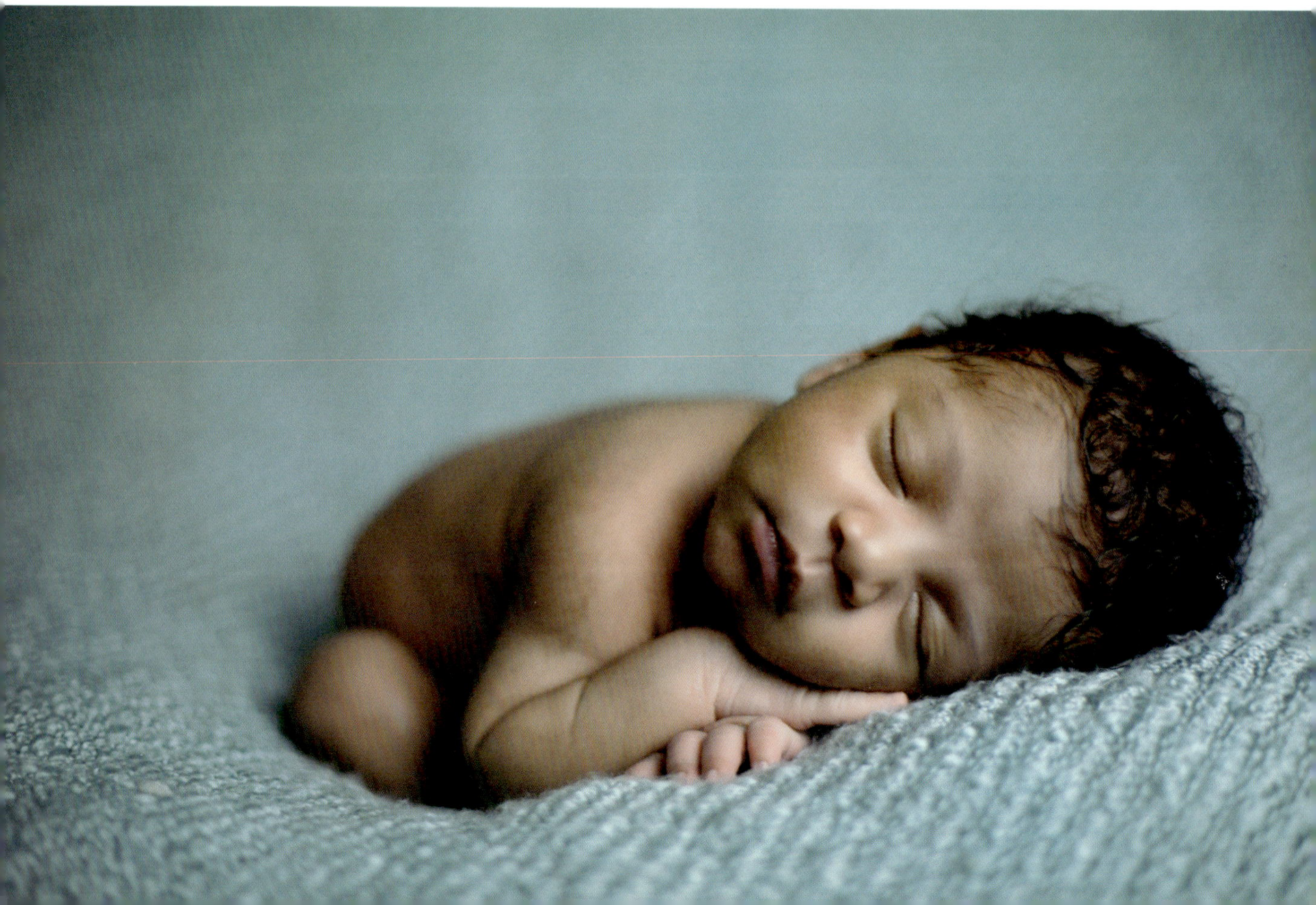

Do you offer in-person sales consultations or do you do online sales only?

Amy: I do both but will probably go back to only doing sales in person.

Kelli: I do in-person sales sessions at my studio. I use an iPad to show the parents the photos, then I show them the samples in my studio so they can touch canvases, flip through the albums, etc. I have had many parents tell me that this was much easier than deciding on their own. It's not easy to make such a big decision, so having professional input on what will look best is a service to the client.

Emily: My sessions are all-inclusive, so sales don't enter into my business model. I do offer in-home design consultations for clients who want me to help them design a wall gallery or showpiece, but that's not an integral part of my business.

Sandi: I prefer in-person sales but will do online sales if the clients live far away or are unwilling to return to the studio.

Louise: I really don't like online sales. As a customer, I would not like to spend a few hundred pounds with no advice. My background has been in both art and design along with sales and marketing, so I think I know how to treat my customers.

Melissa: I use an all-inclusive pricing model. I collect a portion of that as a retainer to secure the client's session in my schedule, with the balance due prior to the photo session.

Angela: Roughly 99 percent of my sales consultations are in person. I see an increase in sales when clients come in to order their portraits. I do online sales in certain situations—for instance, if the client traveled over an hour to come to the newborn session.

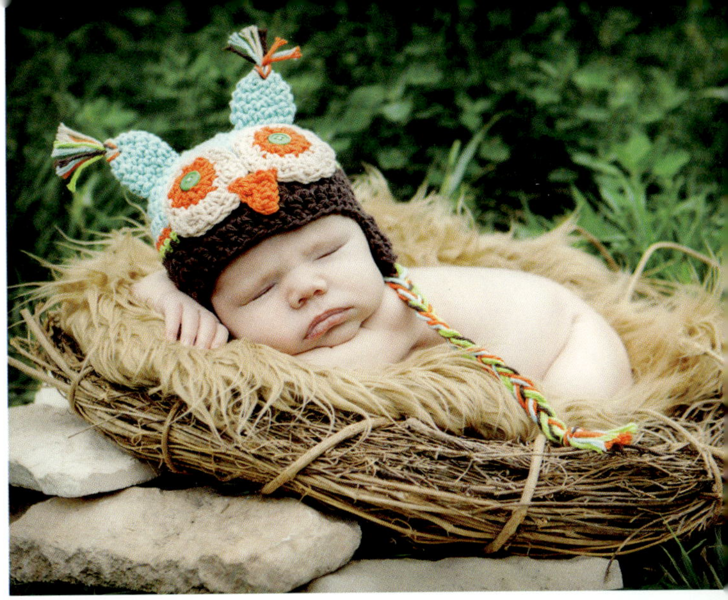

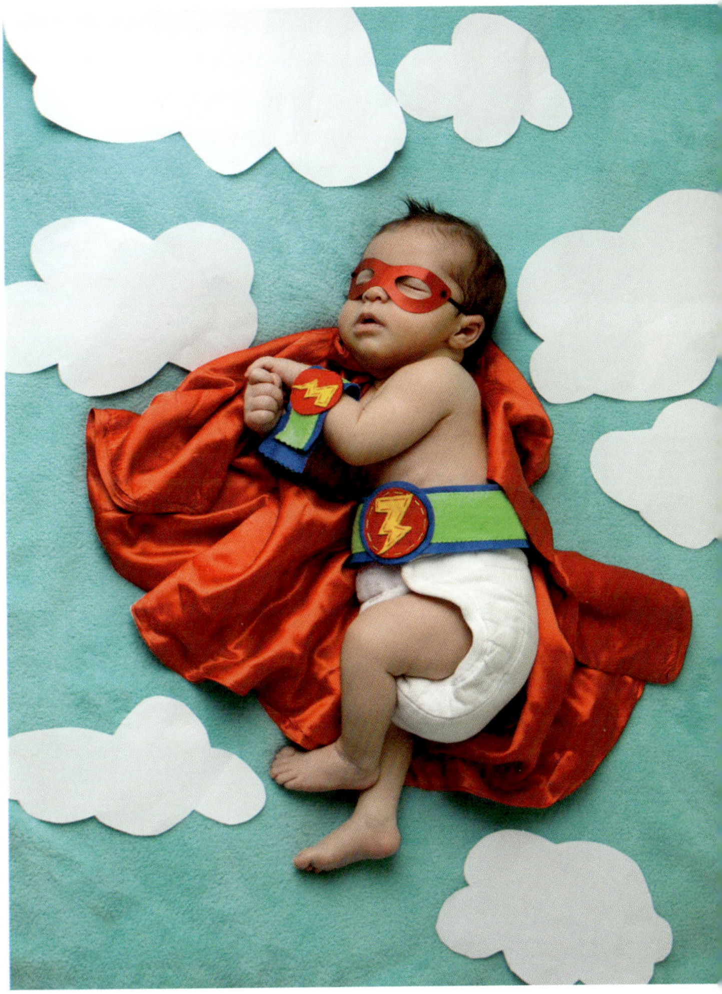

▲ (top) Photograph by Angela Randall.
▲ (bottom) Photograph by Amy Coe.

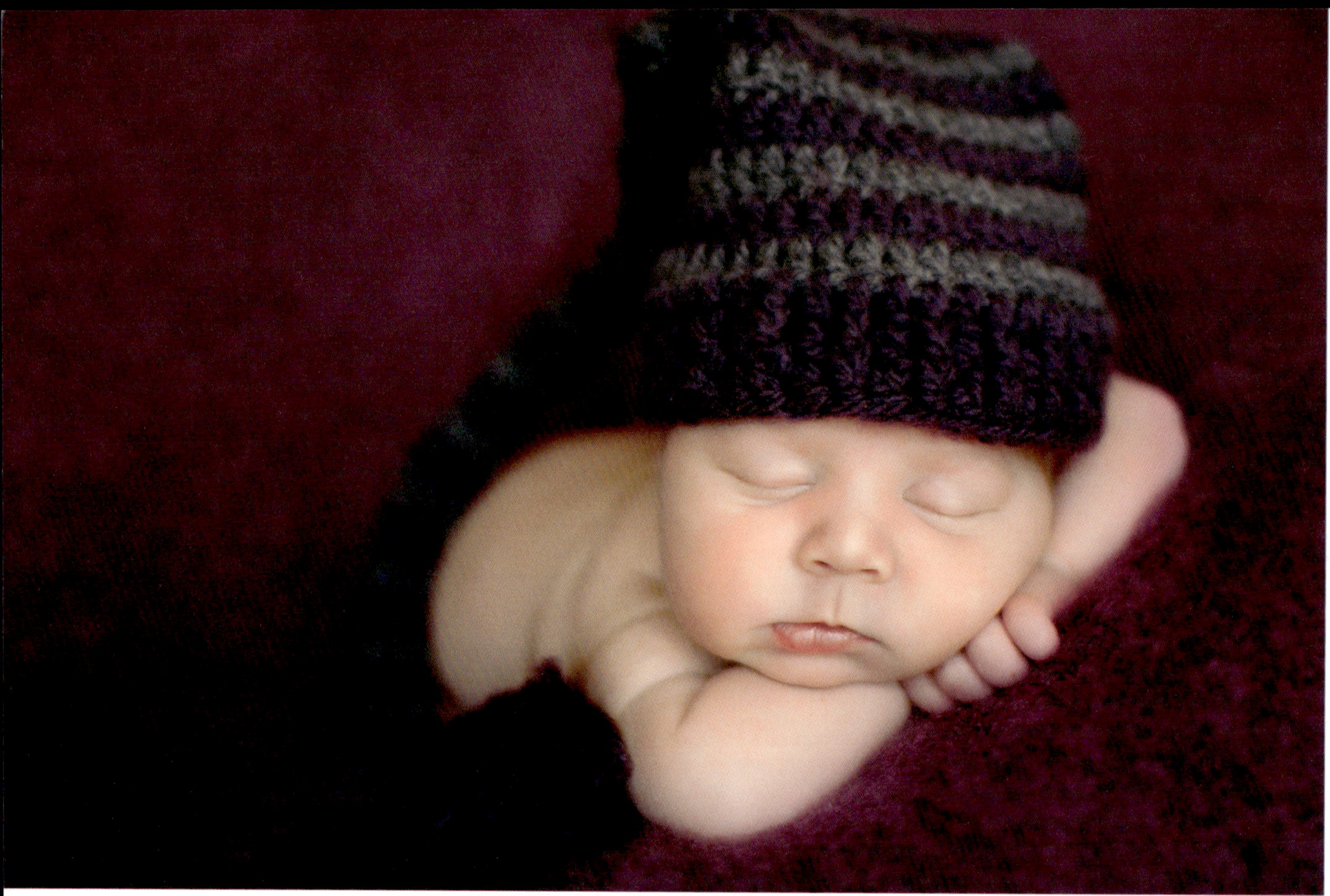

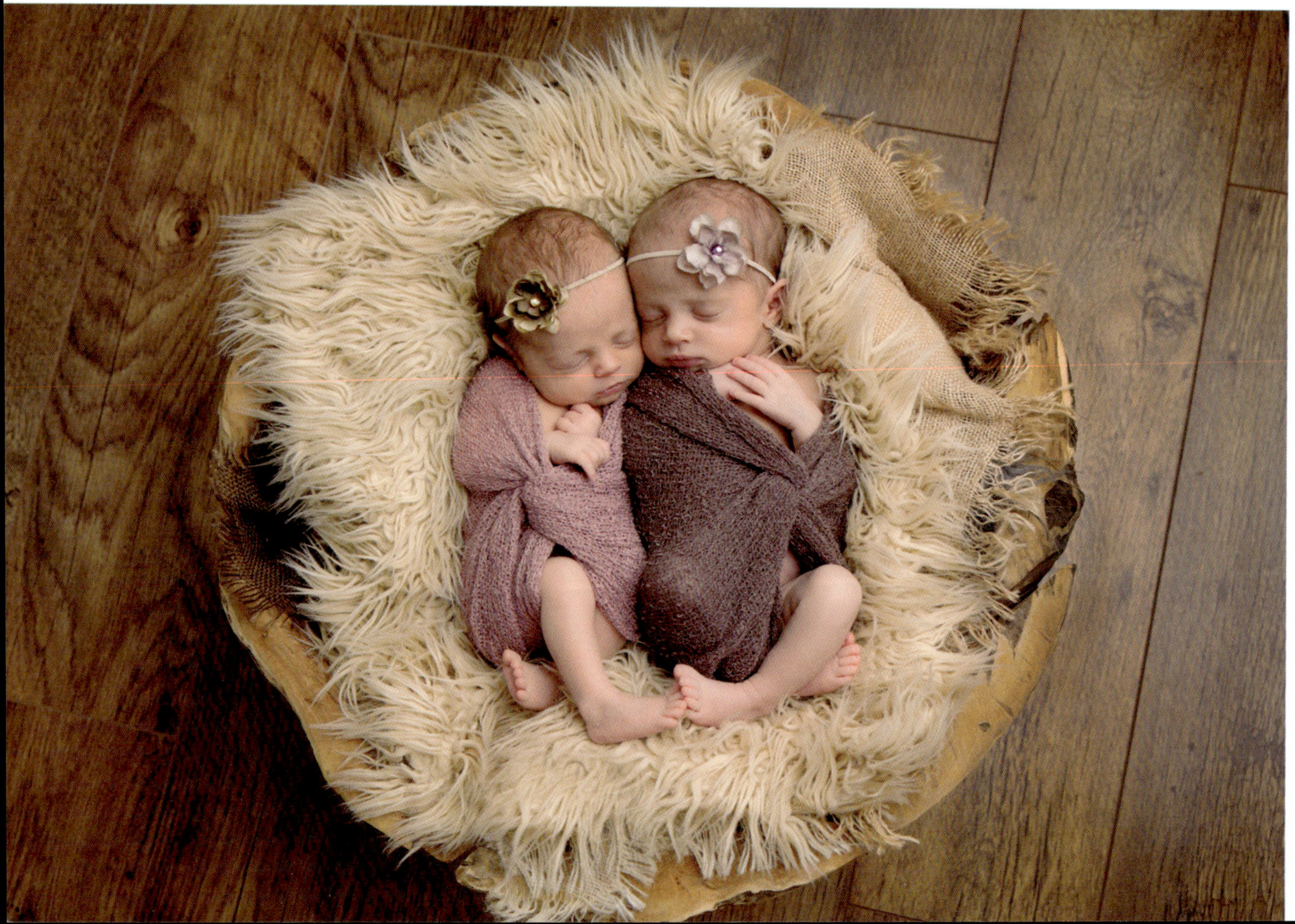

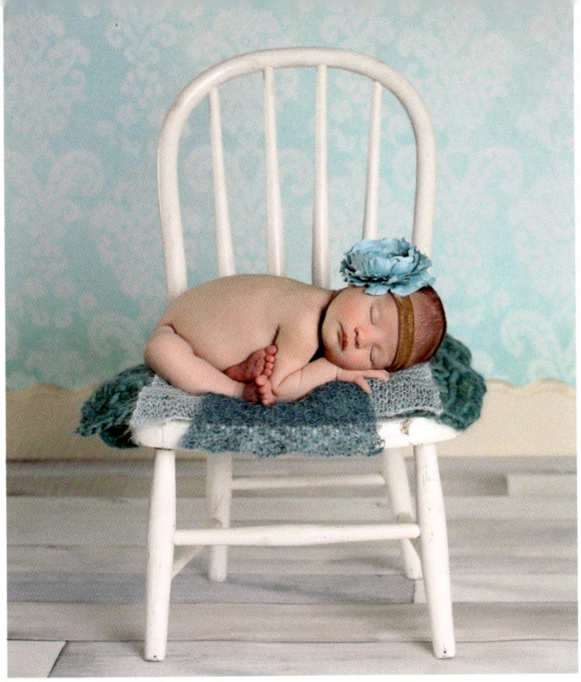

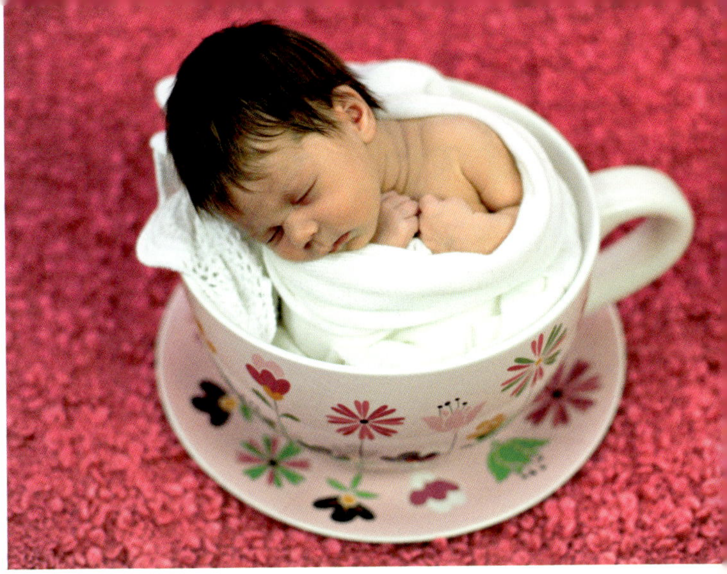

◄ Photograph by Brenda Horan.
▲ Photograph by Louise Fullbrook.

Brenda: My studio favors in-person sales; however, we offer online sales for out-of-town relatives.

Heather: I have done online sales, but I may change to in-person sales this year.

What is your favorite part about being a newborn photographer?

Amy: Snuggling babies fills up my baby want/need. I cuddle them, photograph them, and give them back—then I no longer want to have more babies!

Kelli: Composing the images. I love when I am able to take an idea from my head and bring it to life in an image.

Emily: I love capturing real memories and real life, just the way it is in all its beauty. This is what fills my heart and keeps me going in this business. When a client comes back to me years after their newborn session and tells me they still cry with joy every time they see their images or tearfully thanks me for capturing the things they love most about their beautiful life, my job feels so fulfilling.

Sandi: It really gives you the opportunity to be creative and artistic with portrait photography, and I love giving families these memories of their babies.

Louise: I love meeting wonderful people and I feel proud that they chose me above all others to photograph their precious baby.

Melissa: My favorite part is the challenge. It's hot and dirty and sweaty, and out of it comes the most gorgeous portraits of these little babies. It's not a glamorous job by any means, and it is probably more work than most realize, but the resulting classic, timeless images are worth it to me!

Angela: My favorite part of being a newborn photographer is creating precious memories for each of my clients. I am always amazed that I am creating a portrait that is going to hang in someone's home and that they will cherish it and how small their little one once was. Babies grow way too fast, so to capture this time is simply amazing. I also love all the

◄ (top) Photograph by Kelli Annison.
◄ (bottom) Photograph by Sandi Ford.

cuddle time I get with each of my tiny clients.

Brenda: I love the entire process, from styling the session to photographing the baby, to editing the images. Nothing beats a beautiful baby!

Heather: The best part is seeing the happy expressions of the parents when I'm working with their newborn and handling the babies!

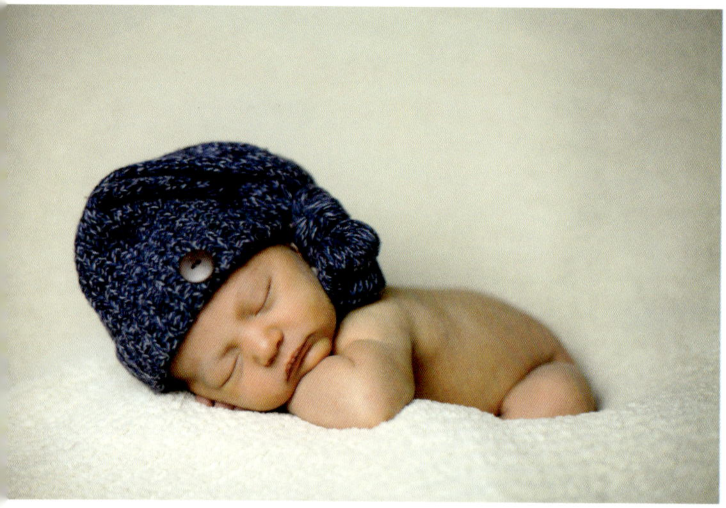

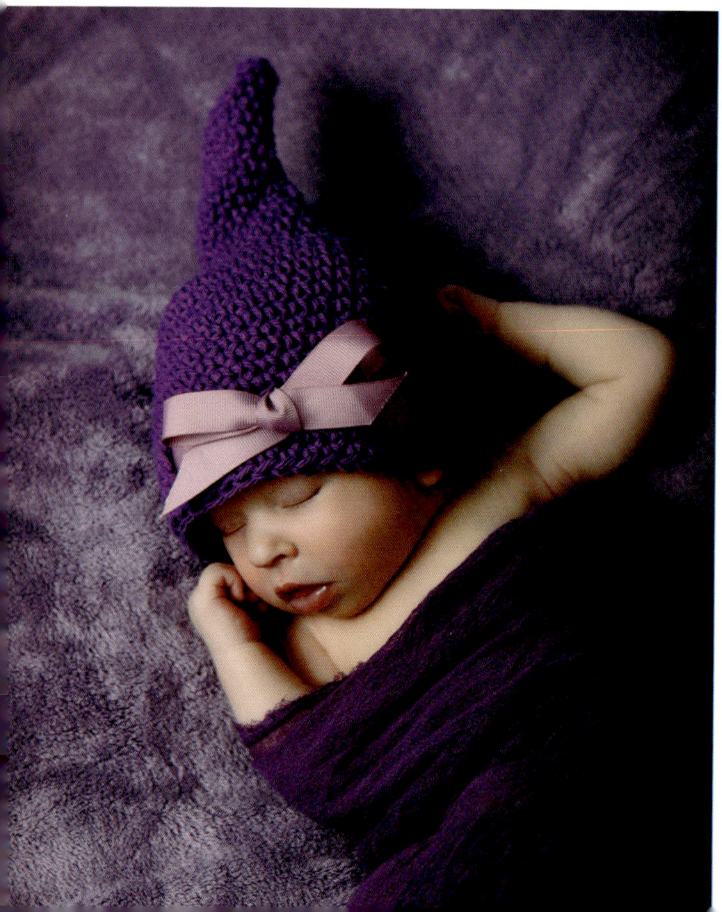

What are your favorite and most effective methods of getting business?

Amy: I use my website, Facebook, and word of mouth. Now, Pinterest is huge for driving traffic to my website!

Kelli: I get about 50 percent of my business through my website and search engines. I believe it is important that your website sells your services and instills trust. I have also spent a good amount of time to make sure my website appears on the first page of the search engine results for my local area. The other half of my business comes from marketing partners. I have made friends with other business owners in the area, and I try to help them in any way I can. When I help community businesses, they often refer their own customers to me. This is different from just putting business cards on someone's counter, though. To get referrals, you must make a genuine connection with the business owner and you must both benefit from the relationship. I think how that happens is different for every business, but if you find a way to help others, they will never forget you.

Emily: Excellent customer service is the best method of generating business. You don't need to spend tons of money on marketing, just be extremely good to your clients. They'll do your marketing for you if you treat them right. Be kind and courteous, underpromise and overdeliver. Wow them with your communication, your promptness, and your above-and-beyond mentality.

◄ (top) Photograph by Kelli Annisson Full.

◄ (bottom) Photograph by Angela Randall.

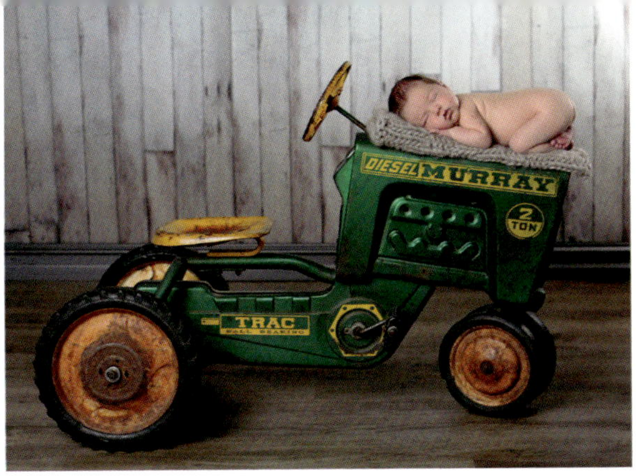

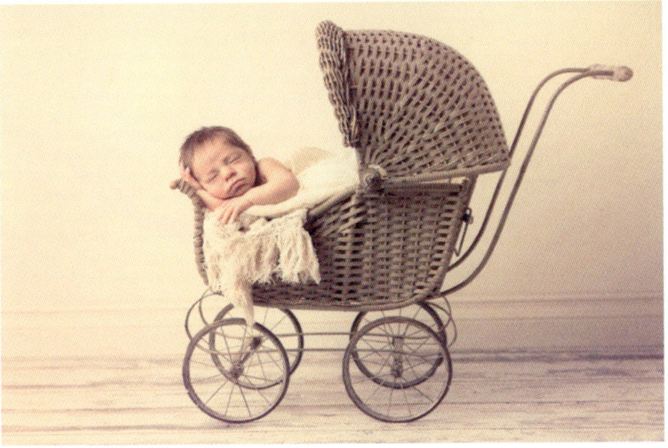

▲ (top) Photograph by Brenda Horan.
▲ (bottom) Photograph by Amy Coe.

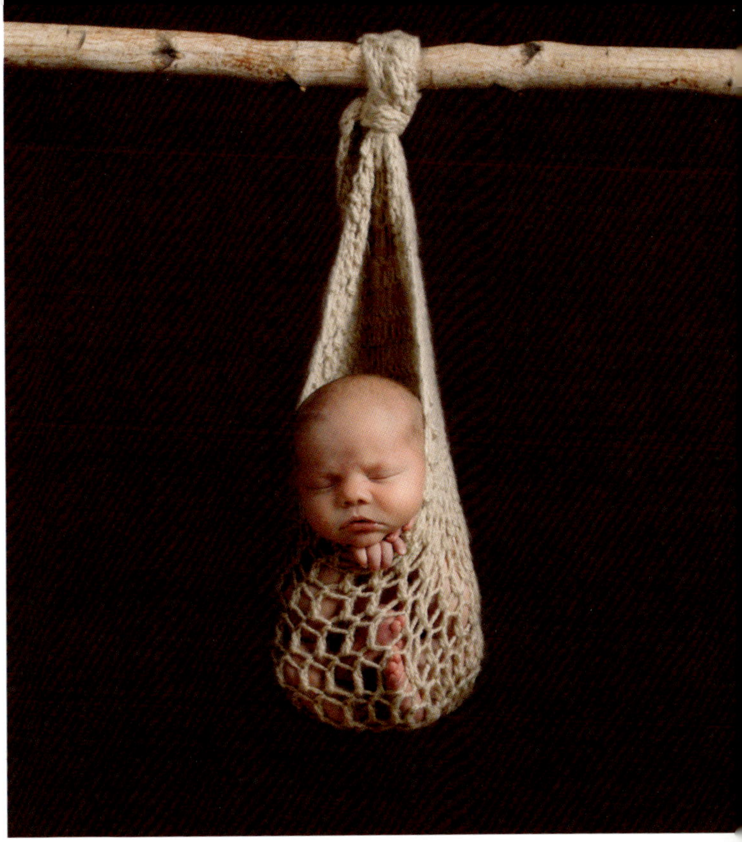

▲ Photograph by Kelli Randall.

Sandi: SEO organic searching is paramount for me. My pricing is quite high, and I personally find that Facebook leads are not always quality referrals. Also I get a lot of word-of-mouth referrals.

Louise: Word-of-mouth referrals work best for me. I get out there and get a few new moms in. If they send me five new moms over the next few weeks, they get a cake smash session for free with one print (not including cake).

Melissa: The majority of my clients come from local relevant Google searches and referrals from previous clients. I find Facebook works better for lower-priced photographers or mini sessions. I don't believe in doing mail-outs. It is not targeted marketing and is usually a waste of money. Make sure your marketing is targeted!

Angela: Most of my clients come from referrals and Facebook. I have done advertising through mail with promo postcards, but I don't see a great turnout for the amount of money being spent. When I post the images my clients have ordered on Facebook, their friends see the images, call me when they need images, and tell me that a friend was a client.

Brenda: Word of mouth is terrific. We use Facebook, Twitter, and Instagram to get that word of mouth going. We do some print advertising in magazines that go directly to our target market.

Heather: I'm slot #1 to #3 on page 1 of the Google search in my area for newborn photographers. My business also comes from referrals, and I advertise with The Bump and mail out postcards.

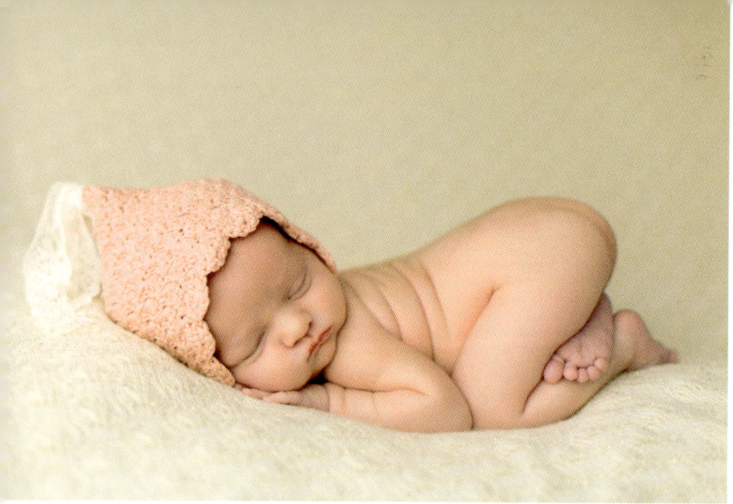

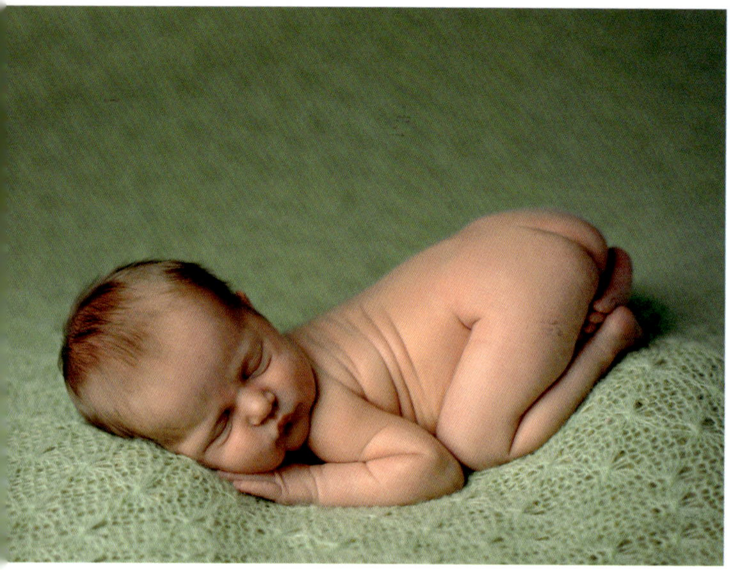

▲ (top) Photograph by Sandi Ford.
▲ (bottom) Photograph by Melissa Morrissey.

What are you favorite props and poses?

Amy: My favorite props are soft blankets, pashmina shawls, baskets, old wooden boxes, and rusty baskets. I make as many of my own props—like hats and headbands—as I can.

Kelli: I like to keep things simple. Small, delicate headbands for girls and a few simple hats for boys. I also love putting Baby in a bucket or basket to show off their tiny size.

Emily: The family's home is my strongest "prop." Putting them against the backdrop of their real lives is a powerful emotional tool, and it helps the clients relax during the photo session.

Sandi: Bottom-up is my favorite pose on a blanket, but I also love simple neutral organic tones, wooden bowls, and flokati rugs.

Louise: I quite like natural poses. I'm not sure about the froggy-type pose. I just don't feel good about the risk involved with placing a newborn in an unnatural position.

I studied horticulture for two years and have a massive love of the outdoors, so I love wood, plants, and other natural elements. I take inspiration from woodland, dreamy but not over-the-top pixie styles, just subtle hints using natural wooden trugs [a shallow wooden basket], etc.

Melissa: My favorite pose is one we call the tushie-up pose. It was basically adapted from the cute way babies sleep with their bum in the air. We newborn photographers exaggerate it a bit to make it a little more dramatic. My next favorite pose is a very simple one—I love a wrapped sleeping baby on their back with a nice tight crop of just their head and shoulders. I adore those stretchy wraps; they are very versatile. Another favorite is the "taco" pose. There are many variations of this pose, and I like them all, but I especially like using the wrap with this pose as well. My all-time-favorite prop, other than the wrap, is the flokati rug. I use it at every single session! I try to keep everything very simple and sophisticated so it has a timeless feel.

Angela: My favorite props at the moment are crochet/knit hats, stretch wraps, and textured fabrics. My favorite poses are those that create all those wrinkles in the side. I get them by placing the baby on their belly and getting the elbow and knee to touch, wrapping them so they are cocooned. I try to get them with their hands under their chin. I always have someone helping me with that particular pose.

Brenda: My favorite prop is my vintage bucket. I use it all the time. I love attaching a tag that I can personalize with the baby's name in Photoshop. My favorite pose is the "taco" pose, although I am really loving the basic "bum up" pose lately.

Heather: I love the froggie, taco, and tushie-in-the-air poses. My favorite props are furs, buckets, tons of backdrops, and all the clothes.

▼ Photograph by Heather Dougherty.

What tips can you offer for soothing a newborn baby and dealing with parents?

Amy: Keep the baby warm! My comfort and the parents' comfort means nothing. I preheat each set with a heating pad so when I position Baby it's super cozy and warm. I also have the heat in the baby room set at 80 to 85 degrees. I use an app I downloaded on my iPhone with soothing baby sounds. The heartbeat option is my favorite. Finally, I make a moderately loud "shhhhh, shhhh, shhhhh" sound near the baby once I have him/her on the set.

Kelli: I think the key to soothing a newborn is patience. Babies can sense when you are

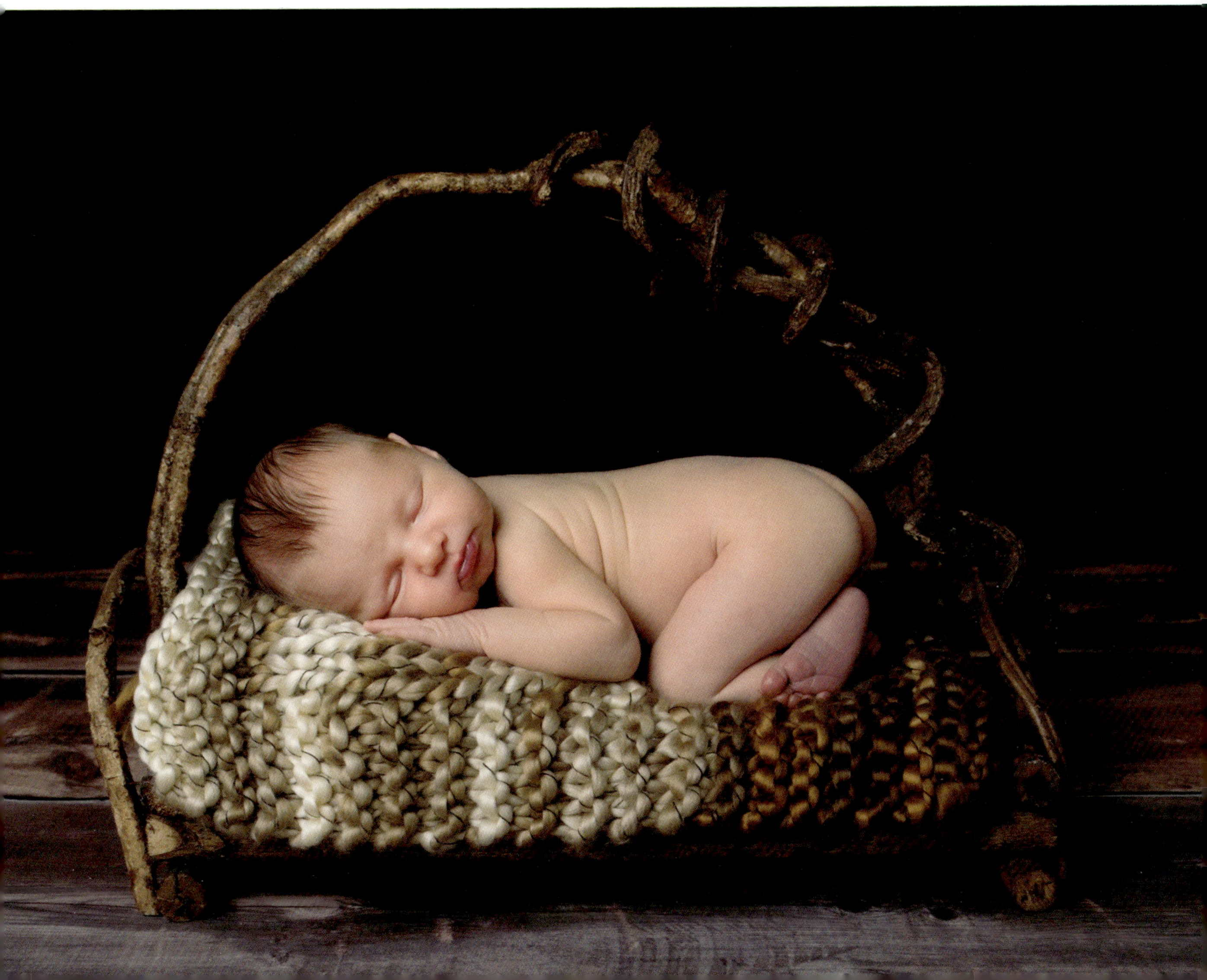

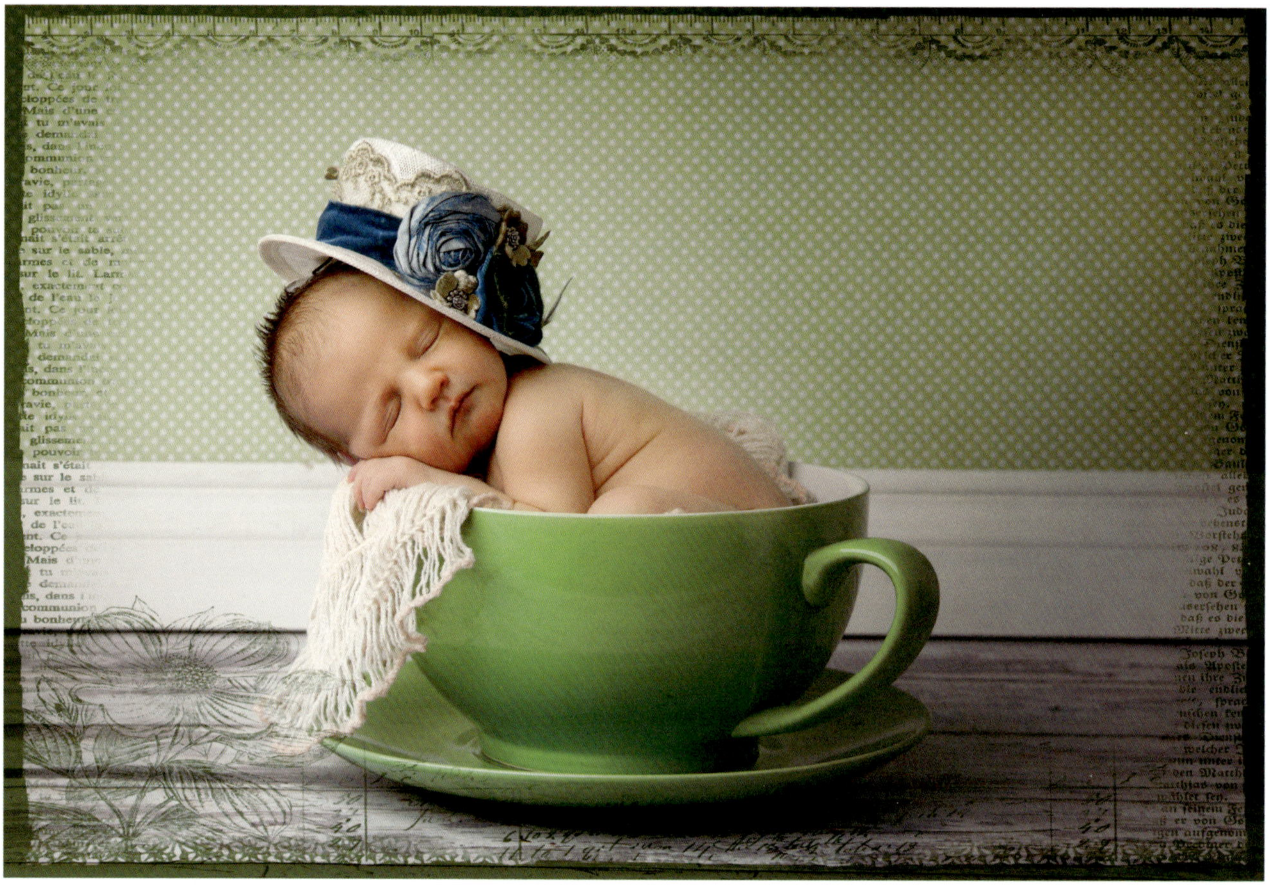

▲ Photograph by Amy Coe.

anxious for them to fall asleep or nervous about getting the shots you want. I like to let it all go and just relax with Baby. If you give yourself enough time for the session, Baby is bound to fall asleep, so relax and be patient. I find that parents feel better when they are given information up front, so I like to call clients a few days before the session. I talk to them about how long the session will take, what to expect, when to feed Baby, etc. Once they arrive at the studio, I am constantly telling them what will happen. I tell them how the flow of the session will go, I tell them why I use a heater and offer them water, I tell them don't worry if Baby pees or poops on my props because it happens on a daily basis, etc. When you keep your clients informed, they feel like you are an expert and are taking good care of their baby.

Emily: It's extremely important to prepare your clients ahead of time so they know what to expect. Many of my clients are first-time parents who book me long before their baby is born, so they not only have no idea what to expect from a newborn session, they have no idea what to expect from a newborn! I tell my clients to turn the thermostat up in their home to help keep the baby calm; to have a soothing playlist of music going; to have all non-immediate family out of the house; and most importantly, to relax. If you are calm, soothing, and in control, your clients (and the baby!) will relax significantly. You set the tone for the session, and that begins in your pre-session communication with the family. For fussy newborns, I make sure my families

▼ (top) Photograph by Louise Fullbrook.
▼ (bottom) Photograph by Sandi Ford.

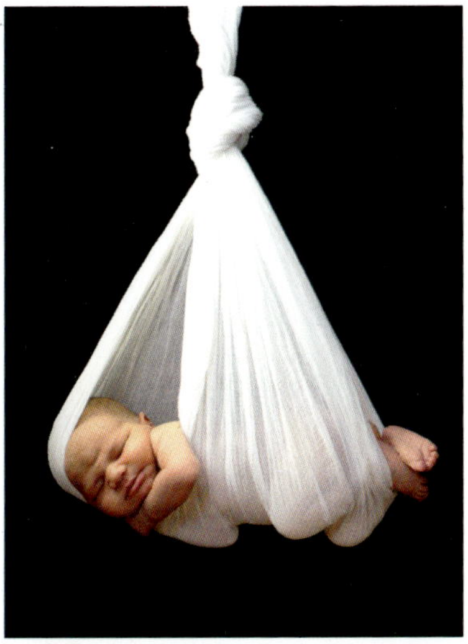

know that nursing breaks, diaper changes, and soothing time are expected and not a hassle. Also, babies need to feel secure. They need swaddling and to be held close. Don't let a need to get "that perfect nude shot" outweigh the real need to make sure the baby is warm, secure, and cozy.

Sandi: Be gentle but firm. Babies take comfort in being held with confidence. Be patient and calm, too. Show parents that you are an experienced professional and they will look to you for handling tips.

Louise: The first thing I do is sit down and chat! I talk about having my own children and having photographed over 300 babies. This tells my clients that I know how to work with them. I hold the baby firmly, with little space to move—this is how they would feel inside the womb. Doing so gives the baby a sense of safety. I also do a lot of shushing and rock the baby gently. It always works for me.

Melissa: My secret weapon for soothing babies back to sleep is rubbing their eyebrows—specifically, just the very beginning of the eyebrow. It instantly relaxes them. The other thing I do

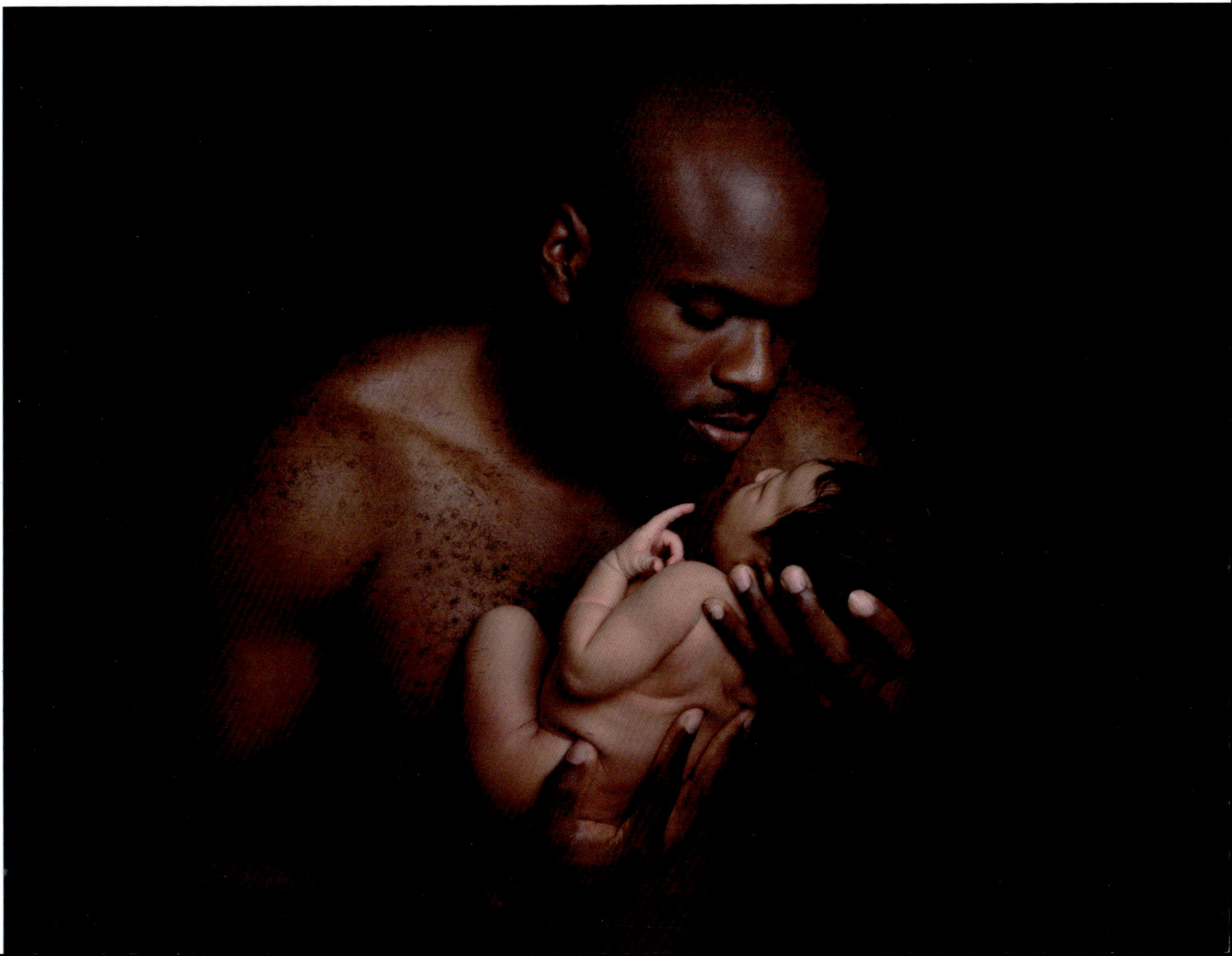

is jiggle them—whether it be their bum or their head, I give them a slight jiggle. When I am putting props under them to adjust a pose, I jiggle as I go! My parents leave their newborn sessions armed with these two little soothing tricks.

Angela: I always tell parents how long they will be at the studio. They need to know that. I tell them what to expect and why the session may take two to three hours. I don't have a problem with the parents because they have been warned!

How do I soothe a baby? I have an iPhone 5 app that plays sounds from the womb or a heartbeat. When baby stirs a little during the session I try to keep limbs from flailing around. If parents allow a pacifier, I will use that. It can be a life saver. When the baby shows signs of being hungry, I will have Mom feed him or her and, when done, I will walk/rock/sway the baby until he or she is asleep, then go back to photographing them.

Brenda: My staff and I are confident in what we do, so we tell parents to sit back and watch the show. They typically enjoy being able to doze off on our comfy couch. We continually tell the baby that he/she is doing a great job, and the parents love hearing that.

Heather: My tips for soothing the baby include a warm room, sound machine, always holding the extremities while transitioning with posing, and moving slowly. When it comes to working with parents, it's important to explain what you are doing. I also tell them I have a medical background. I worked at the number-one children's hospital in Philly as a CT scan technologist.

▼ Photograph by Heather Dougherty.

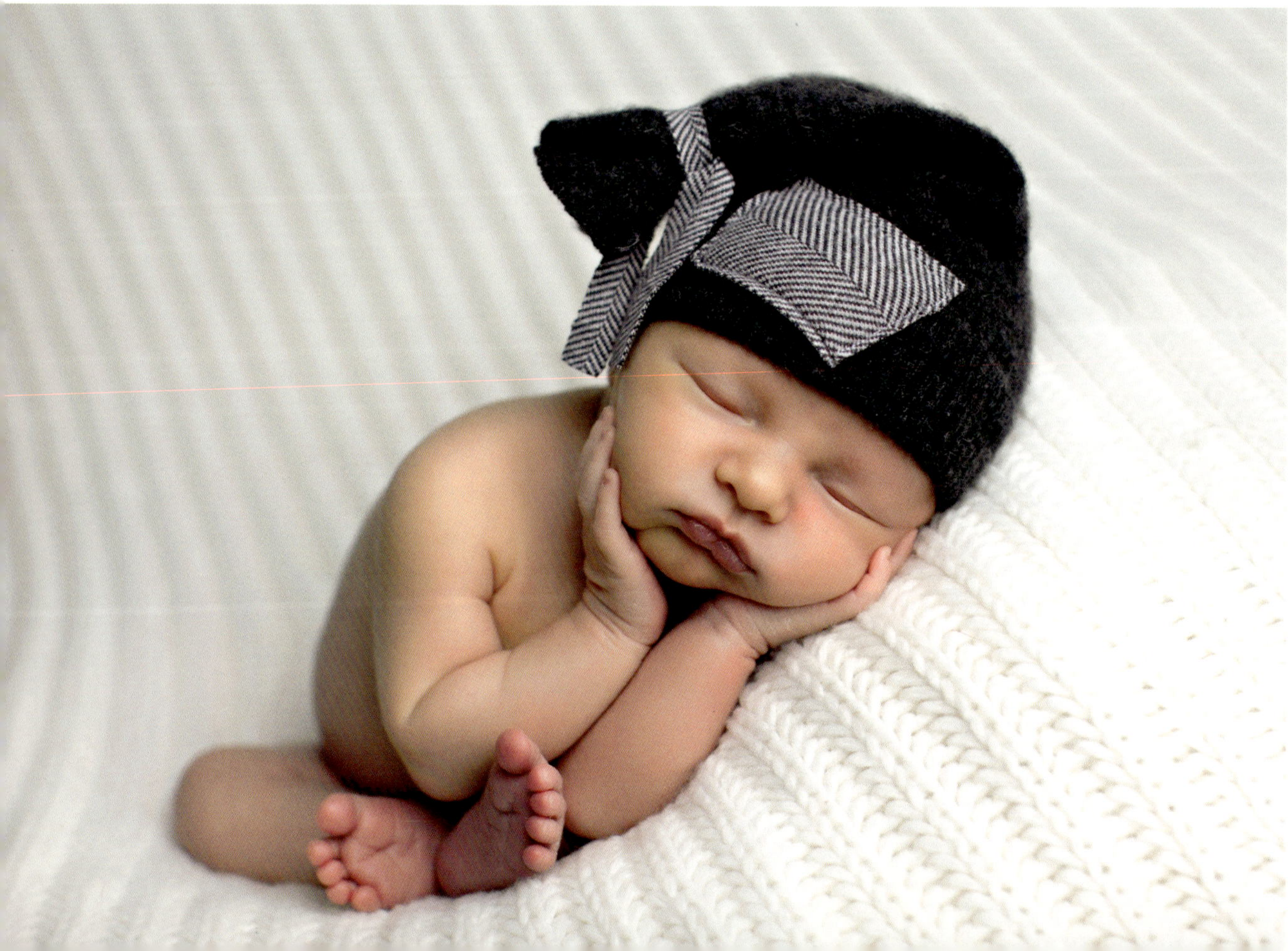

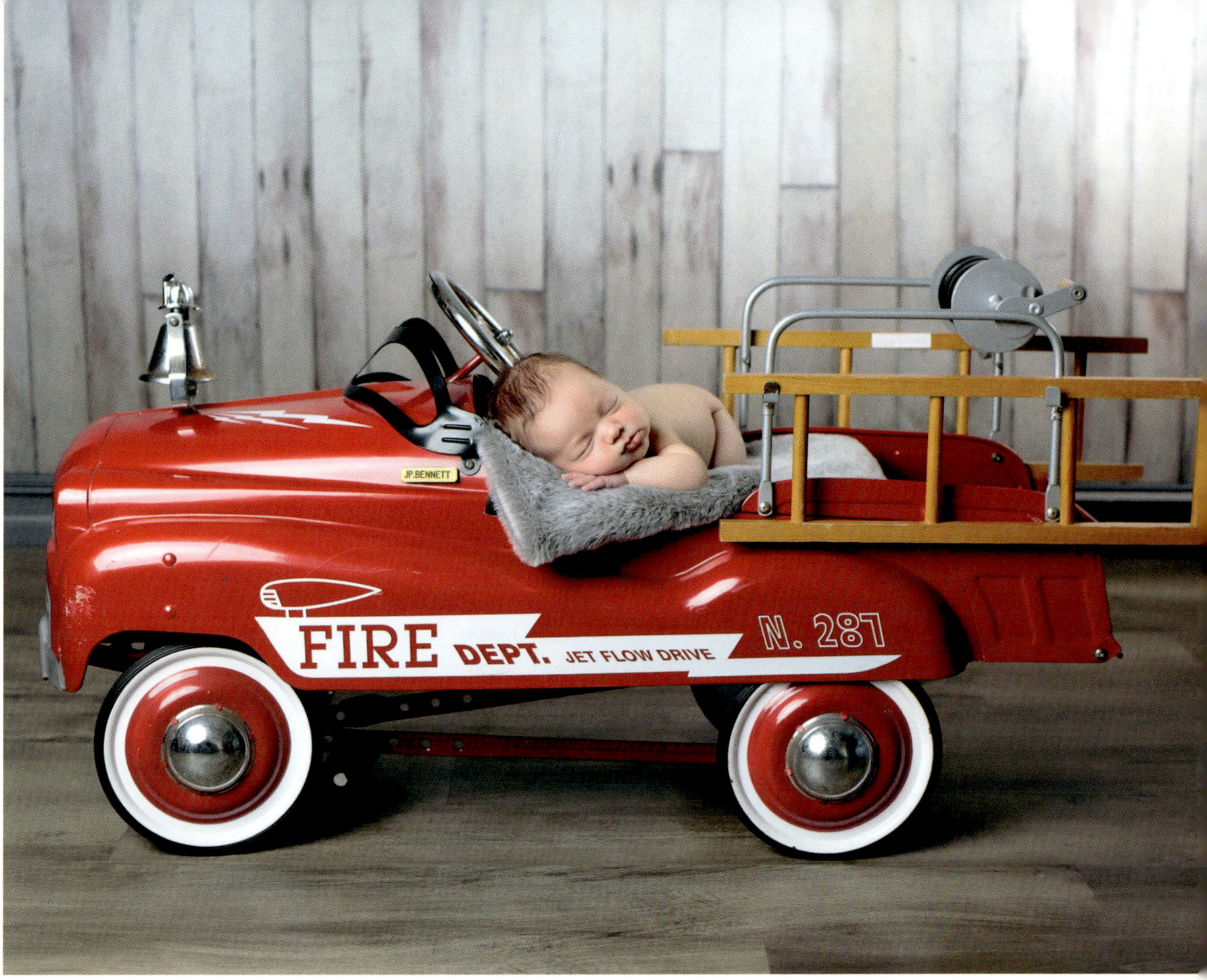

▲ Photograph by Brenda Horan.

What advice can you give photographers who want to get into newborn photography?

Amy: Always think safety first. These little bodies are so fragile. If you can't do something safely or you can't use Photoshop to create a composite, then you don't need to do the shot. It just takes one mistake to ruin lives (theirs and yours) forever.

Start with the simple things. You don't have to invest in hundreds of props. Don't be afraid to look for blankies and scarves at the thrift shop and grab a space heater in the spring when WalMart has them on clearance. Practice your lighting and setups on a doll. I have one of my daughter's old baby dolls so I can try out lighting and posing before I ever have a baby in my studio.

Finally, don't undercut local photographers. If you aren't ready yet, learn your craft before you put yourself out there.

Kelli: I would first tell them not to worry about buying so much stuff! I see new photographers try to overcompensate for their lack of confidence by buying tons of props in an effort to set themselves apart. I would start with just a few basics and practice until perfect. Before I had my first newborn session I actually practiced with baby dolls on the beanbag setup for hours and hours. I studied newborn images that I loved. I tried to see what it was about them that I found so interesting. I found that composition, more than props or anything else, was what I was drawn to. So I started practicing on my image composition.

Of course, there is always the safety concern. I think a new photographer should research the safety issues extensively before ever picking up a baby. There are so many things that can harm these tiny babies: The detergent you use to wash your blankets could cause a rash, you need to have specific immunizations if you plan to handle newborns, and you should never conduct a session while you are ill. If your family members are ill, you could expose the newborn to that illness without having it yourself! There are so many potential safety issues that need to be addressed with newborns. It's a unique situation.

Emily: The most important thing to know for photographers just starting out is that you cannot copy those jaw-dropping Pinterest shots of babies suspended in air, babies holding their head in their hands, etc. Those shots are compiled in Photoshop, not posed. Attempting these poses is a serious danger to newborns. Know your stuff before you dive in!

Sandi: Safety is paramount. Attend a workshop with someone you admire to see how it's done safely. Don't try to perform anything you are not confident with—it's not worth it!

Louise: Pricing! I am so tired of seeing new photographers offering dirt-cheap packages. They don't have insurance and all the other costs established photographers have, so they can do a cheap disc for £100 [roughly $165 as of this writing]. This presents us with many problems as photographers and cheapens the market. It is also hard for those new photographers to raise their prices once they are full-time professionals paying national insurance, tax, public liability insurance, and so on.

It's also important to go to workshops or watch online videos. When dealing with a brand-new baby, safety is of the utmost importance! I have seen new photographers doing things that are just dangerous in an attempt to copy another photographer.

Melissa: The biggest thing I want everyone to do is look past their own nose. You can't improve if you don't put your work out there for critique—whether you do so as part of

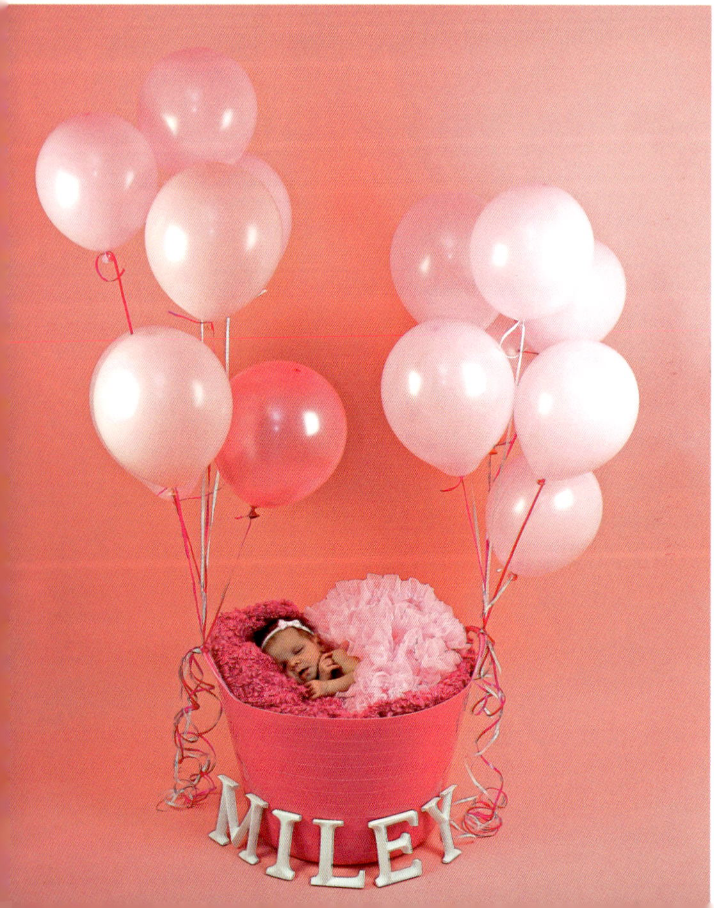

◄ Photograph by Louise Fullbrook.
► Photograph by Amy Coe.

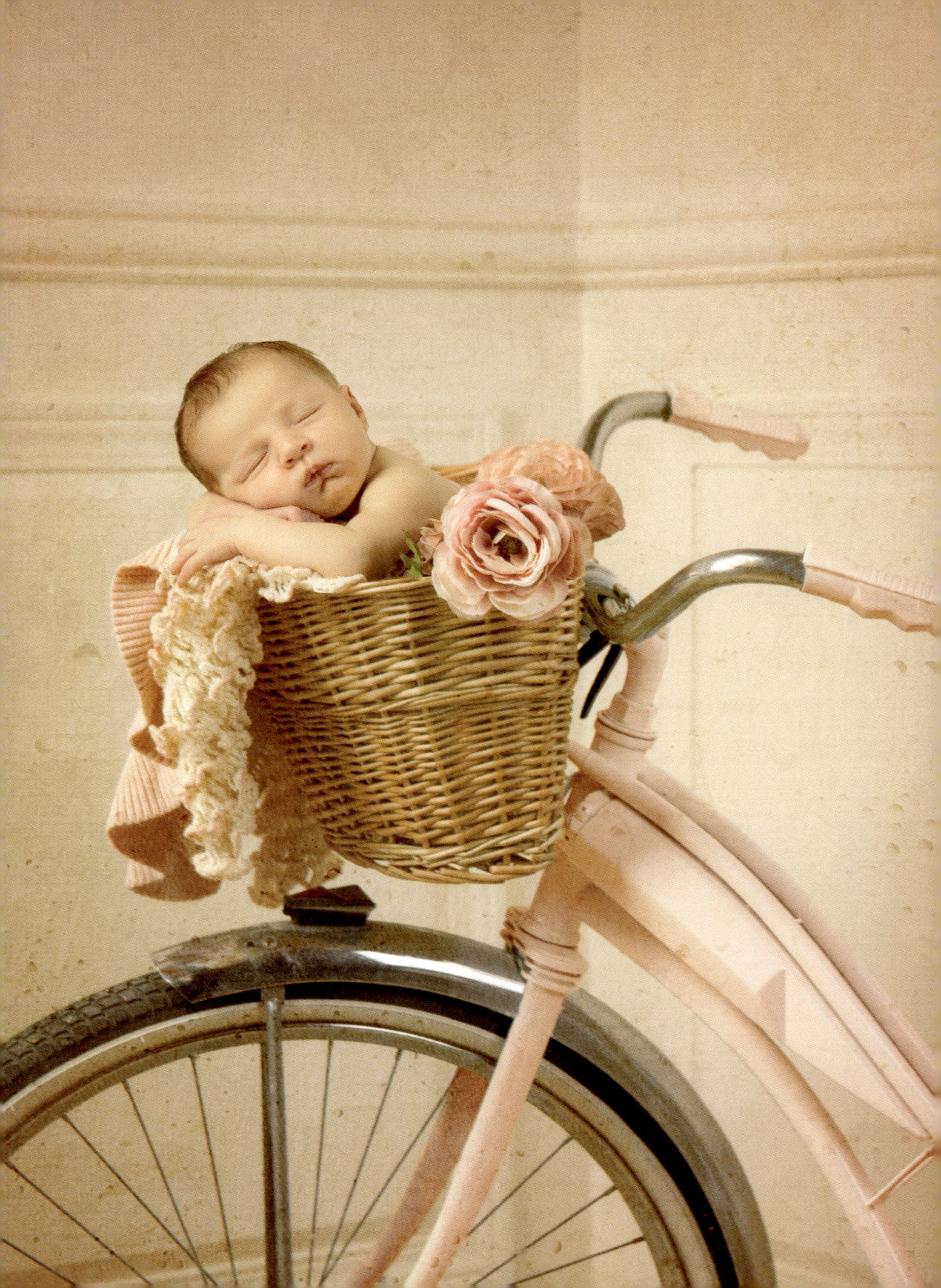

a workshop or mentoring or just an online newborn group for photographers. You have to realize when your skills need improving.

I'd also recommend that new photographers get their prices up as fast as they can, provided their skills allow for it. The higher your prices are, the more value you add to this industry. Try not to offer sales or discounts. Clients will come to expect it.

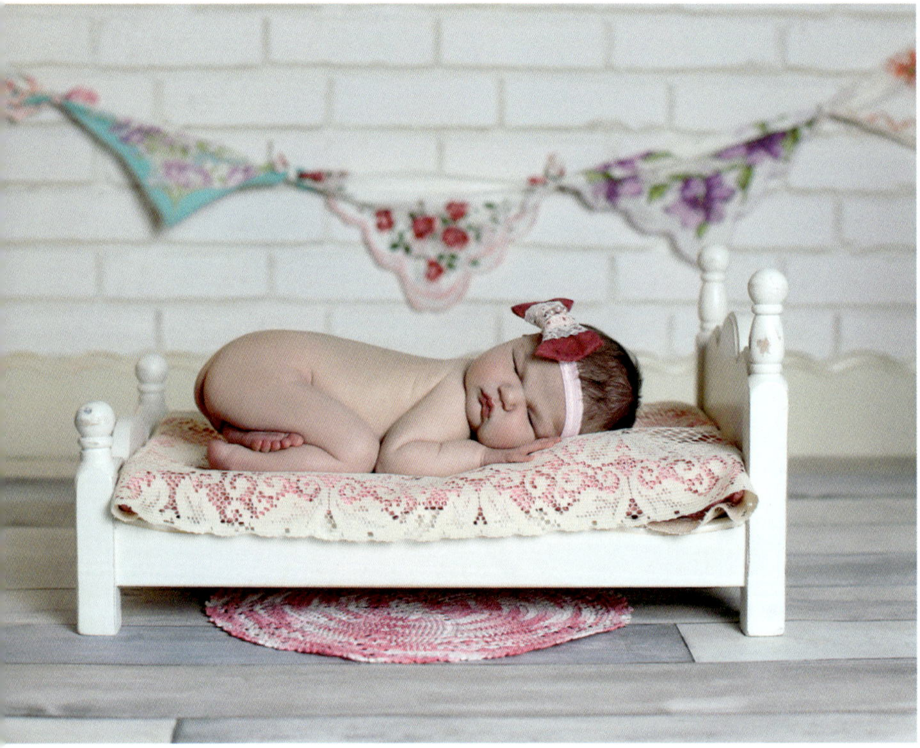

Photograph by Brenda Horan.

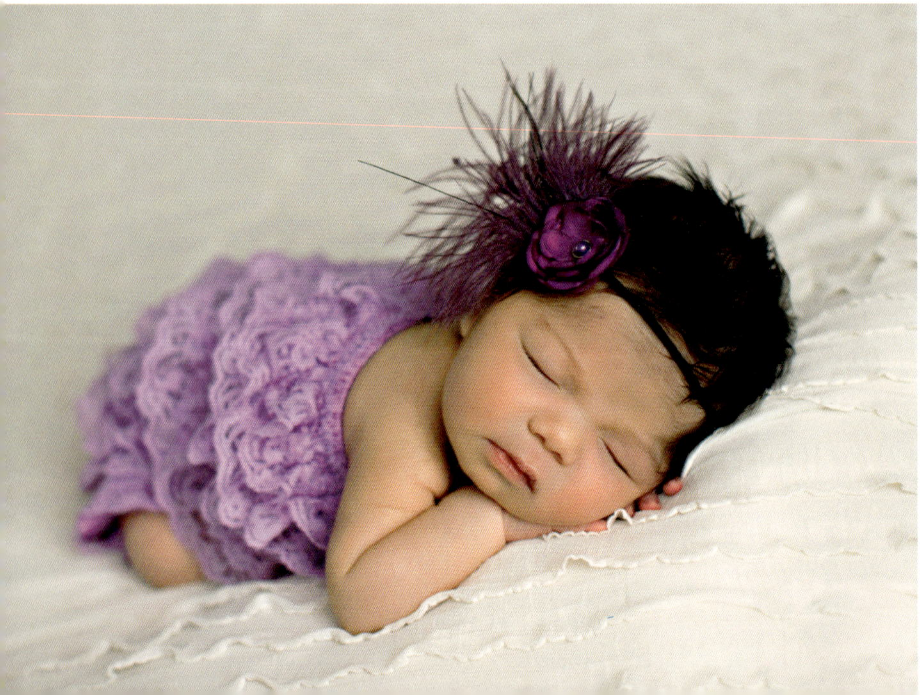

Photograph by Heather Dougherty.

➤ (top) The bottom-up or tushie pose. Photograph by Sandi Ford.
➤ (center) The taco pose. Photograph by Heather Dougherty.
➤ (bottom) The froggy pose. Photograph by Sandi Ford.

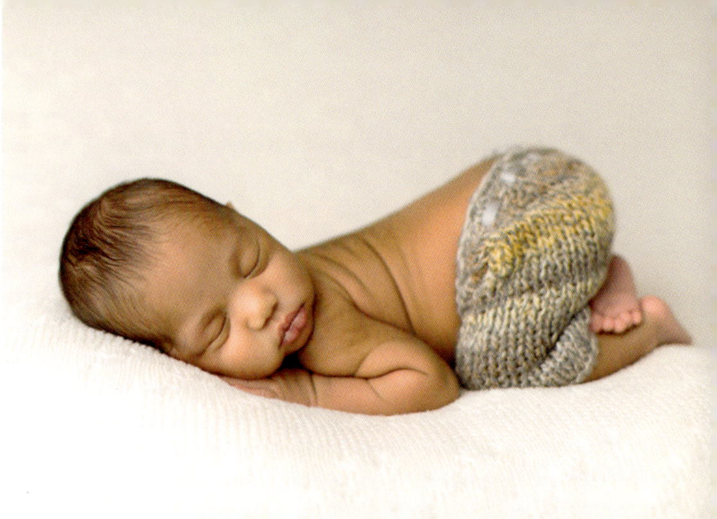

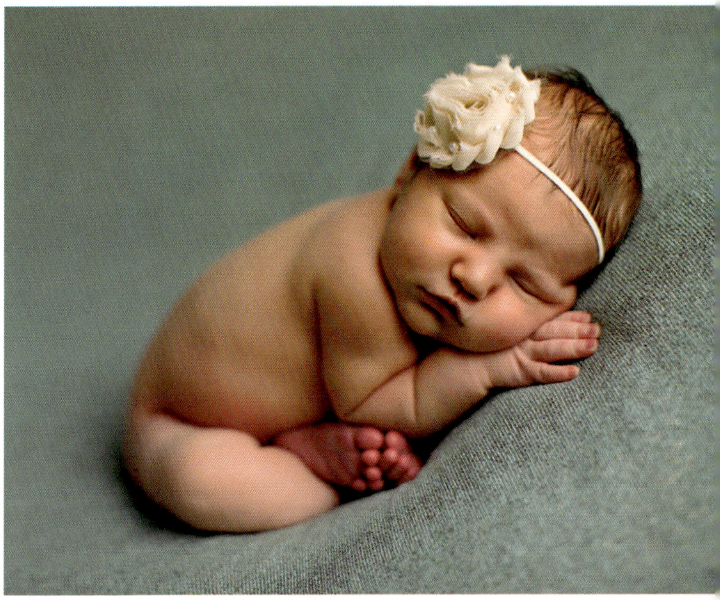

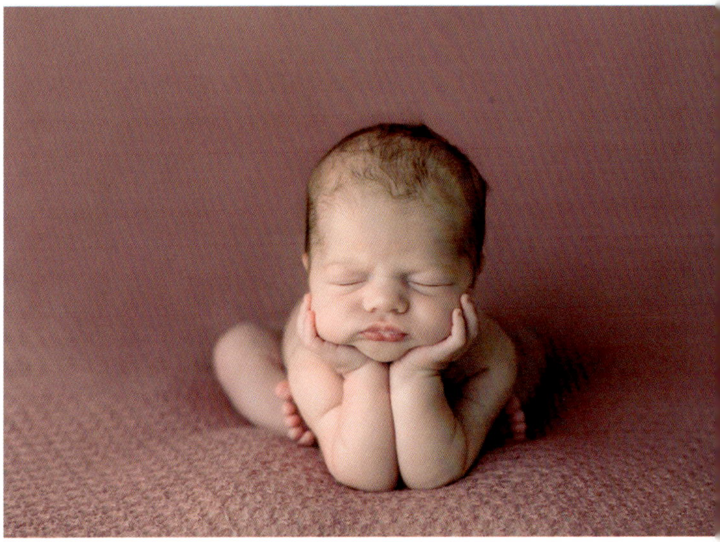

Finally, I don't believe in buying every single thing you think you need to be a photographer. A great full-frame DSLR, two good-quality lenses, and a solid computer are great. I actually use an inexpensive calibrated laptop. I have chosen to save my money in that area, and it works for me!

Angela: My advice to photographers who would like to get into newborn photography is to make sure that Baby's safety is always a priority. When handling a newborn, if you are not sure how to go about certain poses, don't do them without some education first. There are plenty of resources out there. There are other tips I could offer, but safety is and always will be my main priority at my studio.

Brenda: Safety is the most important concern. You are dealing with someone's baby! Don't try to do things that aren't safe. Never leave a baby unattended. Keep that camera strapped around your neck when you do the overhead shots. Take a few workshops to get a good understanding for why photographers do what they do. Don't go to a workshop just to sit back and chat with the other attendees then snap your pictures when the baby is posed. Watch the little details. It's what separates good artists from the mediocre.

Heather: Please do careful research regarding posing. Have an experienced newborn photographer show you the more difficult poses for the safety of the baby.

Charge appropriately. Newborn photography takes so much more time than other genres, and there are more expenses for the photographer.

9. Working with Charities

"There can be no keener revelation of a society's soul than the way in which it treats its children."—Nelson Mandela

I believe as artists we have a duty to use our talents for the good of others. The pursuit of profit keeps us busy most of the year, but we can spare a little time in the pursuit of philanthropy. Helping charities generates goodwill for your business and more love for your brand as you are perceived as generous and authentic.

Over the last seven years, I have been dedicated to donating my services to charitable causes. I focus my efforts to raise funds or provide photography. So far, our cumulative efforts have raised over $10,000 for charity.

Now I Lay Me Down to Sleep is an infant bereavement photography charity founded by renown photographer Sandy Puc'. Grieving parents are provided with images of their dying or deceased baby in an artful and sensitive manner. Now I Lay Me Down to Sleep gently provides a helping hand and a healing heart. This free service is provided by volunteer photographers who give of their time to capture the images and supply a free CD compilation of fully retouched and printable images. Area coordinators deal with requests from local hospitals and call photographers on their list to service requests. The service is required within hours, as babies deteriorate quickly once they pass, so the majority of cases are on a last-minute basis. This service covers stillbirths, early deliveries, and babies taken off of life support.

Many photographers feel they don't have the emotional fortitude to photograph a dying or deceased baby. It takes a strong person with a big heart to volunteer, and although it may seem like you aren't able to do it, you'll be surprised at how far your heart can stretch.

Believe me, the first time is the hardest, but once you realize how truly valuable your services are to the grieving families, you will never look back.

Now I Lay Me Down to Sleep offers help with retouching images if you feel you can't do that. It takes me two to three weeks before I can separate my emotions and look at the images captured during the session so I can edit them. Sometimes the condition the baby is in makes for perfect "sleeping" baby images, and other times you're presented with a deteriorating baby. However, you will surprise yourself with just how strong you can be when you put your mind and your heart to it!

Please visit the Now I Lay Me Down to Sleep's website (www.nilmdts.org) to donate or volunteer today. Thank you for your support!

nilmdts
Now I Lay Me Down to Sleep

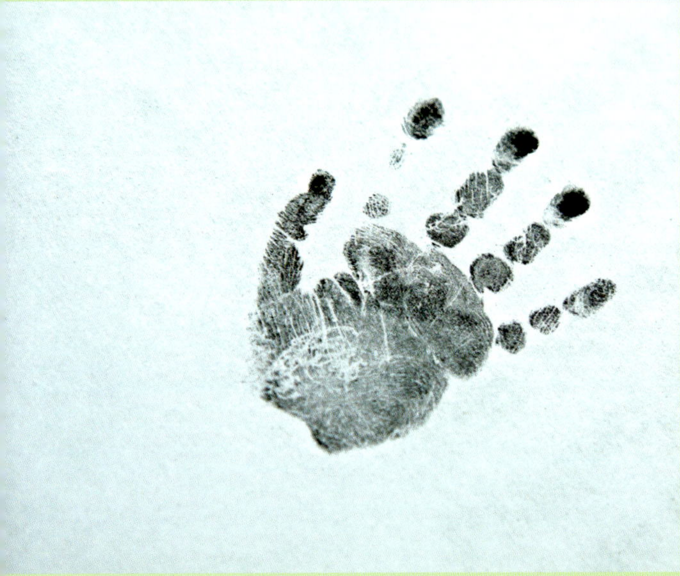

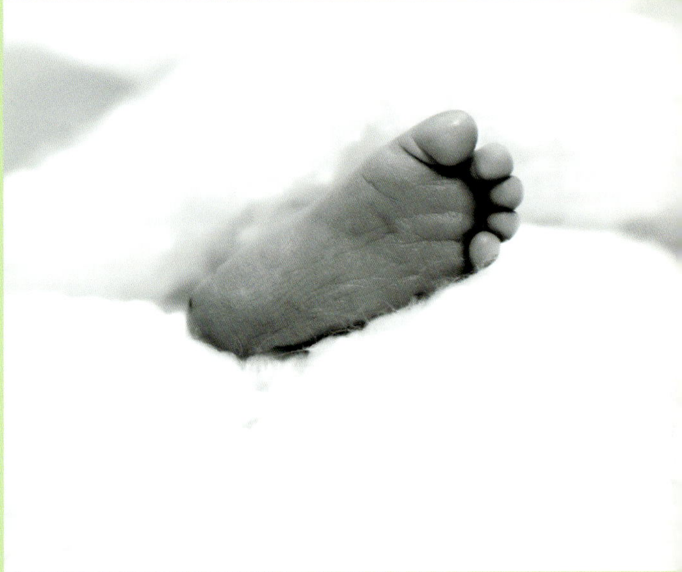

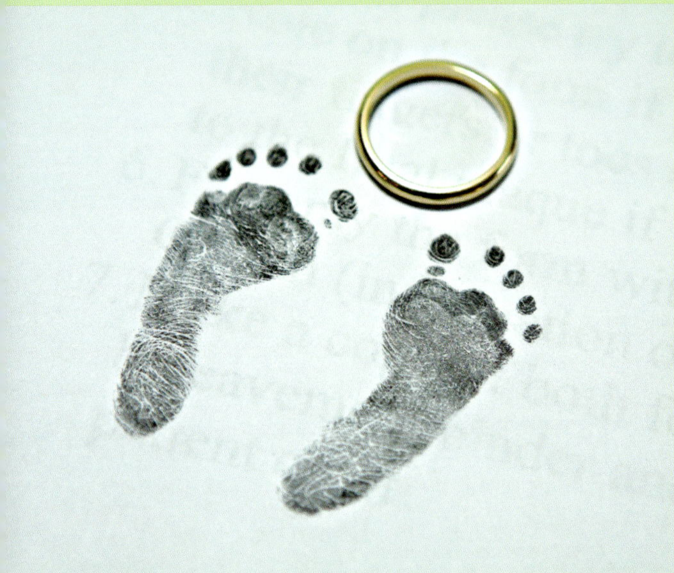

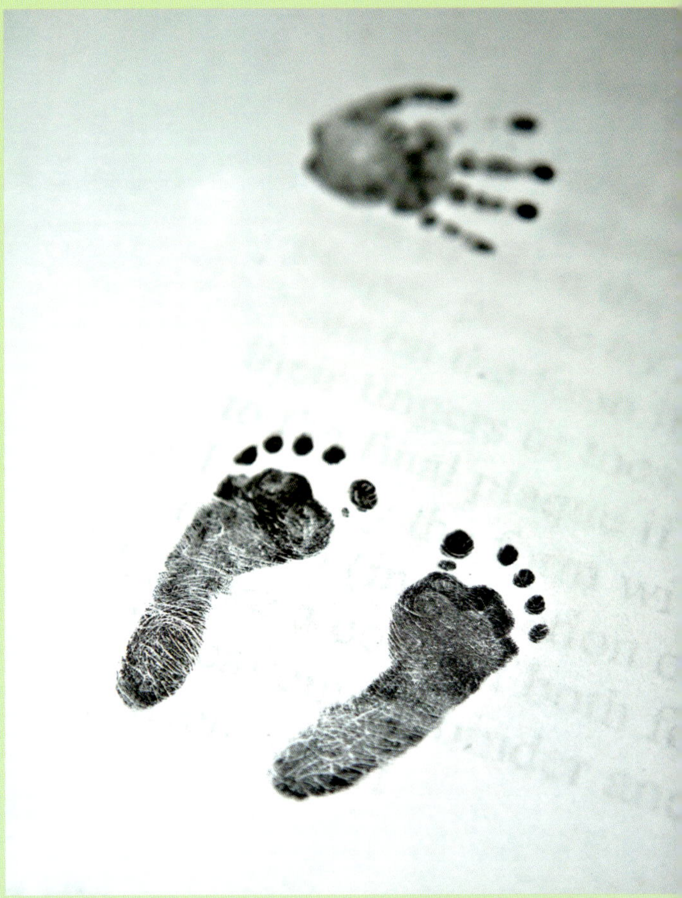

A portion of the proceeds of this book will be donated to Now I Lay Me Down to Sleep.

10. Resources

Associations

Professional Photographers of America
www.ppa.com
Wedding and Portrait Photographers International
www.wppionline.com
National Photographic Society UK
www.thenps.com
British Institute of Professional Photographers UK
www.bipp.com
Clickin Moms
www.clickinmoms.com
Chic Critique Forum
www.chiccritiqueforum.com

Photography Products and Labs

Artsy Couture
www.artsycouture.com
WHCC
www.whcc.com
Simply Color Lab
www.simplycolorlab.com
Miller's Lab
www.millerslab.com

Software

ProSelect (in-person ordering)
www.timeexposure.com
ShootQ (studio management)
www.shootq.com
Successware (studio management)
www.successware.net
Photographer's Wall Display Guides
www.arianafalerni.com/design
Shoot & Sell iPad App
www.shootandsellapp.com
Adobe Lightroom
www.adobe.com
RescueTime
www.rescuetime.com
Portraiture by Imagenomic
www.imagenomic.com
Florabella Actions
www.florabellacollection.com
Ukandu marketing tools by Sandy Puc'
www.ukandu.com

Royalty-Free Music

Triple Scoop Music
www.triplescoopmusic.com (code MIMIKA)
Slideshows by Animoto
www.animoto.com (code HQJRMFWS)
Slideshows by eMotion Media
www.emotionmedia.com (code MIMIKA)

Online Image Hosting and Print Sales

Pictage
www.pictage.com
Zenfolio
www.zenfolio.com
SmugMug
www.smugmug.com

Frames, Albums, and Canvas Suppliers

Simply Color Lab
www.simplycolorlab.com
Organic Bloom Frames
www.theorganicbloom.com
Finao Albums
www.finaoonline.com
GNP Frames
www.gnpframes.com
Wild Sorbet Frames
www.wildsorbet.com
ArtsyCouture
www.artsycouture.com

Social Media

Hootsuite
https://hootsuite.com

TweetDeck
https://about.tweetdeck.com
PinAlerts
www.pinalerts.com
Buffer
www.bufferapp.com

Newsletter Programs

MadMimi
www.madmimi.com
Constant Contact
www.constantcontact.com
Mail Chimp
www.mailchimp.com

Props and Equipment

Design Revolution
www.designrevolutiononline.com
Galpin Studios
www.galpinstudios.com
Photo Prop Floors and Backdrops
www.backdropsandfloors.com

Equipment

Digital Calibration Targets
www.photovisiondigital.com/digital-targets
Elinchrom softboxes, stripboxes
www.elinchrom.us
Reflector
www.larson-ent.com
iDisplay Pro Calibration Kit
www.xrite.com
Spyder4Pro Calibration Kit
www.spyder.datacolor.com

Legal Contracts

The Law Tog
www.thelawtog.com
Photographer's Toolkit
www.photographers-toolkit.myshopify.com

Editing Outsourcing

Shoot dot Edit
www.shootdotedit.com
Michelle Parker Graphics (personally trained by me)
www.michelleparkergraphics.com
Photographers Edit
www.photographersedit.com

Website Design and Hosting

Theme Forest
www.themeforest.net
Go Daddy
www.godaddy.com
99 Designs
www.99designs.com
BlueHost
www.bluehost.com

Customer Service and Networking

Send Out Cards
www.sendoutcards.com/mimikacooney
Contactually
www.contactually.com

Bags and Jewelry

Gina Alexander
www.ginaalexander.com
Kimbra Studios
www.kimbrastudios.net
Kotori Photo Jewelry
www.mykotori.com

Recommended Reading

For my updated list, go to www.mimikacooney.com/book-list.

Start with Why: How Great Leaders Inspire Everyone to Take Action—Simon Sinek (Penguin Group USA, 2011)
Book Yourself Solid Illustrated: The Fastest, Easiest, and Most Reliable System for Getting More Clients Than You Can Handle Even if You Hate Marketing and Selling—Michael Port (Wiley, 2013)
Beyond Booked Solid: Your Business, Your Life, Your Way—It's All Inside—Michael Port (Wiley, 2008)
The E-Myth Revisited: Why Most Small Businesses Don't Work and What to Do About It—Michael E. Gerber (HarperCollins, 2009)
Priceless: The Myth of Fair Value (and How to Take Advantage of It)—William Poundstone (Hill and Wang, 2010)
The War of Art: Break Through the Blocks and Win Your Inner Creative Battles—Steven Pressfield (Black Irish Entertainment LLC, 2011)
Who Switched Off My Brain? Revised: Controlling Toxic Thoughts and Emotions—Dr. Caroline Leaf (Thomas Nelson, 2009)

Switch On Your Brain: The Key to Peak Happiness, Thinking, and Health—Dr. Caroline Leaf (Baker Books, 2013)

Linchpin: Are You Indispensable?—Seth Godin (Portfolio, 2010)

All Marketers ~~Are Liars~~ Tell Stories: The Underground Classic That Explains How Marketing Really Works—and Why Authenticity Is the Best Marketing of All—Seth Godin (Portfolio Trade, 2012)

So Good They Can't Ignore You: Why Skills Trump Passion in the Quest for Work You Love—Cal Newport (Business Plus, 2012)

The Writer's Journey: Mythic Structure for Writers—Christopher Vogler (3rd Edition; Michael Wiese Productions, 2007)

Social Intelligence: The New Science of Human Relationships—Daniel Goleman (Bantam, 2007)

Enchantment: The Art of Changing Hearts, Minds, and Actions—Guy Kawaski (Portfolio Hardcover, 2011)

Renegades Write the Rules: How the Digital Royalty Use Social Media to Innovate—Amy Jo Martin (Jossey-Bass, 2012)

The Icarus Deception: How High Will You Fly?—Seth Godin (Portfolio Hardcover, 2012)

To Sell Is Human: The Surprising Truth About Moving Others—Daniel H. Pink (Penguin Group, 2012)

How to Deliver a TED Talk: Secrets of the World's Most Inspiring Presentations—Jeremy Donovan (McGraw-Hill, 2013)

Spark: How Creativity Works—Julie Burstein (Harper, 2011)

Made to Stick: Why Some Ideas Survive and Others Die—Chip Heath and Dan Heath (Random House, 2007)

The Referral Engine: Teaching Your Business to Market Itself—John Jantsch (Portfolio Trade, 2012)

Duct-Tape Marketing Revised & Updated: The World's Most Practical Small Business Marketing Guide—John Jantsch (Thomas Nelson, 2008)

Switch: How to Change Things When Change Is Hard—Chip Heath and Dan Heath (Crown Publishing Group, 2010)

Brand Sense: Sensory Secrets Behind the Stuff We Buy—Martin Lindstrom (Simon and Schuster, 2011)

Buyology: Truth and Lies About Why We Buy—Martin Lindstrom (Crown Business, 2010)

Clicks, Bricks, and Brands: The Marriage of Retailer and E-tailer—Martin Lindstrom (Kogan Page, Ltd., 2001)

Influence: Science and Practice—Robert B. Cialdini (5th Edition; Allyn and Bacon, 2008)

The Fire Starter Sessions: A Soulful + Practical Guide to Creating Success on Your Own Terms—Danielle LaPorte (Harmony, 2012)

Ignore Everybody: and 39 Other Keys to Creativity—Hugh MacLeod (Tantor Media, 2009)

Who Moved My Cheese?: An Amazing Way to Deal with Change in Your Work and in Your Life—Spencer Johnson (Penguin Group USA, 1998)

Raving Fans: A Revolutionary Approach to Customer Service—Ken Blanchard and Sheldon Bowles (HarperCollins Publishers, 1993)

The Art of Non-Conformity: Set Your Own Rules, Live the Life You Want, and Change the World—Chris Guillebeau (Pedigree Trade, 2010)

59 Seconds: Change Your Life in Under a Minute—Richard Wiseman (MacMillan, 2009)

Trust Agents: Using the Web to Build Influence, Improve Reputation, and Earn Trust—Chris Brogan, Julien Smith (Wiley, John & Sons, Inc. 2010)

The Six Pillars of Self-Esteem: The Definitive Work on Self-Esteem by the Leading Pioneer in the Field—Nathaniel Branden (Random House Publishing Group, 1995)

Brag!: The Art of Tooting Your Own Horn without Blowing It—Peggy Klaus (Grand Central Publishing, 2008)

Master Lighting Guide for Portrait Photographers—Christopher Grey (2nd Ed., Amherst Media, 2014)

The Art of Children's Portrait Photography—Tamara Lackey (Amherst Media, 2008)

The Seven Habits of Highly Effective People—Stephen R. Covey (Touchstone, 2004)

Drive: The Surprising Truth to What Motivates Us—Daniel H. Pink (Penguin Group USA, 2011)

Outliers: The Story of Success—Malcolm Gladwell (Little, Brown and Company, 2001)

Crush It: Why NOW Is the Time to Cash In on Your Passion—Gary Vaynerchuk (HarperCollins Publsihers, 2009)

The Thank You Economy—Gary Vaynerchuk (Harper Collins Publishers, 2011)

The Tipping Point: How Little Things Can Make a Big Difference—Malcolm Gladwell (Little, Brown and Company, 2002)

What the Dog Saw: And Other Adventures—Malcolm Gladwell (Little, Brown and Company, 2010)

Permission Marketing: Turning Strangers into Friends, and Friends into Customers—Seth Godin (Simon & Schuster, 1999)

Little Red Book of Selling: 12.5 Principles of Sales Greatness—Jeffrey H. Gitomer (Bard Press TX, 2004)

Six Pixels of Separation: Everyone is Connected. Connect Everyone to Your Business—Mitche Joel (Grand Central Publishing, 2010)

Index

OTHER BOOKS FROM

Amherst Media®

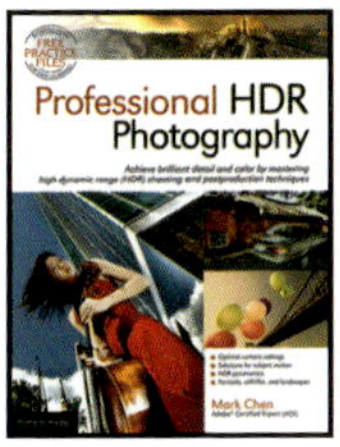

Professional HDR Photography

Mark Chen shows how to achieve brilliant detail and color with high dynamic range shooting and post-production. *$27.95 list, 7.5x10, 128p, 250 color images, order no. 1994.*

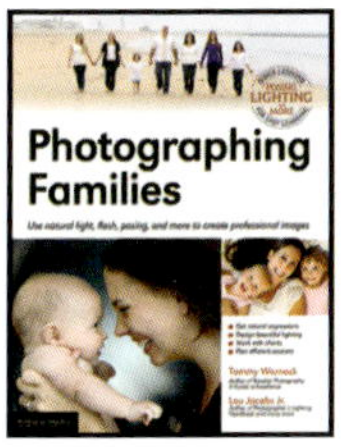

Photographing Families

Tammy Warnock and Lou Jacobs Jr. demonstrate the lighting and posing skills needed to create professional-quality portraits of families and children. *$27.95 list, 7.5x10, 128p, 180 color images, order no. 1997.*

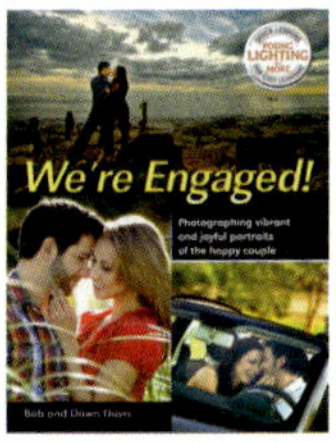

We're Engaged!

Acclaimed photographers and photo instructors Bob and Dawn Davis reveal their secrets for creating vibrant and joyful portraits of the happy couple. *$27.95 list, 7.5x10, 128p, 180 color images, order no. 2024.*

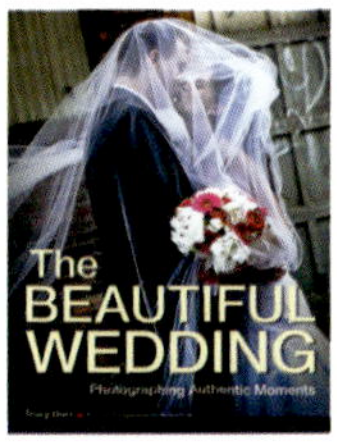

The Beautiful Wedding

Tracy Dorr guides you through the process of photographing the authentic moments and emotions that make every wedding beautiful. *$27.95 list, 7.5x10, 128p, 180 color images, order no. 2020.*

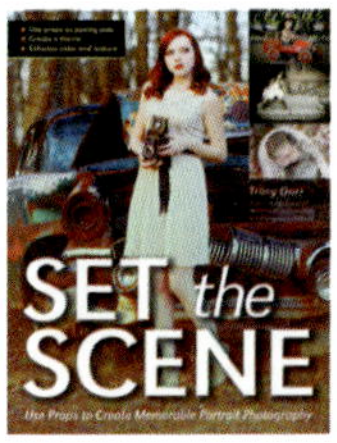

Set the Scene

With techniques and images from nearly a dozen top pros, Tracy Dorr shows you how using props can inspire you to design more creative and customized portraits. *$27.95 list, 7.5x10, 128p, 320 color images, order no. 1999.*

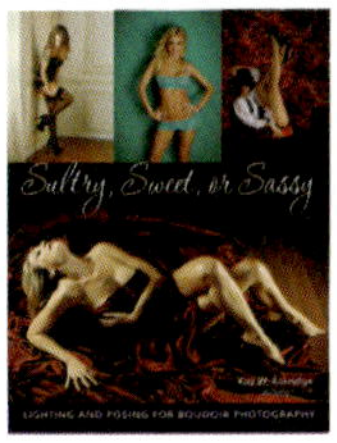

Sultry, Sweet, or Sassy

Kay Eskridge shows you the lighting and posing techniques needed to bring out the beauty and personality of your glamour portrait subjects. *$27.95 list, 7.5x10, 128p,180 color images, order no. 2023.*

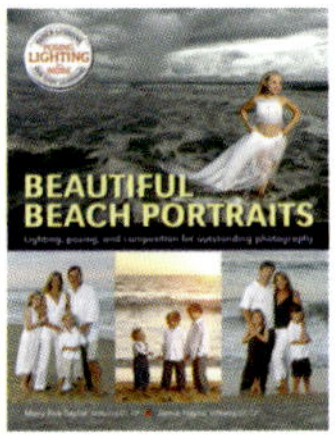

Beautiful Beach Portraits

Mary Fisk-Taylor and Jamie Hayes take you behind the scenes on the creation of their most popular images, showing you how each was conceived and created. *$27.95 list, 7.5x10, 128p, 180 color images, order no. 2025.*

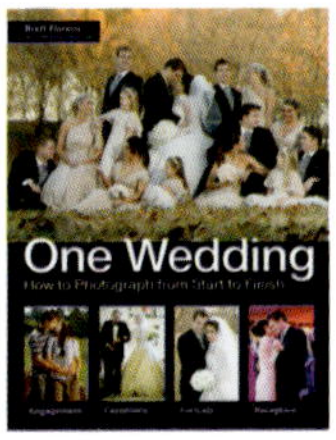

One Wedding

Brett Florens takes you, hour by hour, through the photography process for one entire wedding—from the engagement portraits, to the reception, and beyond! *$27.95 list, 7.5x10, 128p, 375 color images, order no. 2015.*

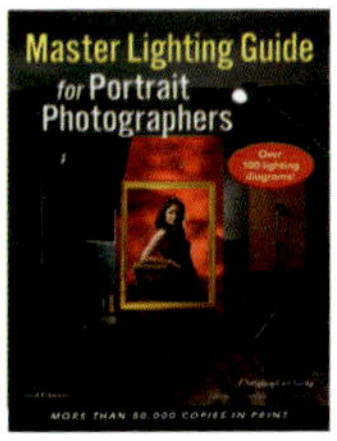

Master Lighting Guide for Portrait Photographers, *2nd ed.*

Christopher Grey shows you how to master traditional lighting styles and use creative modifications to maximize your results. *$27.95 list, 7.5x10, 160p, 350 color images, order no. 1998.*

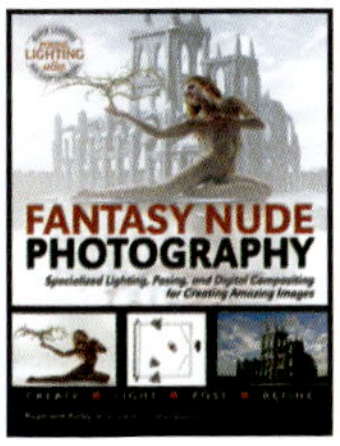

Fantasy Nude Photography

Rayment Kirby guides you through specialized lighting, posing, set design, and postproduction techniques that let you bring to life the images you've imagined. *$27.95 list, 7.5x10, 128p, 180 color images, order no. 2013.*

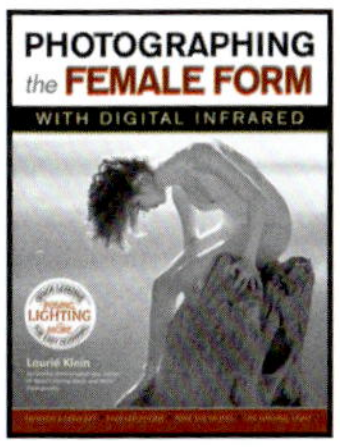

Photographing the Female Form with Digital Infrared

Laurie Klein shows you how to develop a concept, find locations, pose the model, and use natural light. *$27.95 list, 7.5x10, 128p, 180 color images, order no. 2021.*

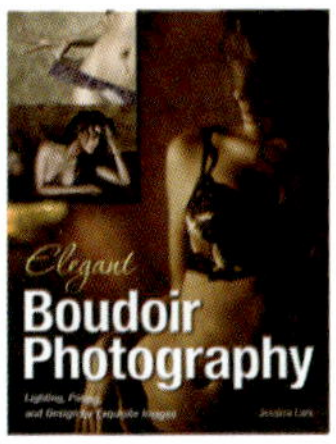

Elegant Boudoir Photography

Jessica Lark takes you through every step of the boudoir photography process, showing you how to work with clients and design images that are more engaging. *$27.95 list, 7.5x10, 128p, 230 color images, order no. 2014.*

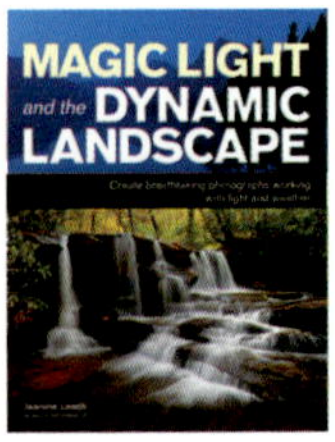

Magic Light and the Dynamic Landscape

Jeanine Leech helps you produce outstanding images of any scene, using time of day, weather, composition, and more. *$27.95 list, 7.5x10, 128p, 300 color images, order no. 2022.*

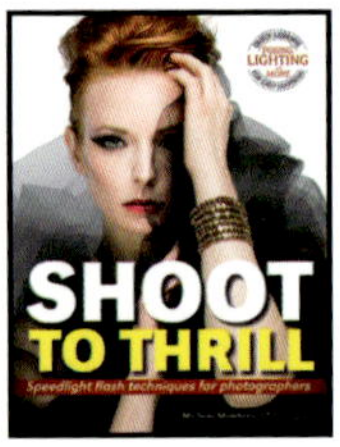

Shoot to Thrill

Acclaimed photographer Michael Mowbray shows how speedlights can rise to any photographic challenge—in the studio or on location. *$27.95 list, 7.5x10, 128p, 220 color images, order no. 2011.*

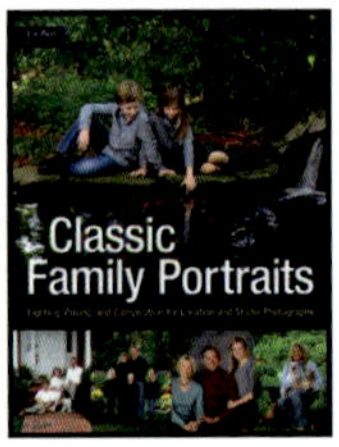

Classic Family Portraits

Ed Pedi walks you through the process of designing images that will stand the test of time. With these classic approaches, photos become instant heirlooms. *$27.95 list, 7.5x10, 128p, 180 color images, order no. 2010.*

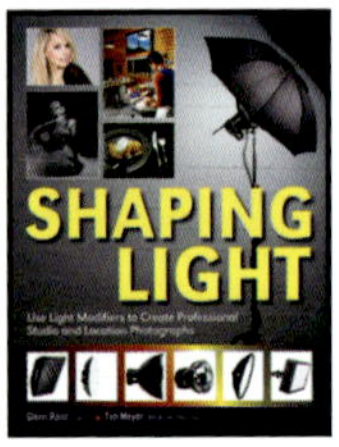

Shaping Light

Glenn Rand and Tim Meyer explore the critical role of light modifiers in producing professional images of any subject, ensuring smart decisions at every turn. *$27.95 list, 7.5x10, 128p, 200 color images, order no. 2012.*

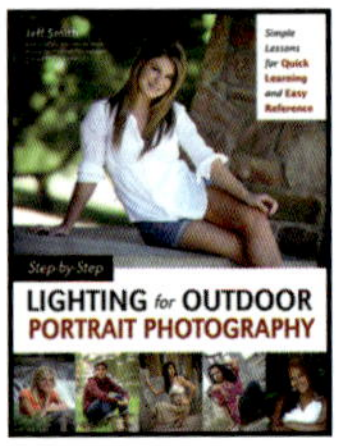

Step-by-Step Lighting for Outdoor Portrait Photography

Jeff Smith brings his no-nonsense approach to outdoor lighting, showing how to produce great portraits all day long. *$27.95 list, 7.5x10, 128p, 275 color images, order no. 2009.*

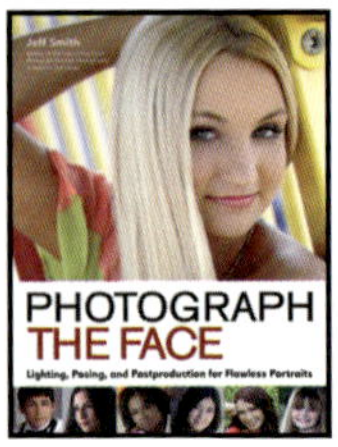

Photograph the Face

Acclaimed photographer and photo-educator Jeff Smith cuts to the core of great portraits, showing you how to make the subject's face look its very best. *$27.95 list, 7.5x10, 128p, 275 color images, order no. 2019.*

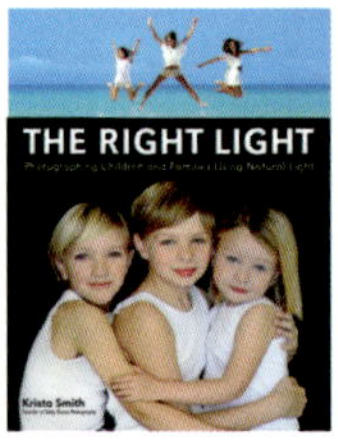

The Right Light

Working with couples, families, and kids, Krista Smith shows how using natural light can bring out the best in every subject—and result in highly marketable images. *$27.95 list, 7.5x10, 128p, 250 color images, order no. 2018.*

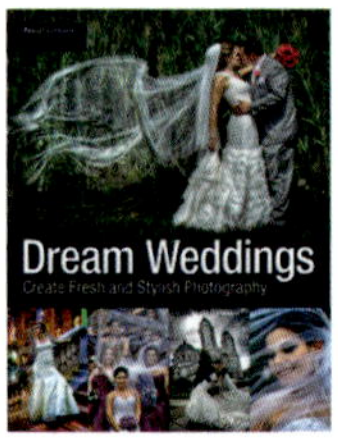

Dream Weddings

Celebrated wedding photographer Neal Urban shows you how to capture more powerful and dramatic images at every phase of the wedding photography process. *$27.95 list, 7.5x10, 128p, 190 color images, order no. 1996.*

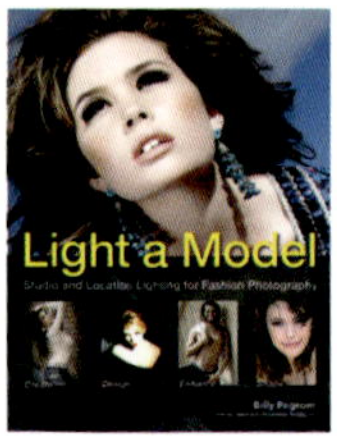

Light a Model

Billy Pegram shows you how to create edgy looks with lighting, helping you to create images of models (or other photo subjects) with a high-impact editorial style. *$27.95 list, 7.5x10, 128p, 190 color images, order no. 2016.*

MORE PHOTO BOOKS AVAILABLE

Amherst Media®
PO BOX 586
BUFFALO, NY 14226 USA

Individuals: If possible, purchase books from an Amherst Media retailer. To order directly, visit our web site, or call the toll-free number listed below to place your order. All major credit cards are accepted. *Dealers, distributors & colleges:* Write, call, or fax to place orders. For price information, contact Amherst Media or an Amherst Media sales representative. Net 30 days.

(800) 622-3278 or (716) 874-4450
Fax: (716) 874-4508

All prices, publication dates, and specifications are subject to change without notice. Prices are in U.S. dollars. Payment in U.S. funds only.

WWW.AMHERSTMEDIA.COM
FOR A COMPLETE LIST OF BOOKS AND ADDITIONAL INFORMATION